THE New Pacific DIPLOMACY

THE New Pacific DIPLOMACY

edited by Greg Fry and Sandra Tarte

Australian
National
University

PRESS

PACIFIC SERIES

ANU PRESS

Published by ANU Press
The Australian National University
Acton ACT 2601, Australia
Email: anupress@anu.edu.au
This title is also available online at press.anu.edu.au

National Library of Australia Cataloguing-in-Publication entry

Title: The new pacific diplomacy / edited by Greg Fry,
                  Sandra Tarte.

ISBN: 9781925022810 (paperback) 9781925022827 (ebook)

Subjects: Diplomacy.
                  Pacific Area--Foreign relations.

Other Creators/Contributors:
                  Fry, Greg, 1950- editor.
                  Tarte, Sandra, editor.

Dewey Number: 327.2

Cover design and layout by ANU Press

Contents

Overview

The Regional Diplomatic System

Fiji's New Diplomacy

NORTHERN MARIANA ISLANDS

Wake Island

Pacific Ocean

HAWAII O'ahu

Hawaii

20°N

GUAM

Caroline Islands

PALAU

FEDERATED STATES OF MICRONESIA

Pohnpei

Kosrae

MARSHALL ISLANDS

Jaluit Atoll

Gilbert Islands

K I R I B A T I

Line Islands

0°

NAURU

New Ireland

Papua New Guinea

Ontong Java Atoll

Phoenix Islands

New Britain

SOLOMON ISLANDS

Santa Cruz Islands

TUVALU

TOKELAU

Marquesas Islands

Torres Strait Islands

Port Moresby

SAMOA

COOK ISLANDS

Society Islands

Tuamotu Archipelago

VANUATU

FIJI

NIUE

TONGA

Tahiti

20°S

NEW CALEDONIA

Loyalty Islands

FRENCH POLYNESIA

AUSTRALIA

Norfolk Island

Lord Howe Island

Raoul Island

Kermadec Islands

Canberra Sydney

Pacific Ocean

NEW ZEALAND

Wellington

40°S

© Australian National University
CartoGIS CAP 00-143

150°E

180°

150°W

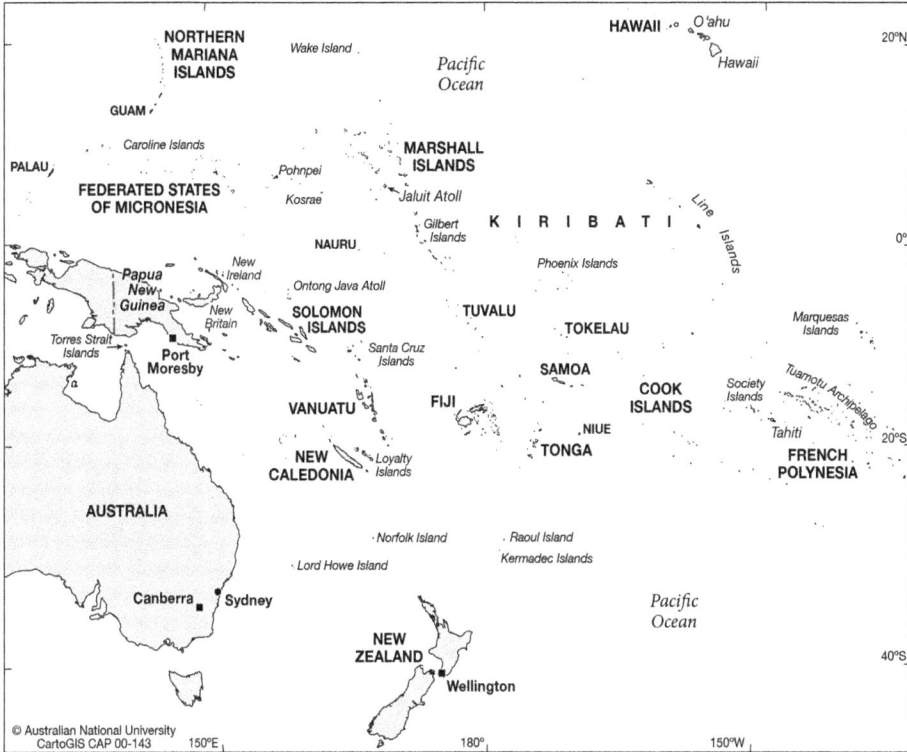

Map of the Pacific islands region

Source: CartoGIS, College of Asia and the Pacific, The Australian National University

Acronyms and Abbreviations

ACP	African, Caribbean and Pacific
ANZ	Australia and New Zealand
ANZCERTA	Australia–New Zealand Closer Economic Relations Trade Agreement
ANZUS	Australia, New Zealand, United States Security Treaty
AOSIS	Alliance of Small Island States
APEC	Asia-Pacific Economic Cooperation
ASEAN	Association of Southeast Asian Nations
BRICS	Brazil, Russia, India, China and South Africa
CANCC	Coalition of Atoll Nations on the issue of Climate Change
CARICOM	Caribbean Community and Common Market
CEPA	Comprehensive Economic Partnership Agreement
CfRN	Coalition of Rainforest Nations
CNMI	Commonwealth of the Northern Mariana Islands
COPs	Conference of the Parties
CRC	Committee on the Rights of the Child
CRGA	Committee of Representatives of Governments and Administrations
CROP	Council of Regional Organisations in the Pacific
CSO	civil society organisation
CVF	Climate Vulnerable Forum

DAWN	Development Alternatives with Women for a New Era
DEA	Department of External Affairs
DFA	Department of Foreign Affairs
DIVA	Diverse Voices and Action for Equality
DSM	deep sea mining
DWFN	Distant Water Fishing Nation
EEZ	Exclusive Economic Zone
EPA	Economic Partnership Agreement
EPG	Eminent Persons Group
EU	European Union
EWTP	Engaging with the Pacific
FAD	Fish Aggregating Device
FAS	Freely Associated States
FFA	Forum Fisheries Agency
FIC	forum island country
FLNKS	*Front de Libération Nationale Kanak et Socialiste* (Kanak and Socialist National Liberation Front)
FPA	Fisheries Partnership Agreement
FSM	Federated States of Micronesia
G77	Group of 77
GDP	Gross Domestic Product
HACCP	Hazard Analysis Critical Control Points
IDEA	Institute for Democracy and Electoral Assistance
IGB	Inter-Governmental Body
ISC	International Sugar Council
JUSCANZ	Japan, United States, Canada, Australia and New Zealand
LDC	Least Developed Country
MCES	Micronesian Chief Executives' Summit
MCT	Micronesian Conservation Trust
MDG	Millennium Development Goal

MOU	Memorandum of Understanding
MPA	marine protected area
MPS	Micronesian Presidents Summit
MSG	Melanesian Spearhead Group
MSG-FTA	Melanesian Spearhead Group Free Trade Area
MSGTA	Melanesian Spearhead Group Trade Agreement
MTEC	Micronesian Trade and Economic Community
NAM	Non-Aligned Movement
NFIP	Nuclear Free and Independent Pacific
NGO	non-government organisation
NSA	non-state actor
NZ	New Zealand
OECD	Organisation of Economic Cooperation and Development
PACER	Pacific Agreement on Closer Economic Relations
PACP	Pacific–African, Caribbean and Pacific
PALM	Pacific Alliance Leaders Meeting
PANG	Pacific Network on Globalisation
PARTA	Pacific Regional Trade Agreement
PCC	Pacific Conference of Churches
PCCR	Pacific Climate Change Roundtable
PCCPP	People's Charter for Change, Peace and Progress
PCRC	Pacific Concerns Resource Centre
PIANGO	Pacific Islands Association of Non-Government Organisations
PIC	Pacific Island Country
PICAN	Pacific Islands Climate Action Network
PICT	Pacific Island Countries and Territories
PICTA	Pacific Island Countries Trade Agreement
PIDF	Pacific Islands Development Forum
PIF	Pacific Islands Forum
PIFS	Pacific Islands Forum Secretariat

PIPSO	Pacific Islands Private Sector Organisation
PLG	Polynesian Leaders Group
PNA	Parties to the Nauru Agreement
PNG	Papua New Guinea
PPAC	Pacific Plan Action Committee
PRNGO	Pacific Regional Non-Governmental Organisation
PRUN	Permanent Representative to the United Nations
PSIDS	Pacific Small Island Developing States
RAMSI	Regional Assistance Mission to the Solomon Islands
REC	regional economic community
REDD+	Reducing Emissions from Deforestation and Forest Degradation
RIF	Regional Institutional Framework
RMI	Republic of the Marshall Islands
ROO	Rules of Origin
ROP	Republic of Palau
SBs	Subsidiary Bodies
SDG	Sustainable Development Goal
SIDS	Small Island Developing States
SIS	Small Island States
SME	small and medium-sized enterprise
SMS	Skilled Movement Scheme
SPARTECA	South Pacific Regional Trade and Economic Cooperation Agreement
SPC	Secretariat of the Pacific Community
SPF	South Pacific Forum
SPNWFZ	South Pacific Nuclear Weapon Free Zone
SPREP	Secretariat of the Pacific Regional Environment Programme
SSC	south–south cooperation
TIS	Trade in Services
TNC	The Nature Conservancy

TTPI	Trust Territory of the Pacific Islands
ULMWP	United Liberation Movement for West Papua
UN	United Nations
UNCITRAL	United Nations Commission on International Trade
UNCLOS	United Nations Convention on the Law of the Sea
UNDAF	United Nations Development Assistance Framework
UNDOF	United Nations Disengagement Observer Force
UNDP	United Nations Development Programme
UNEP	United Nations Environment Programme
UNESCAP	United Nations Economic and Social Council for Asia and the Pacific
UNESCO	United Nations Educational, Scientific and Cultural Organization
UNFCCC	United Nations Framework Convention on Climate Change
UNFCCC COP	United Nations Framework Convention on Climate Change Conference of the Parties
UNFPA	United Nations Population Fund
UNGA	United Nations General Assembly
UNICEF	United Nations Children's Fund
UNOPS	United Nations Office for Project Services
UPLD	*Union pour la Démocratie et le Progrès Social* (Union for Democracy and Social Progress)
USP	University of the South Pacific
VDS	Vessel Day Scheme
WCPFC	Western and Central Pacific Fisheries Commission
WCPO	Western and Central Pacific Ocean
WMCES	Western Micronesia Chief Executives Summit
WPNCL	West Papua National Council for Liberation
WTO	World Trade Organization

Acknowledgements

Most of the chapters in this volume were first presented as papers at the Workshop on The New Pacific Diplomacy held at the University of the South Pacific (USP) in early December 2014. We would like to thank the School of Government, Development and International Affairs at the USP and especially Professor Vijay Naidu, then Head of School, for his support for this project. We would also like to thank Sela Epeli and Annie Kaufonongo for their administrative support for the workshop.

ANU Press has been very supportive throughout the publication process. We would especially like to acknowledge Emily Tinker, Publications Coordinator, and Teresa Prowse who designed the cover. We are also indebted to Duncan Beard for his expert copy-editing and to Beth Battrick for the indexing.

We are especially grateful to Professor Stewart Firth of the State Society and Governance in Melanesia Program at the ANU for his constant encouragement and support for the project and the publication.

We would also like to send a *vinaka vakalevu* to all our students in the postgraduate program in diplomacy at USP who inspired our interest in this topic, not just through their questions and research, but also through our class discussions and debates. Our sincere gratitude also to the various senior Pacific islander intellectuals who addressed our Diplomacy students over the last several years and brought this New Pacific Diplomacy theme to life. They include Kaliopate Tavola, Transform Aqorau, Maureen Penjueli, Dame Meg Taylor, Iosefa Maiava, and Amena Yauvoli.

Last but not least we want to thank Nikolai Tarte and Annie Bartlett for their good-humoured patience and constant love throughout this project.

Greg Fry and Sandra Tarte
Suva, Fiji
12 November 2015

List of Contributors

Transform Aqorau is Chief Executive Officer of the Parties to the Nauru Agreement Office in Majuro, Marshall Islands. Previously, he worked in the Pacific Islands Forum Fisheries Agency as Legal Counsel and Deputy Director, as Legal Adviser to the Pacific Islands Forum Secretariat, and Legal Adviser and Deputy Secretary in the Solomon Islands Ministry of Foreign Affairs. He holds a Bachelor of Law from the University of Papua New Guinea, Masters of Law from the University of British Columbia (Canada), and PhD in Law from the University of Wollongong.

Nicola Baker is Senior Lecturer in Politics in the School of Government, Development and International Affairs at the University of the South Pacific. She was formerly Senior Lecturer in Politics at the Australian Defence Force Academy at the University of New South Wales. Her publications include the co-authored *Making Sense of War: Strategy for the 21st Century* (Cambridge University Press, 2006).

George Carter is a PhD candidate at The Australian National University studying regional blocs in climate change and sustainable development negotiations. He was formerly a Political/State Program Adviser in the US Embassy in Apia, Samoa.

Greg Fry is Academic Coordinator of Graduate Studies in Diplomacy and International Affairs at the School of Government, Development and International Affairs, the University of the South Pacific. He was Director of Studies, Graduate Studies in International Affairs, at The Australian National University from 1988–2011. His publications focus on the international politics of the South Pacific region; the politics of regional and national governance in the South Pacific; and conflict and conflict resolution in the Pacific Island states.

Suzanne Lowe Gallen is a postgraduate scholar in Development Studies at the School of Government, Development and International Affairs, the University of the South Pacific. She was formerly Assistant Director for Compact Management within the Federated States of Micronesia National Government. Prior to this, Suzanne was a Foreign Service Officer and the Deputy Assistant Secretary for American Affairs at the Federated States of Micronesia Department of Foreign Affairs. Suzanne majored in Political Science and International Relations at the University of Hawai'i at Manoa, then later undertook postgraduate studies in Diplomacy at the University of Oxford.

Nicollette Goulding is a postgraduate scholar in Diplomacy and International Affairs, School of Government, Development and International Affairs, the University of the South Pacific. She holds a Postgraduate Diploma in Climate Change from the Pacific Centre for Environment and Sustainable Development at the University of the South Pacific. She is Monitoring and Evaluation Project Assistant for the SPC/GIZ Coping with Climate Change in the Pacific Islands Region Programme at the Secretariat of the Pacific Community.

Makereta Komai is editor of the regional news agency PACNEWS, owned by the Pacific Islands News Association. She is a postgraduate scholar in Diplomacy and International Affairs, School of Government, Development and International Affairs, the University of the South Pacific. She has a broadcasting background, having worked as senior political reporter for Fiji Television (1996–1999) and desk sub-editor for the Fiji Broadcasting Commission (1989–1996). She has been involved with South Pacific Regional Environment Programme's Regional Media Outreach Programme as a trainer and as a mentor for young journalists.

Nic Maclellan is a journalist and researcher. He is a correspondent for *Islands Business* magazine (Fiji) and has contributed as a broadcaster and journalist to Radio Australia, ABC's *The Drum*, *Tahiti-Pacifique*, *The Contemporary Pacific*, and other regional media. He is co-author of *La France dans le Pacifique: de Bougainville à Moruroa* (Editions La Découverte, Paris, 1992), *After Moruroa— France in the South Pacific* (Ocean Press, 1998) and *Kirisimasi* (PCRC, Suva, 1999).

Fulori Manoa is a postgraduate scholar in International Affairs, in the School of Government, Development and International Affairs, the University of the South Pacific. She was formerly a teaching assistant in Ethics and Governance at the University of the South Pacific. Her postgraduate research has focused on Pacific diplomacy at the United Nations, particularly the issue of sustainable development.

Sovaia Marawa is a postgraduate scholar in Diplomacy and International Affairs at the University of the South Pacific, where her research has focused on Melanesian diplomacy on the free trade area. She is also Deputy Secretary of Trade and Investment in the Fiji Ministry of Foreign Affairs and International Cooperation. Prior to her current appointment, she served as Director of Trade.

Litia Mawi has been Fiji's Roving Ambassador/High Commissioner to the Pacific (Micronesia and Polynesia) and Fiji's Special Envoy to the Council of Regional Organisations in the Pacific Agencies since 2011, following a 12-month stint as a UN International Volunteer Specialist in AID Management in the Ministry of Finance of the Government of Tuvalu. Prior to that, she served as Permanent Secretary in Fiji's Ministry of Local Government, Urban Development and Housing, and in the Ministry of Women, Social Welfare and Poverty Alleviation.

Wesley Morgan is the Pacific Policy Adviser for Oxfam, based in Suva. His PhD from the University of Melbourne focused on the Pacific's trade diplomacy.

Tess Newton Cain is an independent Pacific analyst who has lived in Vanuatu and worked in the region for almost 20 years. She is a former lecturer in law at the University of the South Pacific and is currently a Visiting Fellow to the Development Policy Centre of The Australian National University. She is co-author of *Introduction to South Pacific Law* (Cavendish Publishing Limited, 1999), and co-editor of *Passage of Change: Law, Society and Governance in the Pacific* (ANU E Press, 2010) and *A Kind of Mending: Restorative Justice in the Pacific Islands* (ANU E Press, 2010). She is the founder of the Devpacific Thinknet.

Michael O'Keefe is Senior Lecturer in International Relations at La Trobe University, where he is also Convenor of the BA International Relations. He is a regular lecturer in the postgraduate program in Diplomacy at the University of Fiji and an occasional contributor to *Islands Business*.

Maureen Penjueli is Coordinator of Pacific Network on Globalisation, based in Suva. She was formerly a team leader with Greenpeace. Her advocacy and published writing focuses on trade justice, seabed mining, investment and decolonisation.

Henry Puna has been Prime Minister of Cook Islands since 2010. The Hon. Mr Puna studied law at Auckland University and the University of Tasmania before returning to practice law in the Cook Islands. He was chair of the Pacific Islands Forum 2012–2013.

Claire Slatter teaches Politics and Governance at the School of Government, Development and International Affairs, the University of the South Pacific. She is a founding member and current Board Chair of Development Alternatives with Women for a New Era, and a founding member of the Citizens' Constitutional

Forum in Fiji. Her research interests include the politics of economic and trade liberalisation in Pacific Island states, regional development, and economic and gender justice.

Sir Michael Somare, GCL, GCMG, CH, CF, KStJ, PC, MP, was Prime Minister of Papua New Guinea from 2002–2011. He had previously been Prime Minister from independence in 1975 until 1980, and again from 1982 until 1985.

Jope Tarai is a postgraduate scholar and Graduate Assistant, School of Government, Development and International Affairs, the University of the South Pacific. His research focuses on Pacific tuna diplomacy negotiations with the United States.

Sandra Tarte is Head of the School of Government, Development and International Affairs, the University of the South Pacific. She specialises in the international politics of the Pacific Islands region and is the author of *Japan's Aid Diplomacy and the Pacific Islands* (Asia Pacific Press, The Australian National University, 1998). She has written widely on regional cooperation in the Pacific, with a focus on fisheries management and conservation.

Kaliopate Tavola is a Fijian consultant and commentator on regional affairs. He was High Level Representative of the Melanesian Spearhead Group, and was Minister of Foreign Affairs for Fiji from 2000–2006. He was Leader of the Forum Eminent Persons Group charged with reviewing RAMSI and lead negotiator for the Pacific group in EPA negotiations with European Union. He began his diplomatic career in 1984 as Counsellor in London, before becoming Ambassador to Brussels from 1988–1998 focusing on Fiji's relations with the EU, and WTO.

Dame Meg Taylor is Secretary-General of the Pacific Islands Forum Secretariat. She received her LLB from Melbourne University, and her LLM from Harvard University. She practiced law in Papua New Guinea and served as a member of the Law Reform Commission. She was Ambassador of Papua New Guinea to the United States, Mexico and Canada in Washington, DC, from 1989–1994. She is co-founder of Conservation Melanesia and has served on the boards of international conservation and research organisations. In addition, she has served as a board member of a number of companies in Papua New Guinea in the natural resources, financial, and agricultural sectors. Meg Taylor was appointed to the post of Vice President of the World Bank Group in 1999.

Anote Tong is President of Kiribati. He studied at University of Canterbury and the London School of Economics. He was first elected president in 2003, and was re-elected in 2007 and 2012.

Overview

1

The 'New Pacific Diplomacy': An introduction

Greg Fry and Sandra Tarte

Since 2009 there has been a fundamental shift in the way that Pacific Island states engage with regional and world politics. The region has experienced what President Anote Tong of Kiribati has aptly called a 'paradigm shift' in ideas about how Pacific diplomacy should be organised, and on what principles it should operate. Many leaders have called for a heightened Pacific voice in global affairs and a new commitment to establishing Pacific Island control of this diplomatic process. This change in thinking has been expressed in the establishment of new channels and arenas for Pacific diplomacy at the regional and global levels, and new ways of connecting the two levels through active use of intermediate diplomatic associations.

This shift to a 'new Pacific diplomacy' is as fundamental as the move by the independent Pacific Island states, four decades ago, to create a postcolonial diplomatic system, through the establishment of the South Pacific Forum (renamed Pacific Islands Forum in 2000) (see Fry 1994). Indeed, in many ways, the current activity is reminiscent of that time — in its assertive attitude, the emphasis on Pacific Island control of the diplomatic agenda, the creation of new institutions, its appeal to regional identity, and its concern with negotiating global agendas that are impacting Pacific societies. It is not, in our view, too dramatic to see this as a time of transformation of the regional diplomatic culture equivalent to the move from the colonial to the postcolonial era, a time that represents a transformation of regional order.[1]

This book brings together a range of analyses and perspectives on these dramatic new developments in Pacific diplomacy at sub-regional, regional and global levels, and in the key sectors of global negotiation for Pacific states: oceans management, fisheries, climate change, sustainable development, decolonisation, seabed mining, and trade.[2] It also examines state and non-government roles in this new Pacific diplomacy. The book also focuses on the question of the significance of these new developments in negotiating global issues of key importance to the Pacific, and the implications for the future of the regional diplomatic architecture. Some of these perspectives are analyses of new developments, others are proposals that can be seen as part of the new Pacific diplomacy. Examples of the latter include the call by Cook Islands Prime Minister Henry Puna to 're-imagine' the region, President Tong's appeal for the Pacific to 'chart its own course', and Ambassador Kaliopate Tavola's proposal for a Pacific-controlled Pacific Islands Forum (without Australia and New Zealand) to better meet the strategic necessities of the Pacific Island states in global diplomacy.

To create a context for considering these perspectives, this introductory chapter explores five questions. Firstly, what do we mean by 'Pacific diplomacy'? Secondly, what are the expressions of the new Pacific diplomacy? Thirdly, how significant is the new Pacific diplomacy? Fourthly, how should we understand its emergence? Fifthly, what are the implications of the new Pacific diplomacy for the negotiation of Pacific Island interests and for the future regional architecture?

'Pacific Diplomacy'

As employed in the following chapters, the 'Pacific' refers to the thousands of islands and island societies scattered across the Pacific Ocean, stretching from the Micronesian islands just south of Japan and east of the Philippines, south to Papua New Guinea and down the Melanesian chain of islands to New Caledonia, then east across the Polynesian Pacific to Tahiti. These societies are politically organised into 14 postcolonial states (Cook Islands, Federated States

---

1   Sandra Tarte makes the detailed case for seeing the new Pacific diplomacy as constituting a shift in regional order (Tarte 2014).
2   Most of these chapters were first delivered as papers to the New Pacific Diplomacy Workshop organised by the School of Government, Development and International Affairs, the University of the South Pacific, Suva, 4–5 December 2014.

of Micronesia, Fiji, Kiribati, Marshall Islands, Nauru, Niue, Palau, Papua New Guinea, Samoa, Solomon Islands, Tonga, Tuvalu, and Vanuatu) and the remaining dependent territories of France (New Caledonia, Wallis and Futuna, and French Polynesia), Britain (Pitcairn Island), New Zealand (Tokelau) and US (American Samoa, Guam, and the Commonwealth of the Northern Mariana Islands). Taking into account its sea area (largely made up of 200 nautical mile exclusive economic zones of the constituent states and territories), this region is roughly the size of Africa.

By 'Pacific diplomacy' we mean the diplomacy pursued by Pacific states in global forums, or in multilateral arenas in which the Pacific bloc is negotiating with just one external power (as in the case of tuna negotiations with the US). This includes negotiations within the Pacific group to determine joint positions to be taken to global talks. It refers to their engagement in the joint negotiation of such matters as trade, sustainable development, climate change, nuclear issues, decolonisation, and fisheries. We also include the diplomatic activity concerned with establishing the diplomatic institutions in which regional diplomacy is carried out and a Pacific joint position is negotiated. Finally, we include in our definition of Pacific diplomacy, the accepted principles, norms and practices which underpin regional diplomacy and might be usefully described as constituting a regional diplomatic culture.

The history of Pacific diplomacy, so defined, begins in a concerted way in the mid-1960s as the first Pacific Island states became independent from colonial rule. The new Pacific states conducted their own foreign policies, but as small island states their capacity for extensive unilateral diplomacy was limited.[3] From the start, there was a commitment to regional diplomacy and joint diplomatic approaches in global forums to effect diplomatic outcomes. In this volume, Transform Aqorau refers to this as 'the diplomacy of the past, the "Pacific Way", and doing things by consensus'.

The key vehicle for this Pacific diplomacy was the South Pacific Forum. It was established partly to promote cooperation on regional ventures but, just as importantly, also to take a Pacific voice to the world. The Pacific Island states were preoccupied with working together to advance their interests in global diplomacy as well as integrating their economies. They did so by creating a regional organisation, the South Pacific Forum. In the 1970s and 1980s, the forum was very active in expressing a Pacific diplomacy on key issues. Their successful joint diplomacy, which took place under the auspices of the forum, culminated in a series of international treaties on resource protection, environmental issues, and tuna access, and prohibitions on drift-net fishing, the dumping

---

3   These constraints are explored in Boyce and Herr (1974).

of radioactive wastes in Pacific waters, nuclear testing, and trade (Fry 1994). They also collectively achieved the reinscription of New Caledonia on the list of territories falling under the oversight of the United Nations (UN) Decolonisation Committee. These were notable achievements for joint diplomacy by the Pacific states as they took on the world's most powerful countries on issues of great concern to the national interest of those powers.

From the mid-1990s the forum was much less active in global diplomacy. Led by an Australian and New Zealand concern with promoting regional integration and a new regional economic order along neoliberal lines, the forum became focused on regional integration (Fry 2005). This was joined by a War on Terror security agenda from 2001, focusing on countering transnational organised crime and terrorism. While there were examples of the earlier diplomacy being pursued by the forum secretariat — on trade negotiations with Europe, and with Australia and New Zealand, for example (as described by Wesley Morgan in this volume) — this had largely disappeared by 2000. By then, the forum appeared to have moved away from its founding objective of assisting Pacific states to negotiate jointly on global issues impacting the region.

The New Diplomatic System

The most dramatic expression of what we are calling the 'new' Pacific diplomacy has been associated with Fiji's activist foreign policy since its suspension from the Pacific Islands Forum (PIF) in 2009. The Bainimarama Government enunciated several new foreign policy principles aimed at circumventing its isolation in regional and global diplomacy: that Fiji should garner and represent a Pacific voice that could be heard in global forums; that Fiji should promote itself as the hub of the Pacific and as a leader of Pacific Island states; that it should engage in south–south cooperation in the Pacific and the wider world; that regional diplomacy and regional institutions should be firmly controlled by Pacific Island states and not constrained by metropolitan powers (especially Australia and New Zealand); and that the Pacific should be better organised to engage in global diplomacy. The Fiji government also introduced the idea of including civil society, the private sector, and dependent territories, alongside independent governments, as equal partners in a new kind of 'network diplomacy'.

Fiji expressed these ideas in a series of major initiatives: in giving leadership to a renaissance of the Melanesian Spearhead Group (MSG); in creating the Pacific Islands Development Forum (PIDF); and by invigorating the existing Pacific Small Island Developing States at the UN as a Pacific Island-only bloc to a point where it replaced the PIF as the main representative of the Pacific voice at the UN. These developments in Fiji's new Pacific diplomacy are described and examined in the chapters by Ambassador Mawi and Makereta Komai.

It is, however, a central premise underlying the approach of this book that it would be a mistake to see the new Pacific diplomacy as solely a Fiji phenomenon. Fiji policy and leadership has obviously been the key catalyst, but it is important to note the wider support for these new institutions and ideas across the region as evidenced in the support for a new array of Pacific-controlled institutions.

Significantly, the new Pacific diplomacy has been expressed in the actions of the Pacific Island states since 2009 in developing a new diplomatic architecture outside the PIF system, both to conduct some important aspects of regional affairs, and to represent the Pacific Islands region to the world on the key issues of concern such as climate change and fisheries management. For Pacific leaders, these moves do not represent a wholesale rejection of the PIF; rather they suggest recognition of a need for complementary forums to undertake diplomatic functions and pursue needs which can no longer be met in the PIF system.[4] The new Pacific diplomatic system now handles the core global diplomatic needs of the Pacific Island states in relation to key issues such as trade, climate change, decolonisation, fisheries management, and sustainable development. This new system has worked well to meet those needs, and is widely supported by Pacific Island states.

Pacific Small Island Developing States

One significant institutional development has been the rise of the Pacific Small Island Developing States Group (PSIDS) at the UN. Although this group had existed since the early 1990s in relation to global sustainable development negotiations in the Rio process, the PSIDS has taken on a dramatically new diplomatic role for the Pacific Island states since 2009, to the point where it has all but replaced the PIF as the primary organising forum for Pacific representations at the global level.

The PSIDS has also become the key diplomatic vehicle for Pacific participation in global southern coalitions such as the Alliance of Small Island States (AOSIS) and the Group of 77. It is, for example, the main organising arena for determining and prosecuting Pacific positions on climate change mitigation

---

4   This refers to the forum itself and the other institutions in the Council of Regional Organisations in the Pacific (CROP) such as the Forum Fisheries Agency, Secretariat of the Pacific Regional Environment Programme, and the Secretariat of the Pacific Community.

in the UN Framework Convention on Climate Change, and also in relation to the Rio+20 UN Conference on Sustainable Development in 2012, and the Third International Conference on Small Island Developing States in Apia, Samoa, in 2014. It is important to note that while the enhancement of PSIDS was undoubtedly a Fiji-led initiative, it has been strongly supported by all Pacific Island state UN members. Fulori Manoa explores the significance of this development of the PSIDS at the UN in this volume.

Melanesian Spearhead Group

A second major expression of the 'new Pacific diplomacy' has been the reinvigoration of the MSG and its emergence as a major forum for sub-regional integration, and for diplomacy on decolonisation. Again, although Fiji leadership provided the catalyst for its reinvigoration, it is important to note that all Melanesian countries embraced the new and deeper integration proposed as part of the new MSG since 2009. Papua New Guinean leadership was also very important in this reinvigoration. The achievements have been significant. Most prominent has been the achievement of significant free trade in goods and services, including the movement of skilled labour, which is explored by Sovaia Marawa in this volume. The MSG has been able to achieve a level of integration not yet achieved in the wider PIF grouping in relation to trade and movement of professional workers.

The Pacific Islands Development Forum

The third and perhaps most controversial element in the new regional diplomatic architecture is the PIDF, which was a Fiji-led initiative established in 2013. It developed out of the 'Engaging with the Pacific' meetings, which Fiji organised from 2010 as a means of building ties with its Pacific neighbours following suspension from the PIF. While clearly the flagship of the Fiji government's efforts to lead regional diplomacy after suspension from the PIF, the new kind of regional diplomacy it represented also appealed to many other Pacific leaders. This is described in the chapter by Sandra Tarte.

There were three novel elements of the PIDF that particularly seemed to capture the imagination of Pacific Island leaders. The first was that the new institution emphasised inclusivity, a connection between leaders and society, which had been lacking in the PIF. It brought together civil society groups, the private sector, international agencies and governments in a process that stressed partnerships and network diplomacy. Second is its focus on 'green growth', which seemed to offer hope of overcoming the stalling of regional action in key areas such as climate change and sustainable development. Finally, the PIDF was motivated by the desire for self-determination. At the PIDF secretariat opening in 2014, Prime Minister Bainimarama said the Fiji-based group had a single purpose:

> It is not a question of prestige or establishing yet another talkfest, it is about creating an organisation that is more attuned to our development needs as Pacific countries. It is about creating an organisation that is relatively free of interference from outsiders (Cooney 2014).

Although Prime Minister Bainimarama has said that the PIDF was not intended to compete with the PIF, he seemed to give a different impression in other statements about the organisation's purpose:

> Why do we need a new body, a new framework of cooperation? Because the existing regional structure for the past four decades — the Pacific Islands Forum — is for governments only and has also come to be dominated only by a few (Pareti 2013).

Parties to the Nauru Agreement

The fourth institutional development was the establishment of the Parties to the Nauru Agreement (PNA) Headquarters in 2009. The PNA represented the island states with the region's largest tuna stocks and served as a vehicle for gaining greater control over their shared resource. The tiny but effective Majuro-based secretariat has been highly successful in implementing novel ideas in fisheries management, which have translated into dramatic increases in revenue to the member countries. This development is independent of Fiji's suspension from the PIF, since Fiji is not a member of PNA, and therefore demonstrates a broader assertion of Pacific control over regionalism. The role and impact of the PNA are described in the chapters by Transform Aqorau and Jope Tarai.

New Trade Negotiation Agencies

Finally, Pacific Island states have created new Pacific-run institutions outside the PIF to negotiate trade and economic relationships with Australia and New Zealand, and Europe. In the case of negotiations with Australia and New Zealand on the Pacific Agreement on Closer Economic Relations (PACER) Plus (described in the chapter by Wesley Morgan), they argued for an independent office outside the PIF to provide advice on the negotiations. The Vila-based Office of the Chief Trade Adviser was established in 2009, despite Australian and New Zealand efforts first to oppose its creation, then to dictate who the adviser would be, and finally to sideline it. In the case of negotiations with the European Union over a regional economic partnership agreement, and in relation to developing Pacific positions to take to African, Caribbean and Pacific (ACP) meetings, the

Pacific Island states decided in 2012 to create a Pacific ACP Office based in Port Moresby. The Pacific Islands Forum Secretariat had previously been the responsible agency for this function (Komai 2014).

Pacific Islands Forum

It could be argued that we are now seeing evidence of 'new Pacific diplomacy' ideas in developments within the PIF. Dame Meg Taylor's chapter talks about inclusivity, and making the forum fit for purpose and responsive to critical reviews (allowing the leaders to make effective decisions). Significantly, the forum has also begun to redefine its mandate to include joint diplomacy, rather than just integration and cooperation as in the recent past, and has made new claims to diplomatic agendas, which it had seemingly abandoned in the previous decade. This is partly in response to the new Pacific diplomacy, and indicates the influence of the thinking and ideas shaping the new diplomacy. Whereas the new Pacific diplomacy is in many ways a response to what was seen as the limitations of the PIF (that it was elitist, statist, and unable to act on key diplomatic needs such as climate change), the forum has now sought to remedy some of these areas. As Dame Meg Taylor asserts: 'The forum secretariat must engage with civil society and the private sector more routinely in its work. We need to recognise the important role that civil society plays in the regional space.' As Claire Slatter argues in this volume, the new Pacific framework goes a long way in addressing the key concerns of civil society about inclusion and openness, although she argues it is still too early to judge how substantive these moves are.

A Paradigm Shift?

Underpinning these institutional changes is a new set of ideas about how the Pacific should engage in global and regional diplomacy. The coherence and novelty of these ideas and their departure from prevailing ideas suggests that President Tong of Kiribati was prescient in calling this a 'paradigm shift'. First and foremost of these ideas is that the Pacific should, in President Tong's words, 'chart its own course'. This is reflected in various calls for the development of an effective Pacific voice, in Prime Minister Puna's call for reimagining Oceania and in the founding ideas of the PIDF. This call for regional self-determination is expressed in the creation of new institutions and ventures.

Secondly, there is the claim that the Pacific needs to engage assertively in global diplomacy in relation to key challenges impacting the region; that it should indeed aspire to global diplomatic leadership in key areas such as climate change, tuna diplomacy and oceans management. Thirdly, it is claimed that there should be effective representation of a genuine 'Pacific voice' in global forums and that Pacific Island states need to work together in joint diplomacy at the global level. Fourthly, there is growing recognition and acceptance of the role of sub-regional groupings and initiatives, in line with the view that a 'one-region' approach need not be the best approach. As Aqorau notes in his contribution to this volume: 'Having a single region arrangement is useful for some purposes but not for others.' Chapters by Dame Meg Taylor and Tess Newton Cain also make this argument.

Fifthly, there should be a capacity to participate in southern diplomatic alliances and to leverage Pacific Island positions on the global agenda through these intermediaries. Specifically, Pacific diplomatic architecture needs to be configured to provide the capacity to participate in middle level 'southern' diplomatic alliances, such as AOSIS, the ACP, and Group of 77 plus China. Sixthly, the generation of the 'Pacific voice' needs to be inclusive (of civil society, private sector, and governments).

The Significance of the 'New Pacific Diplomacy'

How then should we assess the significance of this 'new Pacific diplomacy'? As already suggested, we argue that it represents a fundamental transformation in diplomatic ideas, institutions and practices. The transformative nature of this new paradigm and its institutional expression in a new diplomatic system is more clearly seen if we compare the current developments with other stages in the history of Pacific diplomacy. Seen in this historical context, the significance of the current changes is clearly of the order of the shift from the colonial to the postcolonial diplomatic system in 1971.

Those developments set up a regional diplomatic culture with certain assumptions about who should belong, who should speak, and how diplomacy should be conducted. This prevailed until the early 1990s. In the 1990s and 2000s there was a slow unravelling of this regional diplomatic culture, and a move away from the assumptions of equality and respect for self-determination. When compared with the regional diplomatic culture which developed in the 1990s and early 2000s — which was hierarchical and disrespectful to the self-determination principle — the new Pacific diplomacy represents a new regional diplomatic culture. At the same time, because it represents the same values and principles of the original regional political settlement of 1971, it could also be represented as a restoration of the original regional diplomatic culture established by the forum in 1971 (Fry 2015). More broadly, the new Pacific diplomacy can be seen as effecting a fundamental change in the contemporary regional order given its impact on the pattern of power, and the transformation of dominant ideas and institutions (Tarte 2014).

The significance of the new Pacific diplomacy is also accentuated by the lack of attention to the joint diplomacy side of regionalism within the PIF for the last two decades, seemingly encouraged by a definition of regionalism focused on regional integration. This emphasis had overlooked that the forum was established to do both — support regional integration and represent the Pacific interests in global diplomacy. In the first two decades it was not doing well on regional integration, but it was highly successful in collective diplomacy. In the next two decades it focused more on regional integration and less on its role of representing the region in global diplomacy. This makes the emergence of the new Pacific diplomacy, from around 2009, an even more marked development.

Finally, significance is derived from the fact that support for this new paradigm, and the new institutions, has come from across the Pacific. Thus this is not just to be seen as only Fiji-supported, and as therefore disappearing once Fiji re-enters the forum system. The PSIDS, for example, is supported by all Pacific Island states (including Samoa), and the significant MSG achievements since 2009 could only be achieved with the support of all Melanesian states and the joint leadership of Fiji and PNG. There is widespread Pacific support for the principles and objectives of the PIDF. They are not about to be wound back to the status quo ante with Fiji's return to democracy.

Why the New Pacific Diplomacy?

How then to explain this transformative development in Pacific diplomacy since the late 2000s? For many observers, the answer is Fiji. Fiji foreign policy post-2009 was the catalyst for many of the key institutional developments. Suspended from the forum, and from forum trade talks with the European Union, Fiji sought other ways of linking to the world and alternate regional arenas. It obviously had the key role in initiating the reinvigoration of MSG and the establishment of the PIDF, and the development of the Pacific group at the UN was a Fiji initiative. However, other leaders and countries supported Fiji's initiatives and nearly all Pacific Island states signed on to these initiatives.

Other observers have emphasised China's influence or the support of other geopolitical influences as being behind these developments. As argued by Michael O'Keefe in this volume, while the heightened global interest in the Pacific — particularly from China — acted as a facilitating environment for some of these developments, the driving force is provided by Pacific agency.

The changing geopolitics of the region since 2009 has created an enabling context to promote alternative diplomatic initiatives without relying on Australian or New Zealand funding. Chinese, Russian, Indonesian and United Arab Emirates funding is important for PIDF operations, for example.

The driving force for the wider support for the new Pacific diplomacy lies outside these explanations. It lies in a shared perception of an increasing strategic necessity to develop effective diplomatic strategies to deal with key issues of concern to regional leaders around trade, fishing, climate change, and decolonisation. This has been coupled with a realisation that the PIF was not meeting this need.

There were several reasons for this. One was the involvement of Australia and New Zealand in forum deliberations, making it hard to take strong positions on climate change or trade and decolonisation when their positions were antithetical. There has been a building resentment that the forum is no longer a place where the Pacific diplomatic voice can be developed and promoted, and that the regional diplomatic culture has reverted to the kind of hierarchical diplomatic culture that the forum was established to overcome. Rather than a diplomatic forum in which Australia and New Zealand were guests at the diplomatic table of the Pacific Island states, as originally conceived, the forum is now seen as one in which the interests of Australia and New Zealand prevail, to the detriment of island interests in engaging the global negotiations which matter to them.

The most obvious case is climate diplomacy in relation to carbon emissions targets, where the interests of Australia and New Zealand could not be more divergent from that of the island states. Indeed, in many ways climate change has become the nuclear testing issue of the 21st century. It has brought an urgency and united front to island collaboration. Where the Pacific states might in the past have tolerated some frustration with the domination of the regional agenda in the PIF by Canberra and Wellington — to pursue the War on Terror or to promote a regional neoliberal economic order — this tolerance may have reached its limit on the climate change issue.

One can see the rising anger, among the atoll states in particular, on the lack of action by the PIF in representing a joint position on this question because of the restraining influence of Australia and New Zealand on regional positions on emissions targets. For the Pacific Island states it is simply not possible to pursue an AOSIS position on emissions targets through an organisation in which Australia and New Zealand are present and determined to water down any positions that might affect their interests. This concern has been accentuated by the Australian Government's extreme position on the issue. Marshall Islands Foreign Minister Tony de Brum was reported in September 2014 as saying:

he and the leaders of other Pacific island nations were bewildered by what he called 'backsliding' on climate change by Australia, which the region had considered to be its 'big brother down south'. Probably one of the most frustrating events of the past year for Pacific islanders is Australia's strange behaviour when it comes to climate change … Island nations had watched with dismay not only the abolition of the carbon tax in Australia, but also the defunding of scientific advisory bodies … Pacific island nations no longer have time to debate climate change or even to engage in dialogue about how it might be mitigated — they need immediate action. Failure to act for us would mean disappearance under the sea by the turn of the century (O'Malley 2014).

A second reason is that the presence of Australia and New Zealand in the PIF creates a logistical problem for the Pacific Island states in seeking to use southern global coalitions — such as AOSIS and the G77 — to leverage their joint position on key issues such as climate change. With Australia and New Zealand being full members and the main financiers of the forum, the forum is not recognised as a southern grouping by these coalitions. This unnecessarily limits the bargaining power of Pacific states.

Thirdly, as we have seen, since the mid-1990s the forum had largely abandoned the field of joint diplomacy for a focus on regional integration. This emphasis culminated in the Pacific Plan of 2003 to 2013, which was a technocratic plan around an Australia–New Zealand agenda of pooling and integration either to secure the region in the War on Terror or to lower tariff barriers and harmonise laws in accordance with a neoliberal economic agenda. This was a far cry from the assertive Pacific voice of the 1980s dealing with the big issues confronting the region. Significantly 'joint diplomacy', or representing a Pacific voice, no longer appeared as part of the forum's definition of regionalism and its mandate.

A fourth explanation of a region-wide commitment to the new Pacific diplomatic network was the emergence of a more vocal Pacific leadership with a commitment to engage in regional debates more like the 1970s and 1980s. This has partly been due to Fiji's commitment to overcome the isolation imposed by the forum, but just as important have been the efforts of Marshall Islands leaders and President Tong of Kiribati to give leadership in climate change diplomacy in the region, and even globally, and the political will of the O'Neill Government in Papua New Guinea to work with Fiji in promoting the MSG, and an independent Pacific ACP secretariat.

Implications of the New Pacific Diplomacy

The new Pacific diplomacy represents an assertion of regional independence as well as a means for achieving more effective outcomes in regional and international forums. This has seen some marked successes: unprecedented financial returns from tuna access agreements as described by Transform Aqorau and Jope Tarai; reinscription of French Polynesia on the UN list of non-self-governing territories (see Nic Maclellan's chapter); the inclusion of 'stand-alone' sustainable development goals on oceans and climate change by the UN (as described by Fulori Manoa); and more coordinated advocacy on global climate policy by Pacific states (see George Carter's chapter). Meanwhile, members of the MSG continue to take significant steps towards regional integration (described in chapters by Sovaia Marawa, Wesley Morgan, and Tess Newton Cain) and the promotion of south–south cooperation. Pacific states have also successfully navigated what Dame Meg Taylor describes as 'a crowded and complex geopolitical landscape', in order to leverage recognition for their own development agenda (as evident, for example, in the broad support for the establishment of the PIDF).

These successes and achievements vindicate and validate the shifts that are underway in Pacific diplomacy, including the use of alternative, island-only groupings, and the forging of closer relationships with non-traditional partners. They also lend momentum to President Anote Tong's call to 'engage even more aggressively internationally'. Perhaps most significantly, given the current trends in Pacific regionalism, these successes can inspire greater political commitment to 'act regionally'. Ultimately, it is not frameworks or plans that matter to the leaders and their people, it is the results of regional endeavours that count.

The transformation of the regional architecture is central to the new Pacific diplomacy, but it remains an unfinished journey. As various chapters in this volume indicate, it is by no means obvious where this journey will end. Dame Meg Taylor refers to 'a complex regional architecture where geopolitics and finance play an important part'. The influence of these factors will continue to challenge Pacific regionalism, whether or not Australia and New Zealand play a different role in the PIF in future, and whatever role the PIDF assumes in the regional system. Tensions over policy positions on issues such as decolonisation and climate change are also likely to deepen in the future.

What the contributors to this volume all point to — from their various perspectives and positions — is the way the new Pacific diplomacy is creating opportunities and avenues for island countries to influence the regional order, in line with their own interests and aspirations. This will perhaps have most impact and resonance on future efforts to shape an approach to regional integration and diplomacy that will deliver fully on the expectations of the people of the Pacific.

Organisation of the Book

The book begins with an overview vision statement by President Anote Tong of Kiribati, which expresses many of the key ideas which motivate the new Pacific diplomacy. His plea for the Pacific to 'chart its own course' reflects the central importance of the promotion of regional self-determination at the centre of the new developments. A second theme with wider resonance is that the Pacific states should pursue this in unison. There is, he argues, a need for Pacific solidarity. Thirdly, he contends that Pacific leaders need to act from necessity and survival to confront new global forces threatening their way of life. They need to not only assert themselves 'aggressively' but to aspire to 'global leadership' in key diplomatic domains such as climate change, oceans management and sustainable development. To achieve this they need to change their mindset away from the view that small island states are necessarily dominated by developed countries and find confidence in the fact that they are large ocean states. He both recognises, and calls for, a paradigm shift in Pacific diplomacy.

The importance of President Tong's vision is reflected in the recognition given to them by Australia's Foreign Minister, Julie Bishop, when she argued that any review of regional architecture needed to take this sentiment into account. During her visit to Papua New Guinea in December 2014 she said, 'it was time for Pacific leaders to chart their own course … I really think it's time the Pacific leaders determine what they want for the 21st century and I'm hoping that Australia will be able to host that' (Wroe 2014).

The first section of the book focuses on the recent developments in the regional diplomatic system. These institutional developments and their underlying principles are what have caught peoples' imagination that something significant has been under way. Kaliopate Tavola's chapter presents the case for a radical restructuring of the Pacific Islands Forum without Australia and New Zealand. His considered case for an all-island state forum provides the economic and political logic for the Fiji Government position that it will only return to forum membership if Australia and New Zealand are asked to leave.

The New Pacific diplomacy was initially seen as in opposition to the Pacific Islands Forum system dominated by Australia and New Zealand. But as evident from Dame Meg Taylor's chapter, the forum is also undergoing major change consistent with many of the principles of the new Pacific diplomacy. This is recognised by Claire Slatter's critical examination of the claims surrounding the new Pacific framework, which she argues do seem to treat seriously the earlier critique of the forum in such areas as inclusion of NGOs. Maureen Penjueli offers a more trenchant critique of both the forum and the PIDF (despite its claims of inclusion) based on the past difficulties of civil society to be heard in Pacific regionalism.

Sandra Tarte then introduces the most prominent expression of the new Pacific diplomacy, the Pacific Islands Development Forum. As seen by many, this is potentially a competing organisation with the Pacific Islands Forum and is to be the heart of a Fiji-led alternative regional system. Fulori Manoa demonstrates that, while less well known, the dramatic rise of the Pacific Small Island Developing States (PSIDS) at the United Nations since 2009 has in many ways been the major success story of the new Pacific diplomacy.

The second section focuses on Fiji's key role in the new Pacific diplomacy showing its major role as a catalyst in key developments since 2009. Ambassador Mawi provides a government perspective emphasising the south–south aspect of this new regional foreign policy while Makereta Komai provides an analysis of the origins and implications of Fiji's new policies since 2009.

The third section deals with the geo-political context in which the new Pacific diplomacy emerged and developed. Michael O'Keefe argues that the changing geo-political context, including the rise of China and the entrance of new interests such as Russia and UAE, has provided an enabling environment for the new Pacific diplomacy but does not devalue 'the issues, trends and agendas that have shaped the evolution of a new approach to diplomacy from within the region'. Nicola Baker explores the dominant managerial role of Australia and New Zealand in Pacific regionalism, which is seen by many to provide the major stimulus to the development of a reactive new Pacific diplomacy. She argues that it is a mistake to lump together these two influential neighbours as if they are a joint actor or to assume that New Zealand simply follows Australia's lead.

The fourth section focuses on developments in sub-regionalism and the question of how they articulate with the broader regional diplomatic system. Tess Newton Cain explains the nature of the renaissance of the Melanesian Spearhead Group and highlights the issues provoked by its new prominence. Sovaia Marawa examines what is arguably the most impressive achievement in this recent renaissance — the negotiation of a Melanesia Free Trade Area — and why this was successful in contrast to the experience in the broader Pacific Islands region. Suzanne Lowe Gallen reviews the untold story of Micronesian diplomacy at the sub-regional level and how this complements Pacific regional diplomacy.

In the final three sections, the authors examine the key areas of contemporary Pacific diplomacy. Nicollette Goulding and George Carter introduce us to the complexity of Pacific approaches to climate diplomacy on the road to the 2015 Paris conference; Transform Aqorau and Jope Tarai examine new developments in tuna diplomacy; Wesley Morgan explores the assertive Pacific diplomacy in relation to Europe and Australia and New Zealand on trade; and Nic Maclellan examines the recent record of Pacific diplomacy on pushing for decolonisation in the case of French Polynesia and West Papua.

References

Boyce, P. and R. A. Herr, 1974, 'Microstate Diplomacy in the South Pacific', *Australian Outlook* 28(1), pp. 24–35.

Cooney, C., 2014, 'Fiji Shuns Pacific Forum Membership unless Australia and New Zealand are Expelled', ABC News online, 29 April. Available at: www.abc.net.au/news/2014-04-29/fiji-shuns-forum-membership/5418014, viewed 23 February 2015.

Fry, G., 1994, 'International Cooperation in the South Pacific: From regional integration to collective diplomacy', in W.A. Axline (ed.) *The Political Economy of Regional Cooperation*, Pinter Press, London, pp. 136–77.

Fry, G., 2005, 'Pooled Regional Governance in the Island Pacific: Lessons from history', *Pacific Economic Bulletin* 20(3), pp. 111–19.

Fry, G., 2015, 'Recapturing the Spirit of 1971: Towards a new regional political settlement in the Pacific', SSGM Discussion Paper 2015/3, The Australian National University, Canberra.

Komai, M., 2014, 'Reconfiguring Regionalism in the Pacific', PACNEWS, 9 April. Available at: www.pina.com.fj/?p=pacnews&m=read&o= 137809727550b7cea62a2839b85457.

O'Malley, N., 2014, 'Australia is a Pacific Island: It has a responsibility', *The Canberra Times*, 21 September.

Pareti, S., 2013, 'Fiji Pushes for Alternative to Pacific Islands Forum'. ABC News online, 6 August. Available at: www.abc.net.au/news/2013-08-06/fiji-forum/4867748.

Tarte, S., 2014, 'Regionalism and Changing Regional Order in the Pacific Islands', *Asia and the Pacific Policy Studies* 1(2), pp. 312–24.

Wroe, D., 2014, 'Foreign Minister Julie Bishop Backs Summit to Plan New "Regional Architecture" in the Pacific', *The Canberra Times*, 14 December. Available at: www.canberratimes.com.au/federal-politics/political-news/foreign-minister-julie-bishop-backs-summit-toplan-new-regional-architecture-in-pacific-20141214-126wh0.html.

2

'Charting its Own Course': A paradigm shift in Pacific diplomacy[1]

H.E. President Anote Tong

Our Pacific countries have come a long way as communal societies. Since the beginning of time, we began as very insular, traditional communities living together and sharing resources available to us from nature, until our recent history when we came into contact with the outside world through whalers, traders and missionaries, among others. This contact introduced our societies to the outside world, and there began our engagement in international relations, which has become so globalised and interdependent that we no longer can live in isolation. What happens in other parts of the world affect the lives of our communities. Climate change, world economic crises, food and fuel prices, conflicts and others are just some examples of the interdependent nature of the world we live in today. As we progress further into the 21st century we see the value of replicating communal systems at the regional and international levels as crucial to our advancement as a region and as a people.

[1] Keynote Address by President of Kiribati at the Launch of the Pacific International Relations Forum of the School of Government, Development and International Affairs of the University of the South Pacific, Holiday Inn, Suva, 9 October 2012.

I believe relationships, including international relations, are always about people. Yes, textbooks may define international relations as relations among states but what are states without people? International relations is therefore about managing relations among the peoples of our region and of our world. And, depending on how well we manage our relations, it is about living in harmony or otherwise with each other. It should be about helping each other. But we know very well from experience that that is not always the case.

I have just come back from the 67th United Nations General Assembly, the premier venue and forum for international relations, where I had the opportunity to meet, engage and relate with fellow leaders from around the world and from our region. We were all there to share our challenges and to share our visions on how this could be a better world for all.

But the question is: How effective is such a forum in dealing with global issues which require credible solutions? Do we really engage in dialogue with each other and do we really listen to each other's stories? As nation states we gather in New York every year to tell our own individual stories, and to listen, and assess who will deliver the most provocative statement this time. The challenge is how to get the world to not only hear our stories but support our efforts in delivering on those stories — that is, in making this a better and more secure world for all.

I do not pretend to be able to answer these questions, but I shall be happy to share with you my own experiences at the different UN meetings as well as within the region itself and elsewhere. At the last general assembly, I was very happy to note a number of developments which indicated the increased engagement of our region in some significant groupings within the United Nations: the Republic of the Fiji Islands is Chair of G77 and China, a grouping which is an influential negotiating block within the United Nations system; the Republic of Nauru is Chair of the Alliance of Small Island States, another influential negotiating group within the United Nations system; and the Independent State of Samoa will be hosting the Global Small Island Developing States Conference in 2014 — all demonstrating that even small island states can be relevant in international affairs.

In 2011 and this year we also had high-level visits into our region from the UN Secretary General: to the Solomon Islands, Kiribati, and then to the Pacific Islands Forum Meeting in Auckland. There were also visits from the European Union President, the Vice-Minister from the People's Republic of China, the Foreign Minister from Russia, and more recently the US Secretary of State. All these visits clearly indicate interest on the part of these countries in engaging with our region.

This is a new experience for our region and, quite frankly, I for one have not been able to fully analyse the reason for this new level of engagement on the part of these countries, and the implications for our foreign relations as individual countries and as a region. I must, however, be honest in saying that I find these initiatives most welcome indeed and worthy of close scrutiny. It is nice to be relevant.

But as we focus our attention on our relations beyond our region, we need also to look at how we relate with each other within our own region. There can be no doubt that there is greater strength in regional solidarity. This has been clearly demonstrated in many areas, including regional fisheries, trade negotiations, environmental management, climate change, and so on. But let me refer to the more recent initiative on ocean management — the Pacific Oceanscape. This was initiated in 2009 but is already gathering such strong momentum, reaching global proportions by the Rio+20 UN Conference on Sustainable Development with the launch of the World Bank initiative on Global Partnerships for Oceans on the margins of that conference.

Following the designation of marine protected areas (MPAs) by a number of Pacific countries, it was considered that, rather than embarking on fragmented management of these MPAs, it would be logical to link them up in order to coordinate and share experiences in their management — hence the Pacific Oceanscape. Since its formal endorsement by the Pacific Islands Forum in 2010, several countries have declared new and increasingly larger MPAs, including Cook Island, New Caledonia, Tokelau, and Australia. Other Pacific Island countries are also exploring their options for doing the same. However, the point that I wish to make here is that even though we may be small island states, we are large ocean states, and with a great deal more relevance in international affairs than we realised. The Pacific Ocean under the jurisdiction of Pacific Island countries is a significant portion of the earth's surface, and I believe it is important to keep reminding ourselves of this fact, especially in our foreign policy analysis.

The last issue on the international agenda that I wish to touch on is climate change. I have deliberately left it till last, because it is by far the most challenging issue in international relations, one which threatens the survival of a number of countries within our region and beyond, and indeed the planet as a whole. I have no desire to delve into the science except to say that every time new science comes up it is more alarming than the last one. The scenarios put forward guarantee that some countries will not have much of a future even if greenhouse gas emissions were reduced to zero. So that poses serious challenges for countries like Tuvalu, Marshall Islands, Kiribati, etc.

I have been quoted as saying many things about adaptation measures in response to the impacts of climate change. I have, time and time again, expressed my deep disappointment at the apparent lack of care by the many countries which can do the most to do something about this global scourge. I have even questioned the effectiveness of our international governance system in dealing with what is unquestionably an issue of survival which can only be addressed at the international level. How can we, in all conscience, and with all the science available to us, continue to regard this issue as a matter of sovereign right? Until we as a global community can commit to addressing this greatest moral challenge, there can never be any credibility or sincerity in any of our other initiatives.

Tonight's launch is timely, for I believe the Pacific is now entering a new phase — a new paradigm shift where the Pacific needs to chart its own course and lead global thinking in crucial areas such as climate change, ocean governance, and sustainable development. For a long time, we have been branded as 'small island developing states', since we emerged into the global stage as independent and sovereign states. Our mindset and vision of ourselves and the world has been influenced by this doctrine. More often than not, we see a world where developed countries will continue to dominate global politics and economics, whether we have a say in it or not. How much longer must we continue to remain pacific? Our very survival is in question.

Therefore, the message I wish to leave with you excellencies, ladies and gentlemen, but most especially with our Pacific International Relations Forum, is that we have no choice but to engage even more aggressively internationally, because the key to our survival will depend on whether international action is taken on climate change or not. I also wish to add that our strength is in our solidarity. We can and must continue to work diligently together to influence world opinion on these issues, because they matter to us.

The Regional
Diplomatic System

3

Towards a New Regional Diplomacy Architecture[1]

Kaliopate Tavola

Introduction

This paper makes the case for a new regional diplomacy architecture centred on a reformed Pacific Islands Forum (PIF). It does so on the strength of two existing developments that are clearly pointing in this direction. The first is the new evolving Pacific diplomacy and its overwhelming demand to create a Pacific voice for the Pacific Small Island Developing States (PSIDS) to best address the issues that genuinely matter to them. Such a voice will render legitimacy to the utterances of the PSIDS on global issues in the global arena; it will be conducive to creating and fostering genuine partnerships with development partners that have an interest in the Pacific; and it will ensure that PSIDS' own interests are not compromised by the national, international and geopolitical interests of Australia and New Zealand. This voice is already being expressed in real

---

1   Some of the ideas developed here were first developed in a series of seminar presentations: 'What We Have Learned About the Factors that Shape the Regional Institutional Structure and How Might this Structure be Optimised for the Benefits of Pacific Island Countries', What Can We Learn Symposium, 6–8 November 2012; 'PIDF and the Future of Regionalism', School of Government, Development and International Affairs, the University of the South Pacific, 5 September 2013; and 'Pacific Diplomacy and the Future Regional Architecture', Workshop on the New Pacific Diplomacy, University of the South Pacific, 4–5 December 2014.

developments in PSIDS at New York, and in the revitalisation of the Melanesian Spearhead Group (MSG) and the creation of the Pacific Islands Development Forum (PIDF).[2]

The second discourse is associated with Fiji's response to the invitation to return to the PIF after suspension: that as a condition of re-entry, Australia's and New Zealand's membership status in the forum should be reconsidered in the light of their development partner status, and the significance of other development partners in the region. This Fiji position is prominent and relevant in driving the need for a debate over a suitable architecture to meet future needs of the Pacific Island states. The Fiji case is a political imperative in the region. If it is not addressed with wisdom and foresight, the implications for Pacific regionalism — its unity, solidarity and utility — could be serious indeed. Regional PSIDS leaders have their work cut out. Australia and New Zealand in particular should be forward-looking.[3] There is little to gain from trying to retain the status quo when it has proven not to be delivering the goods. There is everything to gain, however, by looking through a fresh lens to a reconfigured regional architecture that promises better outcomes for all concerned, even to the extent of losing membership in an existing forum that has become outdated.

These two developments point to the need for a dialogue about reconfiguring the regional political architecture, and in particular to the membership and governance of the PIF. In this chapter, I develop a rationale for undertaking such a reconfiguration based on an assessment of the achievements of Pacific regionalism since 1971. I argue that Pacific regionalism has been disappointing: it has under-delivered in many areas. The assessment points to the constraining nature of the regional architecture. The membership of Australia and New Zealand in the current regional architecture creates a dichotomy and an over-diversity of membership that has not supported the optimisation of benefits from regional initiatives. This points to the need to move to a PIF without Australia and New Zealand, in order to bring about the optimisation of benefits that have long evaded the PSIDS. Increased benefits need to accrue to the PSIDS for Pacific regionalism to be worthwhile, useful, and meaningful, to bring about economic and social development to the PSIDS and to facilitate their integration into the global economy.

---

2   These institutional developments are detailed in Tarte (2014).

3   Greg Fry has just released a paper, 'Recapturing the Spirit of 1971: Towards a new regional political settlement in the Pacific' (2015a) which is intended to inform the proposed meeting in Sydney. He raised five areas of discussion in the paper. His third point is directed at Australia and New Zealand: 'recognising the need for Australia and New Zealand to return to a 1971 interpretation of equality and partnership within the PIF with possible consideration of a reintroduction of the island caucus system of the first PIF'. This chapter goes further, not only in recreating an island caucus, but formalising it into a forum which is formally and contractually linked to Australia and New Zealand.

However, given the continued significance of Australia and New Zealand to the PSIDS, and given our shared regionality, this chapter argues that Australia and New Zealand should still attract a special place in the new regional architecture. Furthermore, the need to reflect on the role of other development partners vis-à-vis the new regional architecture is not only an acknowledgement of global reality, but also a firm statement of PSIDS' own strategy in wanting to create its own Pacific vision in response to the increasing global focus on the region.

The Rationale for an All-PSIDS Forum

New Pacific diplomacy, whatever field it is conducted in, inevitably points to the need for a PSIDS-only forum. Utterances from an all-PSIDS forum will be seen as more legitimate, and consequently increases the audience and adherents of the PSIDS globally. An all-PSIDS forum will protect the integrity, coherence and sustainability of its critical issues. This avoids the current situation where these issues can come under pressure from Australia and New Zealand, with their often contradictory views, risking compromise of these issues and/or lowered prioritisation. An all-PSIDS forum will be most conducive for the growing south–south partnerships and is likely to benefit maximally from such partnerships. Such a forum can also benefit appropriately from north–south partnerships, especially if it repositions itself strategically in the global arena, driven by transformative leadership and backed by committed interlocutors who can bring energy and dynamism into their work. The partnerships for cooperation, rather than for dominance, are essential for the PSIDS.

An all-PSIDS forum is likely to effectively advance the evolving new Pacific diplomacy in all areas of significance to the PSIDS — climate change, environment, seabed mining, oceans and fisheries — and it may reclaim its place, which it seemed to have lost due to an increased focus on regional integration in recent times. An all-PSIDS forum will be a natural source of regional mandates for the PSIDS in the UN. This is critical, given the increasing impact of the PSIDS in the UN. The PSIDS group in the UN will play an important role in identifying and securing future partners and resources for the PSIDS, especially given the naturally high budgets that would be required to operate the new forum.

Regional Cooperation Lessons

Successful regionalism from the perspective of group (or club) membership is addressed in 'Toward a New Pacific Regionalism' (Asian Development Bank– Commonwealth Secretariat 2005, p. xv). It promotes having to draw lessons from the economic theory of clubs, and it draws two lessons: (i) a club must be self-sustaining; and, (ii) a club must provide a large pool of net benefits for each of its members. Understandably, the success or failure of a club depends on its benefits exceeding its costs. The Pacific Plan, which was developed to take the region 'toward a new Pacific regionalism', lost its way in the process. Political economy aspects — dominance of donors and development partners over the aspirations of the final beneficiaries, for instance — contributed to the malaise that drove the plan off course.

The existing regional architecture has under-delivered on regional cooperation. It is logical, therefore, to revisit the regional architecture for better delivery of critical regional issues. The need to increase benefits to members points to the need to reform the membership of PIF to bring about commonality, similarity of developmental status, interests, expectations, and aspirations. Such commonality will decrease the over-diversity of the group, especially the dichotomy of membership between the island states and their large, developed neighbours. This naturally leads to the reform to establish a PSIDS-only forum, without the participation of developed Organisation for Economic Cooperation and Development (OECD) countries. Such a reform is logical, given similar regional groupings around the world and their respective membership composition — for example, the Caribbean Community and Common Market (CARICOM) and a host of African regional economic communities (RECs). The current PIF stands out due to its mixed membership. If such mixed membership were the modus operandi in RECs, what has prevented Australia and New Zealand from inviting the PSIDS to be parties to the Australia–New Zealand Closer Economic Relations Trade Agreement (ANZCERTA)?

Reducing the costs of regional cooperation is problematic for PSIDS. In the first place, conducting regional cooperation in the Pacific is costly for a host of reasons, including long distances, high costs of travel, poor infrastructure, and diseconomies of isolation. There is still scope, however, for cost reduction through more effective and creative economies of scale, and creative application of IT in the conduct of meetings. Increased costs from diseconomies of isolation give rise to the prospect of a sub-regional approach within Pacific regionalism, with the aim of cost-effectiveness through more focused selectivity of issues of interests, economy and complementarity — a trend already evident, although each sub-region may need to be more strategic in terms of its operations and raison d'être.

Costs subsidisation of regional cooperation in the region will abate with increased contributions from PSIDS members over time. Increased contributions are a factor of national and regional development, economic growth, and meaningful and productive integration into the global economy for the PSIDS.

Increased ownership of funding/costs of regional cooperation by the PSIDS will remove the price distortion currently experienced where Australia and New Zealand subsidise regional meetings, and where beneficiaries or participants of regional meetings are not the financiers but are usually incentivised to attend meetings, even if outcomes of the meetings are not immediately relevant. There is, however, a time lag before such ownership can be established. In the meantime, cost-subsidisation is a development cost for the region that needs to be met. This is best promoted in the context of PSIDS being treated as a 'special case'. The UN is united on this matter.[4] As such, it can be envisaged that more flexibility, reduced conditionality and greater creativity in design will be factored into the determination of development funds for the PSIDS.

In promoting the primacy of PSIDS interests in the context of Pacific regionalism, it is imperative therefore to reform Australia's and New Zealand's funding obligations. The reform does not necessarily entail having to sever the funding relationship. The funds are needed. What it entails, however, is the creation of a mechanism that allows Australia and New Zealand to be at arm's length regarding the use of their own funds. This would logically have an impact on the configuration of Pacific regionalism and of the membership of PIF.[5]

Market Integration Lessons

The dichotomy of existing PIF membership, with the developed OECD members (Australia and New Zealand) at one end of the spectrum and the 14 small island developing states at the other end, has not encouraged joint efforts to optimise their economic integration. The preferential and non-reciprocal South Pacific Regional Trade and Economic Cooperation Agreement (SPARTECA), for instance, would have been welcomed for its generous concessions; and the Fijian textile, clothing and footwear industry took full advantage of these concessions to grow the industry. However, the trade agreement failed to address the supply factors of the other PSIDS' principal industries.

---

4   See, for example, A/RES/66/288, Resolution 66/288, 'The Future We Want', adopted by the UNGA, 27 July 2012, paragraphs 178–180 establish the special case for small island developing states. See also UN Economic and Social Commission for Asia and the Pacific (ESCAP) Resolution 68/1, adopted after a strong submission by Pacific leaders at the ESCAP Commission in 2012. See UN ESCAP (2012, p. 6).

5   Consideration of the treatment of Australia and New Zealand differently in the context of Pacific regionalism and as regards PIF's membership is not a totally new subject. A number of regional commentators have given their sides of the story recently. See, for example, O'Keefe (2012), Grynberg (2012), and Tavola (2012). 'Toward a New Pacific Regionalism' (Asian Development Bank–Commonwealth Secretariat 2005, p. 80) had floated a similar sentiment in 2005.

Fast forward to 2015, the reciprocal Pacific Agreement on Closer Economic Relations (PACER) Plus negotiations are struggling to conclude. Two issues of development resources and labour mobility, critical to the PSIDS, are likely to scupper these negotiations, due to the inflexibility of Australia and New Zealand on these issues. An all-PSIDS forum will remove such dichotomy of membership. Members of the new PIF will have the same interests, in that they are all developing countries, notwithstanding their geographical diversity, and are all trying to integrate successfully into the global economy while trying to manage the overwhelming onslaught of globalisation. Market access and other concessions offered by developed economies will still be available and welcome under the proposed new regional architecture. However, their conduct will be guided by the provisions of the overarching agreement that will be negotiated in good faith.

A major constraint to regional cooperation and the delivery of outcomes under market integration is the lack of national capacity. This remains a challenge notwithstanding the efforts that have been directed at human resources development. This problem will not disappear by reconfiguring relations with Australia and New Zealand. What can happen, however, is that a modality for resolving the problem could be found in the context of an all-PSIDS forum. It is envisaged that much benefit will come through deepened regional integration, but in an unconventional way — through regional integration on the basis of non-trade issues, for example, on capacity building, climate change, and environment. It is further envisaged that since the modality is unconventional, it may not be of interest to Australia and New Zealand. Developed countries like Australia and New Zealand would tend to see more gains and value in conventional regional integration, modelled on the European Union, for instance.

Regional Delivery of Services (Pooling)

Voluntary regionalism is a constraint to regional pooling of resources. The choice to shift away to involuntary regionalism (to introduce degrees of binding into collective decisions), is not going to come automatically to the new PIF, as suggested in this chapter. It is envisaged, however, that the new scenario created in having an all-PSIDS forum will be conducive to redressing the problem vis-à-vis the current PIF. In the first place, the diversity of membership will be reduced. Commonality of interests will therefore tend to be a driving force in decision-making. Secondly, an all-PSIDS forum is likely to learn and adopt lessons from the sub-region that shares the same membership. This is especially so if, for example, a sub-region is to recommend binding decisions after it has been trialled in that sub-region. This is based on the precept that, once trialled in a smaller, more homogenous group, champions from that group can then advocate to the larger group.

Trialling binding of decisions at the sub-regional level can even be part of a larger exploratory intervention on the political economy of the group. It is postulated by a number of commentators of RECs that poor management of the political economy aspects of regionalism has contributed to the poor state of these RECs. For the new regional architecture, supported by a number of existing sub-regions, it is considered best strategy to trial issues of this nature in the smaller group before introduction into the larger group. In any case, studies on the political economy of Pacific regionalism are critical.

Conclusion on Lessons Drawn

If the lessons drawn are taken seriously and implemented effectively, we can anticipate improved results from Pacific regionalism in all its phases. To date, Pacific regionalism seems to be proceeding conventionally — linearly, though in its early stages. Pacific regionalism has to proceed in the collective interests of the PSIDS. Its approach and phases of development, however, will become evident under the new architecture. The prospect of an unconventional approach regarding regional integration on the basis of non-trade issues is flagged in this chapter. It is also relevant to underline that efforts at regional integration should not necessarily displace PSIDS' collective efforts at diplomacy at the regional and global levels, especially diplomacy relating to global issues critical to PSIDS. Since 2002, PIF and PSIDS have devoted a lot of time and effort to negotiating trade agreements such as economic partnership agreements, the Pacific Island Countries Trade Agreement (PICTA), PICTA trade in services, and PACER Plus. This work is still continuing.

The Proposed Regional Architecture

The first step in establishing this new architecture is to declare an all-PSIDS forum without Australia and New Zealand. The designation of PSIDS is the preferred designation under the new architecture for the prospect of strategic linkage to the UN. The 14 PSIDS will immediately constitute the membership of the new PIF. The PIF Secretariat (PIFS) would continue as the secretariat of the new PIF but be subjected to reform in the near future. The question of PIFS being substituted by PIDF has been raised in some circles. This however is not being implied here. The recommended role of PIDF as a Council of Regional Organisations in the Pacific (CROP) agency, providing technical advice to the new PIF, is flagged below.

The second step is to recognise and acknowledge the existing sub-regional bodies as the constituent building blocks of the new PIF. These sub-regional bodies are the MSG, Polynesian Leaders Group (PLG), Micronesian Chief Executives' Summit (MCES), Pacific–African, Caribbean and Pacific (PACP), Smaller Island States (SIS), and PSIDS themselves: members of the Alliance of Small Island States (AOSIS). Sub-regions are to determine the issues that are best handled at that level and those that are best treated at the new PIF level. Criteria of allocation of these issues should be based on value-adding prospects, complementarity, relative efficiency and efficacy, and best trialling prospects of certain issues (binding commitment to decisions made, political economy, and cost benefit analysis of regional initiatives) in the interests of the larger collective. The new PIF should formalise its links to the PSIDS in the UN.

Thirdly, membership of the new PIF is to grow organically to incorporate all 23 Pacific Island countries and territories that are currently members of the Secretariat of the Pacific Regional Environment Programme (SPREP) and Secretariat of the Pacific Community (SPC) — 'organically' being the operative word, implying care, vision, strategy, and utilitarianism. Membership is to also incorporate NGOs and eventually the private sector. This is an important point for Fiji, which has been particularly vocal on this matter. Modality of incorporation of their membership, however, can be informed and prescribed by the lessons from PIDF (an inclusive approach) and from MSG (described as Inter-Governmental Body (IGB) plus, given that its membership comprises governments and a political party). This can also be informed by future conversations on the merit and demerit of the concept of an IGB in the context of being inclusive in the name of sustainable development. Strategically, therefore, we should remain open to all prospects of representation and engagement, including preparatory parallel conferences of different constituencies leading to joint summits.

Fourthly, the establishment of the new PIF should also signal the start of essential reforms in the region. Given the duplication of issues amongst some of the CROP agencies, including PIFS, and the resultant inefficiency and inefficacy in implementation, monitoring and evaluation of these regional issues, there should be a follow-up study to the 2005 Regional Institutional Framework (RIF) study.[6] This is particularly pertinent, since the recommendations of the 2005 study were not fully implemented; some were subsequently misdirected. Politicisation of issues was partially to blame. This follow-up RIF could have an expanded terms of reference to address and rationalise the duplication of issues that exist in the region amongst the CROP agencies, with the aim of bringing

---

6   See Hughes (2005).

efficiency and efficacy in the delivery of services in the region; to review the duties and structure of the secretariat in the context of the new PIF; and to review the optimisation of benefits in all regional initiatives.

Fifthly, the prospect of exploring PIDF as a CROP agency should also be pursued. PIDF has special significance for Fiji, given its conception during the period of Fiji's suspension from PIF. Its significance is also built around the inclusivity of its membership. It is imperative, therefore, that lessons drawn from this inclusive approach, especially the inclusivity applied, should inform future work on membership of the new PIF, as proposed above. The question of PIDF becoming the secretariat for the new PIF does not arise in this reconfiguration of the regional architecture. This chapter presents PIDF as a possible CROP agency. Its competence lies in the proliferation of green growth policies in the Pacific, and here it stands unchallenged as the sole purveyor of green growth technical advice to the new PIF.

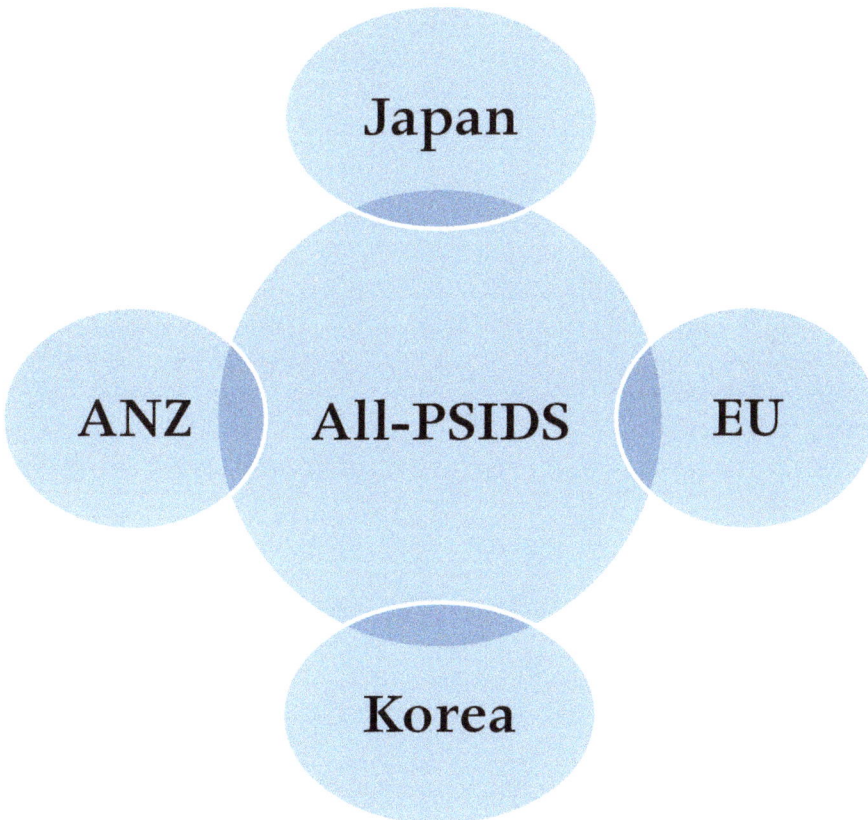

Figure 3.1: Proposed inter-regional structure of new Pacific Islands Forum
Source: Author's research.

The New Pacific Islands Forum and Australia and New Zealand

Any regionalism project is costly. This is particularly true for Pacific regionalism, given the regional geography, the tyranny of distance, and the diseconomies of isolation. Even though the reform calls for a membership reconfiguration without Australia and New Zealand, it is still critical to retain their goodwill and generosity by way of a formally negotiated inter-regional agreement. This is only logical given, inter alia, our shared regionality and history with these two developed countries. The justification of continuing relations and partnerships with Australia and New Zealand goes beyond funding and financial considerations. What is being envisaged is a win-win situation for both parties of the existing PIF. Such an agreement will bind the two parties together in future. The provisions of the agreement will be negotiated in good faith and to focus on areas of need for both sides. The inter-regional agreement would not in any way undermine bilateral relations and could enhance bilateral commitments, by providing a focus on development and funding gaps that can be filled or on areas that can augment or supplement bilateral initiatives. For Fiji, coming out of suspension and sanctions, this bilateral scenario offers exciting prospects.

It is thus proposed that a special agreement be negotiated and established between the new PIF and Australia and New Zealand. Such an agreement would represent an overarching agreement between the two parties and could be modelled on the European Union–Africa Caribbean Pacific Cotonou Agreement. The overarching agreement would include political, economic and development aspects of the new relations. PACER and PACER Plus could be appropriately situated in the agreement. The labour mobility schemes could also be specifically reflected in the agreement. The prospect of an Inter-PIF–ANZCER agreement could also be pursued should it prove imperative for Australia and New Zealand particularly.

The New PIF and Other Development Partners

It is also logical, reasonable and strategic to negotiate and establish similar agreements with other development partners who seek genuine and forward-looking partnerships with PSIDS. It is imperative for PSIDS therefore to identify the relative strengths of prospective development partners and seek, through negotiated treaty provisions, ways and means to take full advantage of these strengths in the resourcing of their development plans.

The overarching agreement between the new PIF and Australia and New Zealand provides a possible template for use in negotiating agreements between the new PIF and other development partners. Agreements are to be negotiated with all current development partners as a starting point. New development partners can be added subsequently. For some partners — Japan, Korea, and the UN — new multilateral/plurilateral agreements can be formulated and built upon on the basis of ongoing unilateral programmes/conferences/summits. Others are to be selected on the basis of their respective benefits (for example, benefits that accrue from pooled services funded from development resources), and their strategic and geopolitical significance (south–south relations, strategic and innovative north–south relations). In all cases, the new PIF is to recognise the strength that each development partner offers and negotiate to take full advantage of that specific strength.

Conclusion

In his Devpolicy Blog, Professor Greg Fry provided four scenarios for the future configuration of regional architecture (Fry 2015b). His third scenario was that of doing nothing and maintaining the status quo. From his analysis of that scenario, he drew the following conclusions: (i) Fiji will not resume PIF membership; (ii) Fiji will continue promotion of PIDF, PSIDS and the MSG; (iii) the region will see the entrenchment of two competing Pacific regional systems with overlapping membership; and, (iv) regional unity will be hampered and scarce human and financial resources will be spread thinly and inefficiently.

I agree with this assessment. To do nothing and simply maintain the status quo will drastically set Pacific regionalism backward and all forum island countries will be worse off. This is the logical conclusion from the analysis of past lessons developed here. Moreover, in Fiji's absence from PIF, the region will also lack a maverick to prick our collective consciences on occasions when we lose sight of our regional diplomatic aspirations.

References

Asian Development Bank–Commonwealth Secretariat, 2005, 'Toward a New Pacific Regionalism', Asian Development Bank–Commonwealth Secretariat Joint Report to the Pacific Islands Forum Secretariat. Available at: www.adb. org/sites/default/files/publication/28797/pacific-regionalism-vol2.pdf.

Fry, G., 2015a, 'Recapturing the Spirit of 1971: Towards a new regional political settlement in the Pacific', SSGM Discussion Paper 2015/3, The Australian National University, Canberra.

Fry, G., 2015b, 'What Now for the Pacific Regional Architecture Debate?' *DevPolicy Blog*, Development Policy Centre, The Australian National University, Canberra.

Grynberg, R., 2012, 'Healing the Forum Divide', *Island Business*, August.

Hughes, A.V., 2005, 'Strengthening Regional Management: A review of the architecture for regional co-operation in the Pacific', report to the Pacific Islands Forum, consultative draft. Available at: www.sopac.org/sopac/docs/ RIF/06_AV%20Hughes%20 Report_CONSULTATIVE_DRAFT%281%29.pdf.

O'Keefe, M., 2012, 'PIF at a Crossroad', *Island Business*, August. Available at: www.islandsbusiness.com/in-print/item/463-pif-at-a-crossroad.

Tarte, S., 2014, 'Regionalism and Changing Regional Order in the Pacific Islands', *Asia and Pacific Policy Studies* 1(2), pp. 312–24.

Tavola, K., 2012, 'Mighty Neighbours to East and West: Impact and Opportunities for Economic Growth,' presentation, Club de Madrid Symposium, Papeete, Tahiti, 5–6 July.

UN ESCAP, 2012, 'Green Economy in a Blue World: Pacific perspectives 2012', ESCAP Pacific Office, Suva, Fiji.

4

The Future of the Pacific Islands Forum and the Framework for Pacific Regionalism[1]

Dame Meg Taylor

Thank you for the opportunity to speak on the future of the Pacific Islands Forum and the Framework for Pacific Regionalism. These are important topics to discuss at an important juncture in our region's history. Allow me to acknowledge the Vice-Chancellor, Professor Rajesh Chandra, and his staff for the warm welcome and for extending the invitation to me. This is the first public lecture that I have been engaged with since taking up office and I am sure it will not be the last. Let me state for the record that I have been in office for five months, so I seek your understanding that anything delivered here comes from within that limited time span.

Since taking up office, I have visited 10 countries and will visit the remaining six before the leaders meeting in September. It has been very useful for me to make face-to-face contact with the leaders, including key officials to whom the secretariat belongs. I also want to state that I have been given a term of three

---

1   Address by Secretary-General of the Pacific Islands Forum Secretariat, Diplomacy Roundtable, School of Government, Development and International Affairs, Faculty of Business and Economics, the University of the South Pacific, 27 May 2015.

years in which to successfully implement the Framework for Pacific Regionalism. Let me assure you that I will be working very hard with my staff at the secretariat to ensure that we deliver on the Framework for Pacific Regionalism.

As a region, we face numerous shared challenges: managing our ocean and fisheries resources, our land-based natural resources, and trying to manage and mitigate the effects of climate change. Economic development remains elusive for the large part across the region, while dependence on development assistance remains high, and in some parts of our region it is necessary for the delivery of basic services.

There is unprecedented interest by a wide range of external actors in our region — some new, some old — and all have combined to present a crowded and complex geopolitical landscape. In addition, our regional architecture is more complex and varied than it once was. Part of this complexity arises from the way in which the regional architecture is governed and financed. Some regional institutions have members who are metropolitan countries and donor partners. Many regional institutions do work encouraged by or in response to their funding sources. These configurations present a complex regional architecture where geopolitics and finance play an important part. It is important that we, as individuals and citizens of the countries and territories of the Pacific, are aware of these complexities.

Against this backdrop, the Framework for Pacific Regionalism presents an opportunity, both for the region and for the Pacific Islands Forum. For the region, it presents an opportunity to work towards the deeper form of regionalism that was always envisaged under the Pacific Plan, but was not delivered on; a regionalism that would acknowledge and recognise our shared challenges, draw on our many shared strengths, build the political will to act collectively, and devise and carry out effective, collective solutions to these challenges — whether through technical or political means.

The Framework for Pacific Regionalism also signals or demands a number of shifts on the part of the Pacific Islands Forum. These include a greater political commitment to regionalism; a more inclusive Pacific Islands Forum; a forum that is open to robust and frank discussion about regionalism; and a secretariat to the Pacific Islands Forum that offers high-level policy advice to support and inform leaders' discussions and decisions.

I will begin this discussion by talking very broadly about the Framework for Pacific Regionalism and some of its key features. I will then say more about the shifts to the Pacific Islands Forum and its secretariat that the new framework signals. First, I will make a few introductory comments.

Introductory Comments

The first is a caveat: that it is important to recognise that regionalism must be about improving the lives of the people of the Pacific, and about fulfilling the goals and objectives set out in the framework. Regionalism cannot be pursued for its own sake. There must be some tangible benefit that it brings about. If regionalism is not doing this, then the strategy must be thoroughly evaluated.

It is worth pointing out that the debate and the discussion about regionalism and its benefit is ongoing. There is never a point where the value of regionalism is assumed. It is continually brought into question and challenged. Regionalism is by no means an assumed good. Regionalism is something that must be revised and revisited and made relevant and appropriate. Our role, and the role of those who work in regional institutions, is to ensure that regionalism remains relevant, and that it delivers tangible benefits to the people of the Pacific.

The second is that the Framework for Pacific Regionalism, and regionalism more generally, is not intended as a replacement for national effort. We will always, first and foremost, think and act as citizens of our own Pacific Island countries, no matter the level of regional integration in the Pacific. There is no doubting the primary sense of identity that we derive from our nationalities, from our culture and custom. There is often a perception that regionalism will somehow displace nationalism or do away with national sovereignty or identity. This is not, by any means, assumed under the Framework for Pacific Regionalism, and it is also worth noting that the priorities that come about through the framework must complement national effort. Any encroachment on national sovereignty under the framework needs to be undertaken with the greatest caution.

Thirdly, in spite of these caveats, there is clearly a role for regionalism. I see our region as being one of great opportunity and promise. I said that we face numerous shared challenges, but that we also possess abundant natural and human resources. Our ability to deliver on our potential depends in large part on our ability to think and act collectively — not only at the political level, but also at the local level. Additionally, our collective voice at the global level on key issues to our region is of continuing importance to our collective well-being.

Fourthly, I earlier made mention of the regional architecture. What I would say in respect to the range of actors in the regional space — whether at regional level or sub-regional level, such as the Melanesian Spearhead Group, the Polynesian Leaders Group and the Micronesian Leaders Summit, or whether they represent special interests as in the case of the parties to the Nauru Agreement — is that our goals and interests are fundamentally one and the same: we all want to improve the lives of the people of the Pacific and we all recognise that working collectively at some level can help to achieve that goal.

Finally, the role of the Pacific Islands Forum Secretariat amongst the range of regional institutions is clear. We have a mandate to carry out the wishes and the decisions of the leaders of the 16 independent forum countries of the Pacific. We also have a responsibility to provide leaders and officials with high quality policy advice in support of their work of making good regional public policy decisions. I am committed to ensuring that the forum secretariat delivers on these expectations, now and into the future. I also want to ensure that we have good working relationships with other regional and sub-regional institutions, to ensure that we are delivering effectively and efficiently on the regional agenda under the framework.

The forum secretariat's position in relation to Fiji is quite clear. Our position is to respect and support the decisions taken by forum leaders. We welcome the recent pronouncements by the Hon. Prime Minister of Fiji regarding their participation in all forum activities at the public service, technical and ministerial levels, and we look forward to advancing the work and development of the region together with Fiji. You would have noted in the media over the past week that Fiji's Supervisor of Elections recently led a Forum Election Observer mission to Bougainville, providing important technical and logistical leadership to the elections observation there. This is indeed encouraging for the forum and its secretariat.

I also wish to remind us of successful examples of regional cooperation where shared commitments and values have led to some tangible benefits. Our very own regional University of the South Pacific is a case in point. This university is not only the place that produces our next generation of leaders and thinkers, but it is a very important hub for interactions between peoples from right across our large and diverse region.

The Framework for Pacific Regionalism

You will recall that the eminent person, Sir Mekere Morauta, and his review team canvassed the opinions of over 700 people across the region and took in over 70 public submissions during the review of the Pacific Plan in 2013. It was a widely consultative process, and one which overwhelmingly called for an overhaul of the Pacific Plan. The review team noted that the plan was in many ways a highly productive regional strategy and that it was not delivering the kind of regionalism that was originally intended. There was little political buy-in from leaders, and the regional agenda was largely driven by officials and regional agencies. As a result, the number of so-called priorities produced under the Pacific Plan was unworkable; in one year alone there had been up to 37 priorities presented to leaders at their annual meeting. In short, regionalism had lost its politics under the Pacific Plan.

One of the review team's major recommendations was to replace the Pacific Plan with the Framework for Pacific Regionalism, which has now been in place since its endorsement in Palau by the Pacific Islands Forum leaders in July 2014. As a strategy for delivering on regionalism, the framework is a flexible one. It contains a vision, and a set of values and objectives, as well as a process for identifying the region's public policy priorities. But it does not prescribe any specific priorities, as the Pacific Plan did. It does not set out a timetable for delivering on regionalism. It does not prescribe a particular form of regionalism for the Pacific to adopt or take up. This flexibility provides space — space for the region's citizens to voice their concerns and raise initiatives for leaders; space for a more robust dialogue at leaders' level about regionalism; and space for regionalism to progress at a pace that is appropriate and suited to the many stakeholders concerned.

A set of tests for regional action is identified in the framework. These tests are central to assessing and selecting the regional initiatives that will be put forward for leaders' consideration and discussion at their forum this year. These tests will help to ensure that initiatives have a regional character, which benefit people, and require political oversight. These tests will provide rigour to regional priorities. The specialist sub-committee on regionalism — with a make-up of representatives from Melanesia, Polynesia, Micronesia, Australia and New Zealand, small islands states, civil society and the private sector, and with the secretary general as chair of the committee — is tasked with selecting a limited number of initiatives, submitted by citizens and organisations from within the region, for leaders to consider at their annual meeting later this year.

Monitoring and reporting on the framework will be a priority. In recognising this, we will need to develop a set of indicators and measures to ensure that we are making effective progress, so as to ensure that these measures are aligned to the sustainable development goals. This reporting will not be confined to the regional initiatives that arise from the framework. Reporting will also be carried out on the framework itself to ensure that we monitor and report on the 'state of regionalism', that is, to ascertain whether regionalism is effective and is delivering on the expected objectives.

I wish to highlight four features of the framework.

An Emphasis on Focused Political Conversations

Out of a recognition of the fact that regionalism had lost its politics under the Pacific Plan, the framework places an emphasis on creating the time and space for leaders to have open and robust discussions about regionalism — about what the regional agenda should be, about what forms of regionalism are appropriate, and about the pace at which regionalism should occur. The opportunity for leaders to discuss the strengths and weaknesses of regional approaches is fundamental to the success of the framework — without these conversations occurring at the political level, regionalism will not progress or deliver on expectations.

Changes to the Regional Architecture

The Council of Regional Organisations in the Pacific (CROP) structure, which is synonymous with Pacific regionalism, is not without its issues. The deeper form of regionalism called for by the framework requires a more coordinated approach and effective regional governance, including a set of financing arrangements, if it is to be effectively realised. At the core of this is analysis of how collective effort and action is best governed and incentivised. In short, we need to interrogate how the network of regional agencies can be better positioned to deliver on the framework, acknowledging that, at an institutional level, their specific mandates are clear.

The secretariat has already started work in this area by reviewing the CROP working groups, to ensure that these groups are well positioned to deliver on the regional agenda under the framework. We will also shortly carry out a review of all meetings that require the attendance of officials, ministers and leaders, to ensure that these meetings are relevant and effective, and worth the time taken by participants to actually attend, and that there is policy cohesion between meetings and the work of regional organisations. Most importantly, we are also conducting a review of the governance and financing arrangements of CROP with the Secretariat of the Pacific Community, to ensure that these arrangements are also positioned to deliver on regionalism under the framework.

Greater Inclusiveness

The process for determining the region's priorities under the framework calls for any and all members of the Pacific Islands Forum community to submit ideas and concepts around key issues for the region. This marks a fundamental shift away from previous practice, whereby priorities were largely determined by officials or regional agencies, with very little consultation of the broader public. From our consultations thus far, the opening up of this process has been largely welcomed by regional civil society and private sector stakeholders.

A Shift in the Development Paradigm

The framework represents a major shift in the development paradigm. We are talking about a process whereby the region's priorities — political, social, economic, and developmental — will, over time, be determined primarily by the Pacific Islands Forum leaders through an open public policy process. This is a change to current practice. Presently, it is an uphill battle for leaders to articulate and put forward their own collective agenda at the regional level, when there are so many actors and partners at the table.

Future of the Pacific Islands Forum

What does the framework mean for the future of the Pacific Islands Forum? I suggest that it signals at least four important shifts for the Pacific Islands Forum.

Political Commitment to Regionalism by Leaders

The Pacific Islands Forum leaders have mandated the implementation of the framework, now it is incumbent on them to drive it forward; our leaders need to make a political commitment to taking collective approaches to addressing common challenges. This requires collective political will to act regionally, recognising the inherent and natural tensions that exist between national and regional imperatives. Ongoing dialogue is important if we are to sustain this collective commitment to regionalism over the long term.

A More Inclusive Pacific Islands Forum

The framework sets out an open, inclusive public policy process — one that seeks the views of those beyond government and the usual set of stakeholders, in a meaningful and practical way. In particular, this process seeks the views of those who did not previously have access to regional priority-setting processes: civil society, the private sector, community groups, academia, and citizens, for example. This inclusive approach requires a shift on the part of the Pacific Islands Forum and its secretariat; it means incorporating the views of those outside the traditional set of stakeholders. There will be some challenges in the short term, and we will have our points of difference around issues, but the fundamental tenet here is that we work together and that we harness the strengths of those in civil society and in the private sector.

Inclusivity, however, cannot be limited to this process. It needs to be more than a buzzword. The forum secretariat must engage with civil society and the private sector more routinely in its work. We need to recognise the important role that civil society plays in the regional space.

I have begun to reach out to a number of regional civil society and private sector organisations, some of whom are in the audience today. We have engaged formally and informally, and I am encouraged by our conversations and interactions.

I also think that there is a role for academia in this new paradigm. The forum secretariat can do more to bridge the divide between policy and research. Sound policy is based in part on robust knowledge and analysis, and I am very interested in developing closer relationships with the University of the South Pacific and other universities and think tanks in the region in order to develop partnerships that support and enhance regional policy making.

A More Effective Post-Forum Dialogue

The framework calls for improved and more meaningful political discussions at the regional level. Some have expressed concerns that the post-forum dialogue is not the productive mechanism for political dialogue that it should be. There are issues with the format of the discussion, and many of our regional partners reduce the effectiveness of the post-forum dialogue by bringing bilateral issues to the discussion table.

The process for priority-setting that the framework calls for needs to be accompanied by an improvement in the quality of our conversations about regionalism, and this includes those conversations with our post-forum dialogue partners. We are already conducting work in this space in consultation with our members, with our post-forum dialogue partners, and with the government of Papua New Guinea, who will host this year's leaders forum.

A Fit-For-Purpose Secretariat to the Pacific Islands Forum

The Framework for Pacific Regionalism calls for some fundamental changes to the Pacific Islands Forum, and there is a need to ensure that the secretariat is fit for purpose in light of these changes. An external review commissioned by senior management has just been carried out in the secretariat, and in response to this review, a change process aligned to the implementation of the framework is now in place, to ensure that we have the right institutional set up within the secretariat to deliver on the framework over the short- and long-term future. The framework demands a number of important and fundamental changes for the secretariat, so it is important that we look at ourselves to see whether we are fit-for-purpose to deliver.

The secretariat will also have to position itself to provide responsive, high quality, and high-level policy advice to the leaders in support of their discussions and decisions on regional issues. This policy advice should not only be about issues, but also about the state of regionalism, and the extent to which regionalism is valued. Leaders' decisions on regionalism will be enhanced and strengthened by quality policy advice.

The forum secretariat also needs to find its optimal position in relation to other CROP agencies. The secretariat's role is primarily political and policy-oriented, although it is the case that we currently implement projects and activities. The way in which we align ourselves and work with and support our fellow CROP agencies will be vital in delivering effectively on the regional agenda under the framework.

Conclusion

In summary, the framework calls for a Pacific Islands Forum that is willing to embrace a deeper level of regionalism; that incorporates and harnesses all perspectives and opinions within the regional community; and that is willing to take a leadership role. It will lead to a strengthened Pacific Islands Forum — one that provides genuine regional leadership, that responds to the challenges of the region, and that embraces and practices the principles of inclusivity. I believe that it is important for the Pacific Islands Forum to continue to play a leadership role in the regional space, given it is the only political grouping comprising all 16 independent Pacific Islands countries. However, it is important that the Pacific Islands Forum make the kinds of shifts that the Framework for Pacific Regionalism demands, to deliver fully on the expectations that the people of the Pacific have of us and of regionalism.

5

The New Framework for Pacific Regionalism: Old kava in a new tanoa?

Claire Slatter

In October 2005, in Port Moresby, Pacific Island leaders adopted the Pacific Plan. Described as 'the master strategy for strengthening regional cooperation and integration in the Pacific', it was greeted with much criticism from academics, non-government organisations (NGOs) and citizens' groups in the region.[1] The outcome of an Eminent Persons Group (EPG) set up by the Pacific Islands Forum in 2003, the Pacific Plan was first of all seen as the brainchild of New Zealand, particularly several senior civil servants from New Zealand including Department of Foreign Affairs and Trade personnel, who were part of the team supporting the EPG, were believed to have largely authored it. The plan was criticised for paying lip service to Pacific values and cultures, while primarily endorsing a neoliberal economic agenda that ran counter to Pacific peoples' interests. Critics argued that it failed to address the needs of Pacific people, particularly the poor and marginalised, and was out of touch with the lived realities of Pacific Islanders (Coates 2006, p. 3).

---

1   Oxfam New Zealand's Executive Director at the time, Barry Coates, cited the following criticisms of the Pacific Plan by civil society organisations, academics and community representatives: 'a lack of genuine consultation, the lack of focus on the needs of those who suffer hardship and injustice, and insufficient connection to the reality of people's lives' (Coates 2006).

The 2013 review of the Pacific Plan offered an opportunity to imagine a future desired by Pacific Island people, and to create an authentically Islander-centred development framework. Public submissions received by the review team, headed by former Papua New Guinea Prime Minister Sir Mekere Morauta, reportedly included 37 submissions from civil society organisations (CSOs) and/or leaders, out of a total of 65 submissions. Delivering the final report to Pacific leaders on 31 October 2013, Sir Mekere Morauta called for 'a new level and quality of political debate, policy and cooperation at the regional level'. The report contained 36 recommendations to Pacific leaders, and a draft New Framework for Pacific Regionalism. The draft framework was widely circulated for feedback before a finalised version was adopted by Pacific leaders in Palau in July 2014.

How new is the New Framework for Pacific Regionalism? How different is it from its earlier iteration? Does it reflect any of the concerns and ideas expressed in civil society submissions to the review team? Does the New Framework for Pacific Regionalism inspire confidence in Pacific leadership and ownership of our leaders' vision? Or does it sorely disappoint by offering Pacific Island people more of the same?

This chapter examines the New Framework for Pacific Regionalism and assesses the extent to which it reflects alternative views and visions of a Pacific future that have been gaining currency over the last two decades. The chapter begins by revisiting the strong criticism that emerged within the region almost ten years ago in response to the Pacific Plan, and situating the Pacific Plan within the broader programme of economic restructuring and trade liberalisation in the region of which it is an integral part. It then examines the extent to which the new Pacific framework responds to these criticisms.

Revisiting Criticisms of the Pacific Plan

In her trenchant critique of the Pacific Plan, Elise Huffer (2006a) began by tracing its origin to the 2003 proposal by the then New Zealand Prime Minister Helen Clark, as Chair of the Pacific Islands Forum, for a review of 'the role, functions and Secretariat' of the Pacific Islands Forum. As such, in Huffer's view, the Pacific Plan was 'intimately tied to the redefining of the Pacific Islands Forum', a body which she criticised as representing 'only heads of governments and states', which did not 'create space for wider discussion of important regional matters by citizens of Forum Islands Countries', and whose secretariat was 'distant from the peoples of the region, as well as hierarchical and technocratic' (Huffer 2006a, p. 159).

An EPG, led by Sir Julius Chan, former prime minister of Papua New Guinea, had been tasked with the job of reviewing the Pacific Islands Forum (PIF) and had produced a report titled 'Pacific Cooperation: Views of the region' (EPG 2004). The report alludes to modernisation and globalisation as if they were autonomous forces that, despite 'bringing wonders to our shores', had 'exposed the vulnerability of our small island states … threatened our family and community bonds and values, weakened our ability to live off the land and sea, and upset our harmony with the natural environment'. Apparently denying any agency on the part of states and governments in exposing island states to these threats, the report asserted a will to 'stand strong to preserve our region, our heritage and the best aspects of our traditions, and enhance them for the benefit of future generations'. 'The bottom line', it revealingly declared, 'is that future inter-country relationships will need to be closer and more mutually supportive *if the region is to avoid decline and international marginalisation*' (emphasis added). What was really meant, in keeping with the predominant orientation of the regional economic and trade policy agenda, was the promotion of economic integration. The report's inclusion of a proposal for a Pacific Plan, 'to create stronger and deeper links between the countries of the region' made this purpose crystal clear.

The rhetoric in the EPG report became the main focus of criticisms of the plan. Huffer, for instance, highlighted the EPG's stress on the need for a 'focus on people' in the regional plan, noting particularly its pronouncement that 'together we shall work to ensure that this is a region where people matter more than anything else, and where every person feels loved, needed and able to enjoy a free, responsible and worthwhile life' (Huffer 2006b, p. 44). That the resulting Pacific Plan endorsed by the Pacific leaders in 2005 bore little resemblance to the EPG's poignant reflections was explained by the fact that the Pacific Plan was drafted by a Pacific Islands Forum Secretariat (PIFS) supported taskforce which based its approach on a technocratic Asian Development Bank report, titled 'New Pacific Regionalism', written by the one-time head of the forum secretariat's trade division, economist Roman Grynberg. According to Huffer, the taskforce identified three 'quite different concepts of regionalism — regional cooperation, regional provision of public goods and services, and regional integration', and advocated shifting from regional cooperation to either of the other forms of regionalism on the basis of a cost/benefit analysis — 'regional approaches to overcoming capacity limitations in service delivery at the national level, and increasing economic opportunities through market integration' were expected to bring the highest gains (Huffer 2006b, p. 44). Huffer rightly perceived the Pacific Plan as setting:

an agenda for new levels of regional integration whereby Pacific Island countries will gradually relinquish sovereignty over certain areas of governance, economic policy and security. As such it sets the framework for a new political and economic order, even though the latter may be introduced incrementally (Huffer 2006a, p. 158).

NGO criticisms of the Pacific Plan similarly highlighted the disjunction between the rhetoric in the EPG report, and the Pacific Plan. Following a regional NGO meeting in Port Moresby in October 2005, Greenpeace Oceans campaigner Lagi Toribau said that, despite considerable rhetoric about security, the Pacific Plan failed to address 'true security for Pacific Island communities, such as health, food and real energy security' (Hamed 2005). NGOs at that meeting also berated the Pacific Plan's drafters for failing to consult Pacific people. They called for a two-year moratorium on the plan to enable 'a more comprehensive and genuine consultation process' to take place and 'informed consent' to be obtained from Pacific people (Pacific Magazine 2005). A subsequent meeting of Pacific NGOs in Nadi in October 2006, convened by Oxfam New Zealand, reiterated civil society criticisms of the Pacific Plan, and particularly of 'planned trade deals'. Slatter and Underhill-Sem dubbed the Pacific Plan 'a neoliberal framework for regional market integration', noting its coherence with PIFS' regional economic and trade liberalisation agenda, and its substitution of 'political regionalism' (organised resistance by Pacific Island states to powerful outside interests that pose threats to Pacific Islands interests) by the new regionalism of market integration (Slatter and Underhill-Sem 2009, p. 197).

There was little doubt about which of the plan's four pillars — sustainable development, economic growth, good governance, and regional security — lay at its core. Indeed, stripped of the rhetoric, the Pacific Plan was revealed as little more than a road map for regional market integration. Market integration or economic integration is 'tradespeak' for free trade. Amongst other things, the Grynberg report had proposed a broadened Pacific Agreement on Closer Economic Relations (PACER), with investment, services and labour mobility added to free trade in goods, and a binding legal instrument involving trade, aid and governance commitments for forum island countries (FICs).[2] These far-reaching proposals for the proposed free trade agreement between Pacific Island states and Australia and New Zealand, which subsequently came to be called PACER Plus, were anticipated to meet considerable opposition from 'the few losers', who the Grynberg report described as 'often well-organised, vocal, and in a position to effectively oppose reforms' (Asian Development Bank–Commonwealth Secretariat 2005, p. 148).

---

2   The Grynberg report proposed a binding agreement on good governance undertakings for Pacific Island states, in return for a renewable five- to 10-year aid and trade agreement (Asian Development Bank–Commonwealth Secretariat 2005).

Regional specialist Greg Fry aptly termed the exogenously conceived and neoliberal-inspired new Pacific regionalism 'hegemonic regionalism' (Fry 2004, p. 11). The hegemonic framing of regional priorities was not surprising as PIFS had been occupied for more than a decade in facilitating an externally driven, region-wide, economic restructuring and trade liberalisation agenda. The overweening role of New Zealand and Australia within the Pacific Islands Forum, which derived in large part from their almost total financing of the PIFS[3] and effective control of key positions, had helped make it a conduit for regionally implementing donor-driven reforms.

Submissions to the Review Committee by Non-State Actors

Although 37 NGOs and CSOs were reported to have made submissions to the Pacific Plan Review Team, 18 of these submissions were made by international NGOs, 17 by individuals, and four by private sector non-state actors (NSAs). Highlighted below are the submissions made by regionally-based NGOs and CSOs which critiqued the development model embraced by the Pacific Plan and offered an alternative development vision. Submissions from non-regionally based NSAs which shared this critique, and its alternative vision, are also mentioned.

The Pacific Regional Non-Governmental Organisation (PRNGO) alliance, representing 13 regional NGOs 'backed by strong networks across the Pacific', confined its submission to concerns about the inadequacy of the PIFS Framework for Engagement with NSAs. It said some NGOs had limited access to regional meetings convened by PIFS and CROP (Council of Regional Organisations in the Pacific) agencies, but this was 'based on personal relationships and remains this way because credible and sincere engagement with regional NGOs is not institutionalised'. It alleged that private sector NSAs were accorded 'preferential treatment.'

The Pacific Islands Association of Non-Government Organisations (PIANGO), a regional coordinating body of umbrella NGOs in 21 Pacific countries, titled its submission, 'The Pacific We Want: A new Pacific regional architecture' and called for both 'formal institutional recognition of CSOs as legitimate development actors', and 'a rethinking of development and reshaping of the Pacific we want'. PIANGO did not support a continuing focus on economic growth and regional integration in the Pacific Plan, saying there was now

---

3   According to Greg Fry (2015), based on 2013 figures, Australia and New Zealand contribute 94 per cent of the PIF core and regular budget bill, while FICs contribute a mere 5 per cent.

'strong consensus that economic growth does not necessarily lead to improved human development and sustainability', and that the Pacific Plan must deliver 'a transformative development agenda which is human development centred' (Pacific Plan Review 2013a).

The Pacific Network on Globalisation (PANG) submitted that 'the emphasis in the Pacific Plan's economic pillar on neoliberal economics must be re-thought' and framed with consideration of Pacific peoples' right to economic self-determination. It referred to 'growing evidence of the negative impacts of the neo-liberal economic model promoted by the Pacific Plan on the lives and livelihoods of Pacific peoples', and suggested that alternative models of development could be 'derived from embedded traditional communal values such as stewardship, sharing, caring and reciprocity'. The challenge lay in 'having the courage to step forward on such a path and define regionalism on our own terms' (Pacific Plan Review 2013a).

A statement adopted by a meeting of Pacific Young Women Activists on Gender, Economic and Climate Justice, convened in September 2010, submitted to the review team, called for 'development alternatives, policies and programmes that empower communities, families and individuals'. Another statement, from a meeting of Pacific feminists and activists in Nadi in February 2013, reminded Pacific states of their obligations and accountability 'to translate gender equality and human rights commitments into law, policy and budget allocations, and to make these norms and standards the guiding principles for contemporary Pacific societies, to be reflected in … the Pacific Plan Review' (Buadromo et al. 2013).

Two NSA submissions by organisations based outside of the Island Pacific shared the alternative visions of regionally based NGOs. Oxfam New Zealand said the Pacific Plan review 'needs to be framed with the Pacific's people at its core', and future plans should 'build on the Pacific's strengths' of 'social cohesion and resilience, respect for tradition, vibrant cultures, equity and fairness and livelihood opportunities for all'. These foundations, it submitted, 'should not be sacrificed in ambitious plans for economic growth for the few, or economic infrastructure'. World Vision called for 'sustainable management of natural resources including protection of biodiversity; security of land rights of communities and indigenous peoples, especially in the face of extractive industries and infrastructure projects; and ensuring lands and vital resources of communities are free from security risks'.

A personal submission by Noelene Nabulivou, Development Alternatives with Women for a New Era (DAWN), proposed binding development safeguards for all peoples of the Pacific, and highlighted the incoherence in policy between setting up marine protected areas on the one hand, and working towards deep sea mining on the other.

Several NSA submissions called for gender equality targets, including targets and indicators for combating gender-based violence. Pacific Women's Parliamentary Partnership, in a submission signed by New Zealand MP Louisa Wall and Samoan Government Minister Fiame Mata'afa, called for indicators and measures for good governance at the judicial and local government levels. They proposed 30 per cent parliamentary representation for women in Pacific Island states and national progress reports on implementation of PIF's Declaration on Gender Equality.

Four submissions raised specific attention to the need to prioritise human rights protection in the revised Pacific Plan. Diverse Voices and Action for Equality (DIVA) called for the inclusion of two rights-based principles — non-discrimination and right to security of the person — with special attention to the rights of Pacific intersex and trans* people and lesbian, bisexual and trans women.

In summary, the NGO submissions highlighted partnership with NSAs, economic self-determination, people-centred (as opposed to economic growth-centred) development, Pacific values, the need to safeguard land and other resources, gender equality, and protection of human rights for all people in Pacific Island states.

The Pacific Plan Review Process

In response to the barrage of criticism, the Pacific Plan was flagged as a 'living document'. In 2009 it underwent a review by an independent consultant, Makurita Baaro, following which the sustainable development pillar was broadened to include responding to climate change and improving livelihoods and well-being. Five themes and 37 priorities were adopted. The subsequent comprehensive review of the Pacific Plan, which resulted in its recasting as the Framework for Pacific Regionalism, began in December 2012, with the appointment of the review team led by Sir Mekere Morauta.

In contrast to the top-down process of formulating and adopting the Pacific Plan, the Pacific Plan review process was widely consultative, participatory, and transparent. Given the harsh criticism of the Pacific Plan by NGOs, academics and other stakeholders, there was a clear intention to provide NSAs with the opportunity to contribute to revising the plan. From January to May 2013, the review team held country consultations and received public submissions. In all, the team made 18 country visits (including to New Caledonia and French Polynesia), consulted 700 stakeholders, and received almost 70 online submissions (65 of which were made available online with the consent of those who submitted), and commissioned studies on some specific issues. A regional consultation workshop was convened in May 2013, together with a special session of the Pacific Plan Action Committee. Further consultations followed in June and July before the annual meeting of the Pacific Plan Action Committee in August considered review working papers. In October 2013, following the leaders meeting in Majuro the month before, the Final Pacific Plan Review Report, comprising 36 recommendations, was submitted.

The full report was made publicly available in December 2013, following discussion by the Forum Officials Committee. At a special leaders retreat on the Pacific Plan Review in May 2014, the Pacific Plan was recast as the Framework for Pacific Regionalism.

Unpacking the Framework for Pacific Regionalism

According to Sir Mekere Morauta, the Framework for Pacific Regionalism should be viewed 'as a framework for advancing the political principle of regionalism through a robust, *inclusive process of political dialogue*, the expression of political values about regionalism and sovereignty, and the decisive implementation of key, game-changing, drivers of regional integration' (cited in PIFS 2014).

Pacific Plan Adviser at the PIFS, Seini O'Connor, elaborated on the framework at a Pacific update meeting in Canberra, June 2014, confirming the clearly intended involvement of NSAs in the process of deciding regional priorities. The framework, she said, would:

> support a tighter, more focused forum agenda, with space for just a few 'big issues' to be discussed by political leaders at their annual retreat. It will promote the development of large-scale initiatives that bring together development partners, regional agencies and non-state actors with plans of action, rather than just good ideas. It will complement effective sub-regionalism. And it will support recognition for leadership to be shown in other areas: for ministers to drive regional cooperation through decisive collective action, for officials to provide direction to their regional organisations when they sign off on annual work plans, *and for the vast range of actors outside of government to be involved in proposing and deciding what the region should focus its efforts on* (O'Connor 2014).

Essentially, the framework consists of a brief vision statement (of a 'region of peace, harmony, security, social inclusion and prosperity, so that all Pacific people can lead free, healthy and productive lives') and six values, which cover:

1. the integrity of our vast ocean and island resources;
2. the diversity and heritage of the Pacific and inclusivity;

3. good governance, democratic values, the rule of law, human rights, gender equality and just societies;

4. peaceful, safe and stable communities and ensured full security and well-being for Pacific peoples;

5. full inclusivity, equity and equality for all people of the Pacific; and

6. effective open and honest relationships and inclusive and ensuring partnerships based on mutual accountability and respect with [sic] each other, within sub-regions, within the region, and beyond.

There are also four stated objectives, which elaborate concisely but more explicitly the objectives of the four original pillars of the Pacific Plan: sustainable development 'combines economic, social and cultural development in ways that improve livelihoods and well-being and use the environment sustainably'; economic growth is 'inclusive and equitable'; good governance is 'strengthened governance, legal, financial and administrative systems'; and regional security is holistically defined in terms of ensuring 'stable and safe human, environmental and political conditions for all'.

The framework includes a matrix of six different 'forms of regionalism' or of regional collective action, which can be adopted by Pacific countries to support a regional initiative that has been proposed and adopted by Pacific Island countries (states or non-state actors) following a carefully elaborated process for priority setting. Prioritisation of a regional initiative and progress reports on its implementation will be evaluated against six criteria or tests for regional action, namely:

1. a market test (the initiative should not involve a service which markets can provide well);

2. a sovereignty test (it should involve no loss of national sovereignty);

3. a regionalism test (it should satisfy one of seven criteria — for example, establish a shared norm or standard, establish a common position on an issue, deliver a public good which is regional in scope, realise economies of scale);

4. political oversight (it should require the leader's attention and input);

5. a risk and sustainability test (be based on a thorough risk and sustainability evaluation, a sound implementation plan, with funding and human resources capacity); and

6. a duplication test (it should not be already in progress by another organisation or duplicate another initiative).

The framework proposes no specific regional projects, but sets up a process through which proposals for regional initiatives are received annually from Pacific states and NSAs and assessed by an independent sub-committee, with five proposals selected for implementation each year. This essentially puts the onus on states and NSAs (private sector organisations or individuals, citizen groups, academics, development practitioners, etc.) to propose regional initiatives each year for selection by the committee. All proposals will be posted online for public information, although reasons behind the selection of the five initiatives will not be publicly disclosed.[4]

Pacific Plan Review: Report to Pacific Leaders

Making an assessment of the framework requires examining the Pacific Plan Review Report, which explicitly advocated a particular model of regionalism. It said, 'regionalism is in the first instance a political, not technical, process', and that the overwhelming message from citizens across the region was that 'the right conversations are not being had about the region's new vulnerabilities', and 'citizens' voices are not being heard about what kind of Pacific is emerging in the absence of coherent, effective regional governance' (Pacific Plan Review 2013b, p. 54). The Pacific Plan 'lacked ownership' and there was 'a lack of space in the Forum for the kind of political conversations' needed (Pacific Plan Review 2013b, p. 55). A 'largely officials-led process, in which clarity over who are the principals in, and who are the agents of, regionalism has become confused' had resulted in CROP agencies 'prosecut[ing] their own [largely technical] agendas'. One observer was quoted as having said 'we have created a superstructure of institutions and processes to prioritise, mandate and report on something that is ultimately not widely valued, and which does not effectively drive regionalism'. The review committee had concluded that 'an overhaul of the processes, institutions and governance of the Plan', was needed to progress regionalism.

The kind of conversation the review committee thought was needed, however, was clearly rather different from the conversations amongst non-private sector NSAs. The review report made a number of recommendations, including that 'PIFS works with multilateral finance institutions' to 'offer PICs the opportunity to develop more highly prioritized growth strategies', and that PIFS 'investigates the merits of establishing a self-funding Secretariat to assist PICs with the development of seabed mining'.[5] The report showed no evidence of having taken on board any of the concerns raised in the submissions from Pacific NGOs.

---

4   Interview with Pacific Regionalism Adviser at Pacific Islands Forum Secretariat, Joel Nilon, 8 May 2015.
5   It also recommended PIFS work with multilateral finance institutions to 'examine issues relating to reasonable standard of living' and to 'develop uniquely Pacific indicators of both poverty and progress'.

In a section subtitled 'Paths to Deeper Integration', the report diagrammatically set out 'the sort of path' the review committee had in mind, showing progressive advance from regional cooperation (for example, strong external voice such as statement on climate change), to shared service delivery (for example, the University of the South Pacific or Secretariat of the Pacific Community technical assistance), to economic integration (for example, free trade agreement and labour mobility), to political integration (for example, shared supreme court), to political union (for example, European Union, Organisation of Eastern Caribbean States), to, ultimately, federation (for example, establishing a single political entity, such as united Germany) — 'usually irreversible' (Pacific Plan Review 2013b, p. 88). The given examples of regional integration towards federation reflect an unequivocal emphasis on economic integration features that are consistent with neoliberalism, namely free trade agreement, harmonised business regulation and business law, labour mobility, investment liberalisation, customs union, and common currency. Examples of political and administrative integration towards federation include shared supreme court, central government body to manage the region, shared defence force, transfers between countries, and supra-national law-making and taxation powers (Pacific Plan Review 2013, p. 90). It was acknowledged that it is 'the prerogative of the people of the Pacific and their leaders' to decide how far along this path the Pacific should go — and that leaders had only expressed an interest in discussing further integration, and had made no decision to follow this path (Pacific Plan Review 2013, p. 89).

The emphasis on economic and deeper integration was very pronounced in the first draft of the new framework. It is substantially muted in the final framework, evidently in response to feedback on the first draft, not least from NSAs, and this was very likely motivated in part by a need to avoid being subjected, yet again, to major criticism.

Implementing the Framework

The process of implementing the framework began with the establishment of the independent sub-committee to receive proposals, assess them against the six tests, and select the five for implementation. PIFS called for applications for the sub-committee in December, closing in February. A sub-committee of seven standing members was subsequently appointed by a troika comprising the present, incoming and last chairs of the PIF, and although it was not intended to be a representative body, its membership includes one from each of the three sub-regions of Melanesia, Micronesia and Polynesia, one from a small island state, and one each from the private sector, civil society, and Australia and

New Zealand.[6] Chaired by the Secretary General of PIFS, Dame Meg Taylor, the sub-committee has already met and considered gaps in their expertise and the weighting to be given to each of the six tests. An announcement and explanation of the process, together with a template for proposal submissions, was published in April, under the heading 'Listening to the Pacific', with 12 June 2015 set as the submissions deadline. Apart from providing the chair, the role of PIFS will be confined to receiving proposals and checking for completeness.

How New is the Framework for Pacific Regionalism?

The framework is very focused on processes — for priority setting, testing for regionalism, assessing progress reports, and ensuring that politically sensitive and major regional issues are the focus of leaders meeting agendas. Its open process and inclusivity has been conceived in recognition of some of the failures of the Pacific Plan.[7] This distinctive new feature — openness to and inclusion of proposals from NSAs for priority attention by governments — seems to signify a radical shift from the previous state-centric model of regional agenda setting, and a changed role for PIFS, which has long been facilitating a donor-driven regional agenda of economic reform and trade liberalisation. The new framework's narrowing of priority issues to be given leaders' attention each year to just five, and its vesting of decision-making to an independent sub-committee, are also distinctively novel features.

While it remains to be seen what proposals are endorsed as regional priorities, the framework does respond to concerns raised in NGO submissions in two ways: firstly, by incorporating into the framework values which resonate with those highlighted by NGO submissions; and secondly, by instituting an open and inclusive process in which NGO and government proposals are equally assessed and selected for implementation by an independent body.

It may be coincidental, but the new framework appears to concur with the submission by the International Institute for Democracy and Electoral Assistance (IDEA), an international NGO that made a submission to the review team. IDEA commended the Pacific Plan review ream for seeking first the input of citizens and communities on the development process and political reform agenda, saying: 'when the necessity for regional integration emerges from such input … it will then draw life and legitimacy in a way that is impossible from

---

6   According to an NGO source, neither the NGO nor the private sector 'representative' on the subcommittee are known individuals, and are not known to be connected to established NGO or private sector networks.
7   Interview with Joel Nilon, 8 May 2015.

the more technical model that focuses primarily on leaders, executive arms of government and funding agencies ... The revised Pacific Plan needs not only to address the substantive issues of development, but the *process* by which development priorities are identified and validated — and the process by which their legitimacy and relevance [are] retained and their implementation undertaken, its effectiveness overseen, and its shortcoming identified and addressed' (Pacific Plan Review 2013a).

Through the open, inclusive and independent process of the new framework, PIFS is stepping back from a position of pushing policies, seeking instead broad ownership of the framework by Pacific Island people. Dame Meg Taylor's 'listening tour' of Pacific Island states — since taking up the job of secretary general she has been travelling to each of the FICs to ascertain for herself current thinking on regional priorities — is indicative of the importance of the framework to PIFS. Recent challenges to, and destabilisation of the established intergovernmental regional architecture (see Tarte 2014) have almost certainly impacted on the implementation of the Framework for Pacific Regionalism. Indeed, getting buy-in for the framework and making its inclusivity work may recover legitimacy for PIFS. On the positive side, the framework does open a window of opportunity for NGOs to submit proposals and make a case for priority to be given to some of their specific concerns by aligning proposed initiatives to the framework's vision, values and objectives.

Yet, by remaining silent on calls by NSAs for a fundamental shift in the development model being followed by Pacific Island states, the framework may function to simply divert attention from the main agenda of economic integration. While the values and objectives of the framework resonate with sentiments expressed in a number of NGO submissions, the over-emphasis on economic integration in the review committee's report suggests that this is deeply embedded and will remain PIFS' core aim and objective. PIFS maintains that, although economic and trade proposals may be submitted and selected, there is no bias in the framework towards economic integration.[8]

To conclude, on the face of it, the Framework for Pacific Regionalism appears to be serving up a more palatable kava mix than was offered in the Pacific Plan tanoa. But it is still too early as yet to be able to say whether the new processes of inclusivity will substantially change the focus of regional policy making and the development path along which Pacific Island states are being driven. The selection of initiatives may well include those proposed by concerned civil society actors and thereby address issues they raised in their submissions to the review team, however, it is not clear what the current vision of Pacific leaders

---

8   Interview with Joel Nilon, 8 May 2015.

is. More concerning, there seems to be a very evident disjunction between the elements of the finalised framework and the model outlined in the review team's report. This raises questions about the meaning of selecting five initiatives for the leaders to give attention to each year, if the primary focus of PIFS remains unchanged. For NGOs, the jury is still out on the framework.

References

Asian Development Bank–Commonwealth Secretariat, 2005, 'Toward a New Pacific Regionalism', Asian Development Bank–Commonwealth Secretariat Joint Report to the Pacific Islands Forum Secretariat. Available at: www.adb.org/sites/default/files/publication/28797/pacific-regionalism-vol2.pdf.

Buadromo, V. et al., 2013, 'Pacific Feminists and Activists: Re-framing, Re-articulating and Re-energizing Sexual and Reproductive Health and Rights'. Available at: www.pacificwomen.org/wp-content/uploads/Pacific-SRHR-2013-Outcome-Doc.pdf.

Coates, B., 2006, 'Reorienting Economic Growth in the Pacific Plan: Towards equitable and sustainable development', presentation to Pacific Civil Society Forum, Nadi, Fiji. Available at: www.oxfam.org.nz/sites/default/files/reports/Analysis_PPlan_Oct06.pdf.

Eminent Persons Group (EPG), 2004, 'Pacific Cooperation: Views of the region', The Eminent Persons Group Review of the Pacific Islands Forum. Available at: gsd.spc.int/sopac/docs/RIF/05_EPG_Report_April04.pdf.

Fry, G., 2004, 'Whose Oceania?: Contending visions of community in Pacific region-building', Working Paper 2004/3, Department of International Relations, RSPAS, The Australian National University, Canberra.

Fry, G., 2015, 'Recapturing the Spirit of 1971: Towards a new regional political settlement in the Pacific', SSGM Discussion Paper 2015/3, The Australian National University, Canberra.

Hamed, O., 2005, 'Neo-Colonialism Ratified At Pacific Islands Forum', *Just Focus: Youth focus for a just world*. Available at: www,justfocus.org.nz/articles/2005/11/04/neo-colonialism-ratified-at-pacific-islands-forum/.

Huffer, E., 2006a, 'The Pacific Plan: A political and cultural critique', in J. Bryant-Tokalau and I. Frazer (eds), *Redefining the Pacific?: Regionalism past, present and future*, Ashgate Publishing Limited, Aldershot.

Huffer, E., 2006b, 'Regionalism and Cultural Identity: Putting the Pacific back into the plan', in S. Firth (ed.), *Globalisation and Governance in the Pacific Islands*, ANU E Press, Canberra, pp. 43–55.

O'Connor, S., 2014, 'Session: Regionalism — responding to the Pacific Plan Review'. Available at: devpolicy.org/presentations/2014-Pacific-Update/Day-2/Seini-O-Connor.pdf.

Pacific Islands Forum Secretariat (PIFS), 2014, 'The Framework for Pacific Regionalism' Available at: www.adb.org/sites/default/files/linked-documents/pacific-robp-2015-2017-sd.pdf.

Pacific Magazine, 2005, 'Moratorium Call for Pacific Plan', September 15. Available at: www.pacificislands.cc/pina/pinadefault2.php?urlpinaid=16889.

Pacific Plan Review, 2013a, 'Public Submissions'. Available at: www.pacificplanreview.org/submissions/.

Pacific Plan Review, 2013b, 'Report to Pacific Leaders', Pacific Islands Forum Secretariat, Suva, Fiji. Available at: www.cid.org.nz/assets/Key-issues/Pacific-development/Pacific-Plan-Review-2013-Volume-1.pdf.

Slatter C. and Y. Underhill-Sem, 2009, 'Re-Claiming Pacific Island Regionalism: Does neo-liberalism have to reign?', in K. L. Koo and B. D'Costa (eds), *Gender and Global Politics in the Asia-Pacific,* Palgrave Macmillan, New York, pp. 195–210.

Tarte, S., 2014, 'Regionalism and Changing Regional Order in the Pacific Islands', *Asia and the Pacific Policy Studies* 1(2), pp. 312–24.

6

Civil Society and the Political Legitimacy of Regional Institutions: An NGO perspective

Maureen Penjueli

'Citizens' voices about the kind of Pacific that is emerging are not being heard in the absence of coherent, effective regional governance — Sir Mekere Morauta (Pacific Plan Review 2013).

Across the Pacific, the regional network of intergovernmental agencies is matched by networks of church, non-government and community organisations. The Malua Conference of Churches and Missions, held in Samoa in 1961, led to the founding of the region's largest ecumenical body, the Pacific Conference of Churches (PCC), in 1966. For 25 years, the Pacific Concerns Resource Centre (PCRC) served as a regional hub for the Nuclear Free and Independent Pacific (NFIP) movement. Today, networks such as the Pacific Islands Association of Non-Government Organisations (PIANGO), the Pacific Network on Globalisation (PANG), and the Pacific Islands Climate Action Network (PICAN) campaign on development, trade, oceans and climate change.

In many cases, civil society organisations (CSOs) have initiated or led regional debates on key concerns. The NFIP movement campaigned for a nuclear-free zone for years before governments adopted the Rarotonga Treaty, establishing the South Pacific Nuclear Weapon Free Zone (SPNWZ). Women's organisations have led the regional debate on gender-based violence in the home, workplace and community. Churches and women's groups played crucial roles in peacebuilding during conflicts in New Caledonia, Bougainville, and Solomon Islands, well before regional peacekeeping interventions arrived.

For many years, governments and donors have announced that they value the role of CSOs in regional initiatives. But this commitment is not matched by concrete, ongoing and cost-effective mechanisms for engagement with the diverse range of organisations that are branded as 'civil society' or 'non-state actors'. This chapter is based on the actual experiences of CSOs in their efforts to engage and participate in regional institutions — particularly the Pacific Islands Forum (PIF) and Melanesian Spearhead Group (MSG) — for almost two decades. It highlights what lessons can be offered to the newest regional structure, the Pacific Islands Development Forum (PIDF), in terms of CSO inclusion. The paper uses real examples to show how the politics that keep CSOs out of regional institutions and constrain the openness of debates on key issues have been to the detriment of Pacific societies. It also highlights what CSO organisations offer Pacific regionalism.

The Significant Role of CSOs in Regionalism

It is continually stated (South Pacific Forum Secretariat 2000) that the island economies of the Pacific, because of their size and geographical position, have limited access to the skills, information and finance needed for successful global integration and economic growth. It is commonly argued that regional institutions and organisations are able to overcome such shortcomings by pooling human resources, and attracting and retaining highly skilled personnel. By operating regionally, economies of scale allow for sharing of technology and knowledge, and provide administrative savings.

Regional cooperation can also give island countries a more persuasive voice on the world stage and help secure a more favourable external economic and political relationship, rather than be overwhelmed by large and powerful nations who can dictate the terms of such relationships.

The role and importance of CSOs and their contributions to economic, social, cultural and political development have long been recognised at the global level. The United Nations Development Program (UNDP), for example, argues that CSOs:

1. provide basic services, such as primary education, health care, clean water and sanitation, facilitate participation of communities in local planning and budgeting purposes;

2. advocate for rights; and

3. provide special consideration for marginalised groups through the provision of counselling and support services.

Historically, in the Pacific, social movements supported by CSOs have played a key role in the struggle for the right to self-determination and the pursuit of the region's own development goals. In the Pacific regionalism of the 1970s to the 1990s, there was often political solidarity between Pacific Island governments and CSOs, where external interests were evidently detrimental to the interests of the region. The greatest successes by Pacific Island countries at the international level have been in the pursuit of 'collective diplomacy',[1] where social movements and the state have worked alongside each other to hold overseas governments to account in order to achieve significant wins, such as the Law of the Sea Convention, the London Dumping Convention, and to help secure a nuclear-free Pacific and a ban on drift-net fishing.

Much of this success would not have happened had CSOs not provided support (or even led), and provided technical knowledge, outlined moral obligations, and utilised their networks, communication and advocacy skills. Perhaps most significantly, CSOs often gave regional institutions legitimacy by providing direct links to social movements and their issues of concern.

Lack of Formal Recognition and Inclusive Processes

Despite the obvious successes of collective diplomacy and the contribution of CSOs to that effort, it was not until 1995 that the PIF, the region's premier political body, officially recognised this fact. Since 1995, PIF leaders have expressed a need to engage with CSOs, to widen the field of participation in regional and international matters, beyond the members of the forum donors and development partners known as dialogue partners. Yet despite the numerous declarations by leaders and recommendations by independent reviews of the regional body recognising the importance of CSOs, no effective mechanisms for CSO engagement have been developed.[2]

---

1   In the description used by the University of the South Pacific academic Greg Fry (1994, pp. 70–71).

2   See IDEA (2014). The first substantive review of the Pacific Island Forum Secretariat in 2003 contained a landmark decision in which PIF leaders resolved to see how they could better interact with CSOs. In 2004, PIF leaders acknowledged the views of CSOs in a PIF communiqué. Leaders noted the importance of CSOs again six years later in 2009, and again in 2011 in the Waiheke Declaration.

By Pacific Island Forum Secretariat's own admission (see PIFS 2012) there is no protocol for dialogue between CSOs and the regional institutions that are members of the Council of Regional Organisations in the Pacific (CROP). Although some regional institutions have higher levels of CSO engagement, PIF still lacks a formal policy for interaction and liaison with CSOs in the region. After intensive negotiations between CSOs and the PIFS, an accreditation policy was established. It is focused solely on regulating which CSOs would gain observer status at meetings hosted by the PIFS. In other words, it has focused on who can watch, not on who can participate.

While CSOs face significant hurdles in obtaining the recognition needed to get a foot in the door — let alone a seat at the table — there has been an exponential increase in the number of new associate members, observers, and dialogue partners of the Pacific's political club. This is a growing reflection of the changing geopolitical landscape of the region; powerful forces are at work in the Pacific, which is making the regional institutional political space highly contested.

Today, PIF meetings are open to many observers, including foreign governments as far away as Cuba and Israel, multilateral institutions such as the World Bank, the Asian Development Bank, the Commonwealth Secretariat, and UN agencies, as well as private sector organisations. Private sector organisations, including commercial banks, are enjoying access to forum leaders and in recent years have started to sponsor events at the leaders meetings. Development partners and observers now outnumber Pacific Island governments.

Alarm Bells about Legitimacy of Regional Architecture

Our regional institutions exhibit a clear democratic deficit. Each year the list of observers grows, giving the PIF a sense of global legitimacy while failing to regain legitimacy in the eyes of the peoples of Oceania. A recent review of the PIFS found that even island governments generally feel alienated from the organisation and that there needs to be greater participation and ownership by members (PACNEWS 2015).

Over the last decade, alarm bells have been repeatedly rung by CSOs and many regional observers about regionalism, in particular the legitimacy of regional systems (both technical and political) and whether these spaces are democratic spaces. The 2013 review of the Pacific Plan for Strengthening Regional Cooperation and Integration, led by former Papua New Guinea Prime Minister

Sir Mekere Morauta, noted: 'Citizens feel that the right conversations are not being had about the region's new vulnerabilities — social, economic, political and environmental' (Pacific Plan Review 2013).

Key questions posed by many experts are:

1. Who is Oceania for?
2. What does the community stand for; what are its values, practices and ideas?
3. Who should be regarded as belonging to the community, on what basis?
4. Who should speak for it and determine its practice?

National parliaments appear to have lost part of their power to scrutinise the positions taken by their ministers at the regional level, and there are no functional formal mechanisms to link the views of the people on political matters to the agenda of regional institutions such as the PIF. For too long, the public attitude has been one of 'permissive consensus', meaning that regional policies were taken for granted by the Pacific people as an accepted part of the political landscape.

CSOs, as the alternative voice and the bridge between the broader public view, and regional institutions have for a long time been deliberately kept out by the lack of a formal mechanism for engagement with PIFS.

Critical Moments in Regional Architecture and Diplomacy

The suspension of Fiji from the PIF after its fourth coup set in motion a series of events that challenged existing regional structures. The Fiji government, seizing the moment and the opportunity presented by a perception of an Australia-centric PIFS, deliberately pursued an agenda of regional self-determination and set about reshaping regional diplomacy and architecture based on this principle. In doing so, CSOs were offered a platform on which they could revisit the question of the legitimacy of the regional architecture. At the sub-regional level, Fiji's suspension from the various regional and international clubs only served to strengthen its resolve to work with Melanesian leaders in a 'Pacific way', without the participation of New Zealand and Australia. Fiji's chairmanship of the MSG in 2011 was a turning point for Fiji and the MSG: it signalled that a determined MSG wanted to play a major role in setting the region's development agenda without the formal involvement of their big brothers, Australia and New Zealand.

Australia and New Zealand are full members of the forum and are also the region's major donors. The Fiji government's intervention in regional debates has become a lightning rod for criticism from some regional leaders. But Fiji's suspension from forum activities has allowed it to advance opinions that go outside the forum consensus. Fiji has persuasively argued that Australian and New Zealand foreign policy interests have dominated, at times contrary to the interest of Pacific Island countries, a sentiment that resonates with many Pacific Island governments.

Indeed, we have seen an era of increased pressure from traditional allies, particularly Australia, to undertake extensive market driven economic and political initiatives in regional spaces that Pacific Island leaders have sometimes regarded as intrusive, disruptive, and even hostile (Wesley-Smith 2007).

As a direct response, the Fiji government has participated in other international networks, such as the Non-Aligned Movement (NAM) and the G77 plus China grouping, using these platforms to debate south–south cooperation. Fiji also set up the PIDF, a move widely regarded as setting up a direct rival to the PIFS, premised on the argument that the Pacific needed a space in which Pacific Islands governments could meet to discuss issues of importance to Pacific Islanders without Australia and New Zealand.

After a successful return to democracy with the September 2014 elections, Prime Minister Bainimarama argued that Australia and New Zealand should move from full members to dialogue partners of the PIF, presenting this as a condition to Fiji's re-entry into the forum. While this debate has also opened up a much needed space to debate how to effectively include CSOs in regional institutions and place peoples' issues at the centre of policy-making, it also opens up many dilemmas for CSO participation.

CSOs and the Pacific Islands Development Forum

The PIDF claims it will be an inclusive institution, particularly of CSOs. PIDF's inclusion of CSOs is relatively new and the jury is still out; it remains to be seen whether this is merely lip service. CSOs are not just focused on the domination of Australia and New Zealand, but also on the collusion of powerful interests, including multilateral financial institutions such as the Asian Development Bank (ADB) and World Bank. The ADB and World Bank — as well as many other donors — have been pursuing a very specific neoliberal governance and economic integration agenda in the region that in many ways is unchallenged, and yet is in direct conflict with the interests of Pacific peoples. CSOs seek to act as a counter-influence and alternative voice to these powerful interests.

The litmus test for PIDF is whether it can counter the influence of external non-regional members, particularly China and Indonesia, who will also seek to influence the PIDF in ways that undermine a self-determination agenda for the Pacific. The involvement of Indonesia in Pacific regionalism demonstrates the complexities that can quickly come into play. Indonesia has grasped the significance of being intimately involved in regional power plays, whether through MSG, PIF, or PIDF. The growing public support in the Pacific for the West Papuan freedom movement has, no doubt, played a significant role in Indonesia's foreign policy strategy.

Given the ecumenical movement's long-standing support for churches in West Papua, the PCC's Secretary General has asked: 'What agenda do Indonesia and other development partners bring to the PIDF; are they to replace the dominance that Australia and New Zealand have been accused of within the regional architecture centred in the Pacific Islands Forum?'[3]

Indonesia's intentions were exposed on 13 March 2015, when PNG Loop detailed Indonesia's proposal for the five Melanesian provinces of Indonesia to become a full member of the MSG. This can only be regarded as a direct attempt to block the application for MSG membership by the United Liberation Movement for West Papua, supported by Vanuatu and New Caledonia's Kanak and Socialist National Liberation Front (*Front de Libération Nationale Kanak et Socialiste* (FLNKS)) independence movement.

We can only assume that Indonesia will not stop at the MSG; once it gains membership it would then apply, at the invitation of the Papua New Guinea government, for full membership to PIF and possibly PIDF. Politics makes for strange bed fellows, but the long-term implications of Indonesia being a full member of MSG, PIF, and PIDF need to be seriously considered against a right to self-determination push by Fiji and other Pacific Island nations.

No People's Voice in Regional Institutions

In political science, legitimacy is usually understood as the public's popular acceptance and recognition of the authority of a governing regime (in this case regional institutions), where the authority exercises political power through

---

3   As questioned by the Pacific Conference of Churches General Secretary Francois Pihaatae during the welcoming of the President of Indonesia to open the PIDF meeting in 2014.

consent and mutual understanding, not coercion. Legitimacy assumes popular consent; but who gives consent and on behalf of whom is the consent given in these regional political spaces?

Regional meetings, particularly those hosted by PIFS, are conducted behind closed doors and are increasingly subject to secret diplomacy, without a chance for the people whose lives will be deeply affected to have a direct say. This is particularly worrying when we consider that PIF covers matters that affect the ordinary person on the street. Australian and New Zealand interests are decidedly different from and, in some cases, contrary and even hostile to those of Pacific Island countries, regarding such issues as security, economics and trade, climate change, and decolonisation. Yet, increasingly, at the international level — particularly at the United Nations, the G20, and the World Trade Organization — Australia and New Zealand claim to 'represent' Pacific Island nation views by virtue of their membership in PIF.

Given the growing tensions between members over the PIF's 'consensus' policies on climate, trade and decolonisation, there is growing criticism over the lack of ownership of the forum, not just by countries but also by CSOs. In response to this challenge, PIFS initiated yet another program aiming to promote good governance in the Pacific by strengthening dialogue and engagement on policy development and implementation between the PIF and its secretariat and non-state actors (NSAs).

According to PIFS, there is an acceptance of the criticism of a lack of 'people's voice' in regional policies: 'There is no regional government or parliament for the Pacific. As a result, *if* NSAs wish to contribute to regional policies, they must go through the PIFS, whose membership comprises all the national governments in the region' (see PIFS 2012). (Note the 'if' in this sentence, as though there were any doubt that CSOs wish to engage regional policy-making.)

The analysis states that member states of the PIF generally acknowledge that NSAs have strengths in:

- communicating with and engaging civil society; and
- determining public sentiment concerning the current and potential impacts of policies and ongoing or planned government interventions. Governments also recognise they may lack these capacities themselves.

However, many governments perceive NSAs as activist groups that attempt to raise and exploit public sentiment on certain development issues, in order to promote opposition to government policies and strategies. Accordingly, despite some promising shifts towards greater openness, consultations with NSAs still tend to be limited in practice. The focus on CSOs' roles in carrying government policies to grassroots communities dismisses the fact that CSOs have long been engaging with regional policy issues, either to highlight emerging issues of interest, which governments may not necessarily be aware of, or to bring up issues that many governments would prefer to ignore (such as decolonisation issues in West Papua, French Polynesia, New Caledonia, Guam, and Rapa Nui).

Governments too often regard CSOs as seeking to exploit public sentiments on certain development issues, which are contrary to government policies and strategies such as deep sea mining (DSM). But in the absence of a regional mechanism for accountability, it is the role of CSOs to hold governments to account.

While the PIFS would like to regard itself as the gatekeeper, controlling entry into regional policy-making, the PIFS' delay in developing a formal mechanism for CSO engagement means that many CSOs have already climbed the fence and developed other sophisticated mechanisms for engaging in regional policy-making. This includes participation in national government delegations and policy-making committees, much to the ire of some government leaders and some technocrats at the secretariat.

In many cases, specific issues are allowed to dominate PIF's policy on CSO engagement rather than letting policy dictate the terms of engagement.

There are three immediate examples where our regional institutions — PIFS in particular — are being captured by specific interest groups, whether these are foreign governments, multilateral financial institutions or other technical agencies.

1. Seabed Mining

In recent years, CROP agencies have been working to develop legal frameworks and policy documents to support DSM of strategic minerals in the vast exclusive economic zones of forum island countries (FICs). Through a project at the Secretariat of the Pacific Community's (SPC) geoscience division (formerly SOPAC), funded by the European Union, the mining industry is already being given 'legitimacy' by regional institutions: the CROP debate is focused on how to facilitate seabed mining rather than asking whether it should be?

NGOs around the region argue that the EU-SPC DSM project sets out a number of dubious and unfounded assertions about seabed mining.[4] Working with lawyers, scientific organisations, customary landowners, and community groups, these groups argue that the current initiative contravenes numerous international legal norms, such as the precautionary principle and the right to free and prior informed consent.

The Oceans Declaration signed by forum leaders in Palau in 2014 unfortunately supports the EU-SOPAC DSM project rationale. It has given political legitimacy to the industry to plunder the ocean floor of its wealth, by deliberately weakening any efforts to regulate an untried and untested industry. On this issue, CSOs have real grounds (scientific, economic, legal, social, cultural and moral) to challenge the policy interpretations of the PIF-mandated EU-SPC DSM project. CSOs who argue that the question of 'how' should only be discussed after the question of 'if' has first been debated are routinely excluded. Consultation is only sought on policies for seabed mining rather than questioning whether it should be allowed. The effect of this is that there has been no real debate on seabed mining, and dubious claims to legitimacy under the precautionary principle have, by and large, gone unchallenged.

2. Regional and Economic and Trade Integration

In 2009, the PANG released a report, titled 'Speaking Truth to Power', which documented the Australia's and New Zealand's use of power, aid, and at times coercion, to force the launch of the controversial Pacific Agreement on Closer Economic Relations (PACER) Plus negotiations. The trade talks officially commenced after the Cairns Forum meeting in 2009, even though it was abundantly clear that most Pacific Island governments were reluctant to launch negotiations. PACER Plus was launched amidst a flurry of bullying and cheque book diplomacy. Australia and New Zealand are amongst the biggest aid donors to the region, and FICs are dependent on access to funding, limiting their ability to argue against an agreement that is in Australia's and New Zealand's interests.

As negotiations gather steam for completion by December 2015, the implications are only just becoming clear. PACER Plus is far from being a balanced agreement. FICs are being pushed to make binding commitments, and the vast majority of concessions, in exchange for the status quo on labour mobility and possibly

---

4   CSOs such as Act Now! PNG, Bismarck Ramu Group, Pacific Conference of Churches, Lutheran Church of Papua New Guinea (with a membership of over one million), and Melanesian Indigenous Land Defence Alliance, as well as feminist groups, student movements, and academics have called for a ban on seabed mining in the Pacific.

some extra aid money to assist with structural adjustment. The sad reality is that PACER Plus will constrain the ability of FIC governments to shape our development future.

Pacific CSOs have expressed their deepest concerns at the direction, content, pace and process for consultation of state negotiations toward the proposed regional free trade agreement. The PIFS has organised briefings for NSAs, but CSOs, social movements and community networks that are trying to shine a light on negotiations from the outside are not able to attain even observer status. CSOs have therefore called for:

- the immediate suspension of the PACER Plus negotiations until there has been informed, comprehensive dialogue with civil society to ascertain whether there is a popular mandate for such negotiations;
- the immediate release of all negotiating texts to allow full, comprehensive and informed input from civil society; and
- following the release of the texts a properly funded social, cultural, environmental and human rights impact assessment be undertaken to determine the impacts of any proposed outcome (Pacific civil society organisations 2015).

None of the above requests should cause democratic and transparent institutions any concerns; after all, the agreement is supposed to be for our benefit.

3. Political Self-Determination

Surprisingly, in 2015 Oceania is home to some island nations and territories whose people are still fighting for the right to self-determination, notably West Papua, Kanaky, Bougainville, Tahiti, and Hawai'i. CSOs have a long history of actively supporting and being part of right to self-determination struggles. They have been central in some cases, long after Pacific Island governments changed their policy to 'non-interference' in sovereign matters.

On the issue of West Papua and Tahiti, the Australian government has been largely mute in the face of atrocious human rights abuses, primarily because of their strong bilateral relationship with the Indonesian and French governments. Compare and contrast this stance with Australia's reaction to Fiji's last coup. As pointed out by Nic Maclellan (2002), 'decolonisation might not look like a hot-button issue but after our (Australia's) Security Council win we'll have to start taking it seriously in the Pacific'.

Politics of Inclusiveness

In all of these cases, PIFS seeks to justify its position by reference to its mandate from its member states. At the same time, it openly acknowledges in its own policy documents that there is no peoples' voice in regional policies. CSOs such as PANG and the media have experienced first-hand the extent to which the forum secretariat will go to control access to their closed meetings. At the 2013 forum trade ministers meeting in Samoa, even the small public spaces which CSOs and the media used to access trade officials and ministers were rapidly closed down by secretariat staff (*Samoa Observer* 2013). That the secretariat would even attempt to close down public spaces where officials and CSOs and media could meet speaks to the gatekeeper mentality of some technocrats.

The continued exclusion of CSOs from regional engagement dismisses the technical knowledge (scientific, legal, environmental, social, and cultural), values, and extensive networks that CSOs can bring to the table. This expertise has been the basis of cooperation with governments from independence till today. The reason why it has taken PIFS this long to adequately address the issue of CSO engagement is because inclusiveness is, by its very nature, political. Governments instinctively do not want to work with what they call 'lobby and advocacy groups' that do not toe the line. The emphasis in terms of engagement has been to regulate who, how, when and where CSOs can attend regional spaces. A lack of a formal mechanism for engagement leaves the power in the hands of technocrats to arbitrarily determine who can and cannot attend. This informal mechanism leaves not just CSOs, but also the wider community, at the mercy of technocrats.

Regional institutions often seek to find one CSO network as their favoured interlocutor. This effort is self-defeating; 'civil society' across a region as vast as the Pacific is incredibly diverse, and it is difficult for one organisation to claim legitimacy. Instead, CROP agencies should recognise that the diversity of Pacific churches, NGOs and customary groups as a strength rather than a weakness. Regional institutions should provide a variety of mechanisms to engage with communities in a region noted for its geographic, cultural and political diversity.

More than this, the citizens of the Pacific want more than token, one-off consultations with their regional institutions. Surely, in the 21st century, CROP agencies should recognise that good development practice involves ongoing, interactive and well-resourced engagement with people affected by the policies adopted by governments and donors. Existing attitudes and practices do a disservice to the Pacific and its regional institutions. PIFS in particular is increasingly viewed by many as an organisation seeking to facilitate the interest of those in power or those with money. CSOs argue that an organisation confident in its role and its mandate should welcome all views and seek ways to actively allow those views a space.

Regional CSOs demand a formal mechanism and an honest policy which is applied evenly and openly, regardless of the issue in question. The questions that the region faces are too important to be left in the hands of unelected technocrats, however well-intentioned they may be. PIDF has a unique opportunity to lead the way. Let us hope it has the courage and political leadership to engage all views even those that are contrary to PIDF's position.

The time has come for an honest debate; are our leaders prepared to allow it?

References

Fry, G., 1994, 'Climbing Back onto the Map?: The South Pacific Forum and the new development orthodoxy', *Journal of Pacific History* 29(3), pp. 64–72.

International Institute for Democracy and Electoral Assistance (IDEA), 2014, 'The Pacific Islands Forum and its Engagement with Civil Society Organizations' in R. Cordenillo and K. Gardes (eds), *Inclusive Political Participation and Representation: The Role of Regional Organizations*, International IDEA, Stromsburg. Available at: www.idea.int/publications/inclusive-political-participation-and-representation/upload/Inclusive-Political-Participation-chapter2.pdf.

Maclellan, N., 2012, 'The Diplomacy of Decolonisation', *New Matilda*, 24 October. Available at: newmatilda.com/2012/10/24/diplomacy-decolonisation.

Pacific Island Forum Secretariat (PIFS), 2012, 'Programme for Strengthening Non-State Actor Engagement in Regional Policy Development', unpublished PIFS project document.

Pacific Plan Review, 2013, 'Report to Pacific Leaders', Pacific Islands Forum Secretariat, Suva, Fiji. Available at: www.cid.org.nz/assets/Key-issues/Pacific-development/Pacific-Plan-Review-2013-Volume-1.pdf.

Pacific civil society organisations, 2015, 'Open Letter to Forum Trade Ministers: Pacific civil society urgent open letter. Available at: www.pina.com.fj/?p=pacnews&m=read&o=19175072215548149672bbc2a93d34.

PACNEWS, 2015, 'Donors Influence Development Decisions: Forum SG', *Papua New Guinea Today*. Available at: news.pngfacts.com/2015/04/donors-influence-development-decisions.html.

Samoa Observer, 2013, 'Trade Campaigner Kicked Out', *Samoa Observer*, 18 July. Available at: www.samoaobserver.ws/other/science-a-technology/6051-trade-campaigner-kicked-out.

South Pacific Forum Secretariat, 2000, 'Sharing Capacity: The Pacific experience with regional cooperation and integration', Suva, Fiji. Available at: akgul. bilkent.edu.tr/telekom/sharing-Experience.pdf.

Wesley-Smith, T. 2007, *China in Oceania: New forces in Pacific politics*, Pacific Islands Policy 2, East West Centre, Hawai'i. Available at: www.eastwestcenter. org/fileadmin/stored/pdfs/pip002_1.pdf.

7

A New Pacific Regional Voice? The Pacific Islands Development Forum[1]

Sandra Tarte

Introduction

A new regional body — the Pacific Islands Development Forum (PIDF) — was inaugurated at an international conference organised and hosted by the Fiji government 5–7 August 2013 and attended by around 300 delegates. The conference theme was 'Leadership, Innovation and Partnership for Green/ Blue Pacific Economies' and aimed to advance the vision of a 'United, Distinctive and Sustainable Pacific Society'. The following report examines the processes and outcomes of this event and provides a preliminary analysis of its significance to Pacific regionalism, as well as to the development agenda of Pacific Island countries. It begins with an overview of the origins and background of the PIDF.

1   Reprinted with permission. Originally published as *Pacific Islands Brief* No.4, Pacific Islands Development Program, Hawai'i, 2013.

Background

The immediate antecedents to the PIDF lie in a 2012 Engaging with the Pacific (EWTP) leaders meeting, attended by leaders and representatives from Pacific Island states and territories. It was at this gathering that agreement was reached to convene the PIDF in 2013.

EWTP was a Fiji-led regional process that had evolved since 2010, in reaction to its suspension from the Pacific Islands Forum. The first EWTP meeting had occurred by default in 2010 in place of a cancelled summit of the Melanesian Spearhead Group (MSG), at which the Fijian prime minister was due to assume chairmanship of the sub-regional body. The Fiji government's intention was to turn the MSG meeting into a broader gathering, dubbed MSG Plus. This plan was scuttled at the last minute, reportedly due to Australian pressure on the outgoing MSG chair (the prime minister of Vanuatu) who cancelled the meeting on the grounds of a non-democratically elected leader being unsuitable to assume this position.

The Natadola Communique issued at the end of the 2010 summit established the tone and focus for what would become the EWTP and later the PIDF. This emphasised the need for new modes of regionalism and new international partnerships, as well as new development approaches and new diplomatic strategies to support these. From the outset, it was made clear that the EWTP would emphasise Pacific Small Island Developing States (PSIDS) as the core membership. (This also included Timor-Leste and later Pacific non-self-governing territories.) Pacific regionalism would find its strength in shared interests and common concerns around sustainable development and by renewing 'special cultural bonds' and 'regional kinships'. For Fiji, the underlying agenda was also to mobilise Pacific Island endorsement for the Bainimarama Government's 'roadmap to democracy'.

Despite being dismissed by some observers as a short-lived irrelevance (see Field 2010), the EWTP meeting attracted a large number of participants to its second conference in September 2011. There was also a broadening of its agenda to include self-determination (in this case for French Polynesia which attended for the first time). References to the 'blue/green economy' appeared for the first time, and the meeting endorsed the region's preparations for the 2012 Rio Plus 20 World Summit on Sustainable Development. It is significant that just prior to this EWTP meeting, the United Nations (UN) adopted a new nomenclature that recognised PSIDS as part of the Asia Group within the UN (renamed in brief the Asia Pacific Group). This underscored (and gave impetus to) Fiji's determination to assert the PSIDS membership as the primary basis for regional solidarity and cooperation, which would be carried forward to the global level through the EWTP process.

The momentum continued with the third EWTP leaders meeting in Nadi in 2012, which now also included New Caledonia. As mentioned earlier, this meeting resolved to convene the PIDF, alongside the next EWTP leaders meeting. The proposed PIDF aimed to bring together leaders from key sectors in order to advance 'green economic policies'. The concept of green economy — which had been evolving over several years and was given prominence at the 2012 Rio Plus 20 World Summit — emphasised partnerships among governments, civil society, communities and the private sector. Three organisations that made presentations to the 2012 EWTP meeting around this theme were United Nations Economic and Social Council for Asia and the Pacific (UNESCAP), International Union for the Conservation of Nature (IUCN), and Pacific Islands Private Sector Organisation (PIPSO). All three organisations would become part of the steering committee formed by the Fiji government to conceptualise and plan the formation of the PIDF.

Planning the PIDF

Although initially conceived as a parallel event to the EWTP meeting, within a few months the Fiji government had approved the PIDF as a successor arrangement to the EWTP process. Based on a secretariat established within the Fiji government's Ministry of Foreign Affairs and International Cooperation, work began to more fully articulate the role and purpose of the PIDF and to promote this to the region (governments, civil society, CROP (Council of Regional Organisations in the Pacific) agencies, private sector).

In promoting the PIDF, Fiji government officials maintained that there was a need for the Pacific to 'get our act together in the region if we want to make an effective contribution to the (UN's) Asia Pacific Group'. The PIDF would not have any political or security role, but would be 'totally focused on the Green Economy and sustainable development'. Moreover it would represent and comprise 'only Pacific people and values'.[2]

The inaugural PIDF summit was scheduled for early August 2013 and planning was undertaken by a committee comprising the Fiji government (mainly the Ministry of Foreign Affairs, but including other departments), PIPSO, UNESCAP, IUCN, and the Solomon Islands High Commission in Suva.

---

2   These comments were made to a briefing of the University of the South Pacific staff in March 2013.

Participation/Timing/Funding

During the planning process it was envisaged that participating countries would all be Pacific Island countries and territories (including Timor-Leste). Observers would include existing regional organisations, UN agencies, private sector and NGO umbrella groups, academic institutions, and 'development partners'. The latter was intended to encompass as many countries as possible, both current and potential partner states. Other interested organisations and individuals were also welcome to request observer status.

From the outset there was some ambivalence about the inclusion of the Pacific Islands Forum (and Pacific Islands Forum Secretariat (PIFS)). It is perhaps not surprising that the PIFS was the only key regional CROP agency not represented at the PIDF inaugural summit. Whether or not they were invited remains subject to some dispute. But it is also significant that the PIDF summit occurred in the same week as the meeting at the forum secretariat of the Pacific Plan Action Committee (PPAC) and, following from that, the Forum Officials Committee. In what could be seen as a parallel — if not competing — process, the PPAC (which comprised members of the PIF) was meeting to receive the report of the team that had been tasked with reviewing the Pacific Plan and drawing up a more relevant framework for regionalism and regional integration.

In the lead-up to the August PIDF it was not clear how many countries invited as observers would, in fact, attend. It was apparent that some countries were hesitant to accept their invitations, at least until they knew who else would be attending. The hesitancy on the part of some established regional partners (such as Japan and the United States) pointed to a reluctance to give endorsement to the PIDF and thereby undermine the Pacific Islands Forum as the key political body through which they engaged with the region. In the end they all attended — about 30 countries from Europe, Africa, Latin America, North America, Asia, and the Pacific. Those 'partners' with diplomatic missions in Fiji were represented by their resident ambassadors. Those without missions sent diplomats from neighbouring missions in Australia or New Zealand, or special envoys. This included special envoys of the governments of Russia and China, who each made statements to the summit pledging their respective government's support for the PSIDS and the PIDF.

Perhaps of most importance was the attendance of Pacific Island countries. Of the invitees who accepted, five sent heads of government, heads of state, or deputies (Timor-Leste, Solomon Islands, Nauru, Kiribati, and Federated States of Micronesia). The rest sent ministers and diplomatic representatives. There were four members of the Pacific Islands Forum who were conspicuous by their absence: Cook Islands, Samoa, Niue, and Palau. Two of these (Samoa and Palau) are members of the UN PSIDS group, and Samoa will host next year's Global Summit of Small Islands Developing States. None of these countries had previously participated in the EWTP meetings (Palau apparently still does not have diplomatic relations with Fiji). Of the four, Samoa was the only government to openly criticise the meeting (see Radio Australia 2013).

The absence of the Papua New Guinea (PNG) prime minister also became an object of some speculation. It was suggested that the PNG prime minister had been offended by remarks made by the Fiji prime minister and foreign minister criticising Australia's policy of resettling asylum seekers in PNG (as a deterrent to the flow of boat people heading for Australia) and had subsequently decided against attending. However, the PIDF meeting coincided with Papua New Guinea Prime Minister Peter O'Neill's official visit to New Zealand, presumably planned well ahead. Moreover, the PNG prime minister did not feature on earlier drafts of the conference program. It was the PNG minister for national planning who was on the program and who chaired one of the sessions.

In terms of funding, a press statement released in advance of the meeting by the Fiji government revealed that the governments of Kuwait, China, and the United Arab Emirates had provided financial support (totalling US$689,000), along with a number of 'local business houses'.

Procedures/Presentations

The format of the PIDF conference combined an unconventional mix of diplomatic protocol and creative informality. This owed much to the make-up of the participants: from state leaders and politicians to academics, business leaders, diplomats and civil society representatives. There was less room for formal interventions and more for personal or individual reflections and responses. The bulk of the program comprised plenary sessions addressing the conference theme — leadership, innovation and partnerships — however, half a day was set aside for parallel sessions based on key economic sectors or policy areas (seven in all). Each of the parallel sessions had designated facilitators (from government, CROP agencies, private sector and civil society) and each was tasked with coming up with a short list of policy recommendations and actions that would make a difference in advancing the blue/green economy. These recommendations are contained in the conference outcomes documents (PIDF 2013).

Both the plenary sessions (including keynotes and panels) and the parallel sessions aimed to highlight 'best practices' from across the region and beyond in the area of blue/green economy — initiatives by governments, private sector and NGOs of inclusive and environmentally sustainable development, at the grassroots, national and regional levels. There was some disagreement and confusion voiced regarding the precise meanings of blue and green economy. For the Kiribati president, one simply referred to the marine zone and the other to the terrestrial zone, and the extent to which these were developed in an environmentally sustainable and inclusive manner. However, it was recognised by the conference that there was a need for further clarification, and representatives from the University of the South Pacific offered to provide a paper on this.

Throughout the presentations and discussions, a number of things stood out. There was an emphasis on infusing the PIDF with a 'distinctive Pacific voice' — evident by the opening audiovisual presentation of the South Pacific creed. Speakers, especially national leaders, repeated the call for a 'new development paradigm', based around a 'distinctive Pacific model of green growth in blue economies'. There were frequent references to the need to 'step outside the box' and to reject 'business as usual'. On the whole there was a view that PSIDS needed to take greater ownership over the development process and, in the words of Prime Minister Xanana Gusmao, to be 'agents of our own change'.

A presentation by Fijian entrepreneur Colin Philp on sustainable shipping (using wind/sail power) as an innovation towards achieving the blue/green economy appeared to resonate strongly with conference participants, by highlighting the potential role for traditional knowledge and technologies. This provoked a somewhat passionate response from Marshall Islands government minister Tony de Brum:

> For too long we have accepted down as normal; we have accepted small as normal; we have accepted prescriptions of our development partners as normal — that we must do what we are told to do, not what we want to do. I came to this meeting in the hope that the PIDF will make up for that deficiency in our development; where solutions to our development problems can be reached quickly without multitudes of expensive consultants. The world needs alternative energy technology. This is something that can fit into the agenda of this meeting. We need to do something new about climate change. It is frustrating to Pacific Island countries that hardly anything has been done in that area. This organisation can take the lead in that and stop the rhetoric. PIDF must be outcome driven.

The Way Forward

In the final session, which addressed future institutional and governance arrangements for the PIDF, the way forward was mapped out by Fiji's permanent secretary for foreign affairs. In what had been touted as a surprise announcement by the Fijian prime minister (but which probably surprised few) it was revealed that leaders had agreed to establish a PIDF secretariat, based in Fiji, but no longer within the Ministry of Foreign Affairs. It was later reported that the governments of Russia, China and Kuwait had offered to contribute to the costs of the secretariat, which would operate out of Fiji government quarters in Suva. The secretariat staff would be drawn from the PIDF member countries, on secondment/attachment from government, civil society and the private sector. A working group, also representative of these various sectors, would be established to develop the longer term institutional framework ahead of the next PIDF meeting (which the Fijian prime minister promised would be held in 2014, at a place and time yet to be decided).

It was also announced that the work program of the PIDF secretariat would be developed inter-sessionally and circulated to PIDF countries for endorsement. One of the priorities was to agree on language and indicators for the 'ten big things' necessary to achieve blue/green Pacific economies. In response to this roadmap, country representatives made a number of comments and suggestions, including the need for further consideration of the financial implications of the PIDF, the need for clearer terms of reference guiding participation of various stakeholders, and revisiting the name of the organisation. (Kiribati suggested 'Pacific Islands Sustainable Development Forum', but there appeared to be little support for this.)

The conference was closed formally by the Fijian prime minister who used the occasion to again assert the distinctive Pacific voice and identity of the PIDF, that this was an initiative 'by Pacific Islanders, for Pacific Islanders'. According to Prime Minister Bainimarama, the PIDF was a genuine expression of the Pacific way of consultation and consensus and would be the antithesis of expensive, top-down bureaucracy. It would operate, instead, according to the principle of 'less is more', where the goal would be to 'live within our means'.

Assessment

Although described on a number of occasions by Prime Minister Bainimarama as a development forum, not a political forum, there can be no denying the political significance of the PIDF. Moreover, while questions and uncertainties surround its future structure, processes and outputs, there seems little doubt that the PIDF has sufficient support — both within the region and beyond — to carry it forward. The PIDF could not have occurred without the Fiji government's leadership, but it resonates with broader regional concerns and trends. While a direct outcome of Fiji's suspension from the Pacific Islands Forum, the PIDF is a 'product' of the new fluidity in the international relations of the Pacific region, evident by the large number of states attending the PIDF conference that normally have no presence at other Pacific regional forums. It is also an expression of the disaffection and disillusion among Pacific Island countries with the prevailing regional order and the development outcomes it has delivered (or failed to deliver).

The outcomes document underscores a widely held view that new approaches are needed to meet the challenges posed by climate change as well as to address other social and economic problems. This is reflected in the declared need to assert a Pacific model of 'green growth'. How this translates into policy at the local and national levels remains to be seen, but the PIDF was an attempt to showcase what was possible (both through the conference presentations and on the sidelines with the Pacific Green Growth Expo). In this context, the PIDF may well become the driver of the green growth development agenda in the Pacific.

The PIDF may also become the principal interlocutor for Pacific Island states at the UN, based on its claim to represent the Pacific sub-region of the UN's Asia Pacific Group (minus Samoa and Palau). This will involve formalising links with relevant groups and agencies, including the successor to the UN Commission on Sustainable Development (the High Level Forum on Sustainable Development). In this role, there is obvious overlap with the work of the PIFS and it is not clear how this will be resolved, especially in the lead-up to the 2014 Global Conference on Small Islands Developing States, scheduled to take place in Samoa.

The PIDF reflects a new dynamism that has characterised Pacific regionalism over the past few years, and that has challenged the established donor-dominated CROP system. Within this more fluid environment, Pacific states have sought to take control of regional processes and agendas (whether fisheries, trade, or security) through promoting alternative regional frameworks and alliances. PIDF is the latest and perhaps boldest of these initiatives. Not only is it formalising a new regional grouping of Pacific states and territories (PSIDS), it is also breaking convention by incorporating non-state actors (the private sector and civil society) as full partners.

While eschewing convention (including the bureaucratic formalities associated with existing regional bodies) the PIDF will undoubtedly encounter challenges (the week-long delay in releasing the conference outcome documents is perhaps a precursor of those). But, as the Secretariat of the Pacific Community Director General put it, the PIDF marks 'an important historical journey' and it remains very much a work in progress.

Postscript

Since the inaugural summit, attention has focused on formalising the PIDF's institutional and governance structures. This has meant confronting difficult questions about membership and participation in the quest to include Pacific Island states, non-self-governing territories, civil society, and the private sector. It has also meant finding a funding model and formula that would reflect and reinforce the principles of the organisation. The PIDF Governing Council convened for the first time in 2014, ahead of the second summit. This group, which is chaired by Fiji's prime minister, comprises heads of member governments, the PIPSO and the Pacific Islands Association of Non-Government Organisations. A key challenge facing the governing council has been to formalise a legal agreement establishing the PIDF, which would enable the PIDF to participate in its own right at international conferences. A process which included public and regional consultations led to the formulation of the PIDF charter by the People of the Pacific, to be formally launched at the third PIDF summit in Suva in September 2015. Within this charter is provision for a regional development fund. Institutionalisation has also taken place through the establishment of a secretariat headquarters (which opened in Suva in May 2014), led by an interim secretary general. Applications opened for a permanent secretary general (who could not be a citizen of Fiji), and this appointment was also due to be announced at the third PIDF summit.

As indicated at the outset, the PIDF has become a platform for showcasing new regional partnerships. At the second PIDF, the chief guest was Indonesian President Susilo Bambang Yudhoyono, using his first state visit to the region to pledge support for the green growth agenda and announcing assistance to support capacity-building programs for Pacific Island states. Russia and China have also continued to be strong backers of the PIDF, with China providing a financial contribution towards setting up the PIDF secretariat. The chief guest to the 2015 Summit was Thailand's Prime Minister General Prayut Chan-o-cha, with the Commonwealth Secretary General Kamalesh Sharma also attending. Apart from facilitating new economic partnerships, the PIDF is emerging as an important forum for mobilising diplomatic support on crucial global agendas, primarily around climate negotiations and sustainable development. The 2015 PIDF summit thus aimed to formulate 'key messages' from the people of the

Pacific for the UN Climate Change Conference scheduled for Paris later in the year. In keeping with the 'inclusivity' principle, attendance at the third PIDF summit was 'open and free'.

References

Field, M., 2010, 'Natadola: The disappearing communique'. Available at: discombobulatedbubu.blogspot.com.au/2010/07/natadola-disappearing-communique.html.

Pacific Islands Development Forum (PIDF), 2013, '2013 Pacific Islands Development Forum Outcomes'. Available at: pacificidf.org/2013-pacific-islands-development-forum-outcomes/.

Radio Australia, 2013, 'Inaugural Meeting of the Pacific Islands Development Forum Ends with Allegations of Sabotage', 8 August. Available at: www.radioaustralia.net.au/international/2013-08-08/inaugural-meeting-of-the-pacific-islands-development-forum-ends-with-allegations-of-sabotage/1173012.

8

The New Pacific Diplomacy at the United Nations: The rise of the PSIDS[1]

Fulori Manoa

Since 2009 there has been a marked elevation in the profile of the Pacific Island countries at the United Nations (UN). Nauru's much publicised chairmanship of the Alliance of Small Island States (AOSIS), Fiji's successful chairmanship of the G77 plus China in 2013, and Samoa's hosting of the Third International Conference of Small Island Developing States are the more telling signs of this rise in prominence. In addition, Pacific Island countries are now making it onto important UN committees and taking up leadership roles. Much of this new recognition at the UN can be attributed to the Pacific Island countries organising and working together as Pacific Small Island Developing States (PSIDS). This paper seeks to briefly tell the story of the PSIDS, who they are, why they organise the way they do, and outline some of the successes that they have achieved.

---

1   In June/July of 2014, I was privileged to be able to interview eight Pacific Island Ambassadors to the United Nations, 12 Pacific diplomats, and two advisers. I was able to speak to officials from 11 out of the 12 Pacific Island missions. I am exceedingly grateful to the ambassadors, diplomats and advisers for their time and help in sharing with me the story of the Pacific Small Island Developing States at the United Nations.

The PSIDS comprises 14 Pacific Island countries: Cook Islands, Federated States of Micronesia, Fiji, Kiribati, Nauru, Niue, Palau, Papua New Guinea, Marshall Islands, Samoa, Solomon Islands, Tonga, Tuvalu, and Vanuatu. When discussing the PSIDS in the context of the UN, the Cook Islands and Niue are not included, as they are not UN members; however, their names appear on official PSIDS stationery, their flags are included in the logo, and they are able to be part of group statements. For the purpose of this paper, PSIDS refers to the PSIDS who are members of the UN — the UN PSIDS.

When the idea of forming a PSIDS grouping first materialised, it was envisioned as a collective of the Pacific Island Forum (PIF) countries minus Australia and New Zealand. It initially grew out of a need to raise funds for projects around climate change adaptation and mitigation, renewable energy and pollution, but the structure proved successful and it has been consolidated over the past five years to the point where it has become arguably the most important part of the way in which Pacific Island countries engage at the UN.

The PSIDS is a New York–based, United Nations–specific grouping. This is highlighted by the case of Kiribati. Kiribati joined the UN in 1999, but it was not until September of 2013 that it established a mission in New York. A survey of PSIDS statements to a variety of different forums clearly shows that before the establishment of the Kiribati Permanent Mission, only rarely would Kiribati be included in a PSIDS statement. It was only after September 2013 that it became a 'regular' on the list of countries included in the PSIDS statements.

The PSIDS is founded on consensus; members circulate, make joint statements, and agree on which issues to pursue together. Although they have common interests and are recognised as a cohesive grouping, lobbied by other countries, they are not a voting bloc and pursue their national interests individually.

From the Forum Group to the PSIDS

According to Powles (2002, p. 72), writing more than a decade ago, the Pacific states at that time were organised into a Pacific Group which met once a month, made joint statements, and cooperated closely. The Pacific Group comprised members of the PIF that were also members of the UN. In other words, the Pacific Group comprised Pacific Island countries and Australia and New Zealand. The forum group ambassadors continue to meet, and they do release joint statements from time to time. However, today, the PSIDS is the primary vehicle for advocacy at the UN among Pacific Island countries. A long-serving ambassador put it this way: 'the Forum group still meets but not as regularly as it used to and it does not deliver as many joint statements as it used to. PSIDS, as a group, are making more statements' (personal communication 10 July 2014). The PSIDS ambassadors officially meet once a month, or more often if necessity dictates — if there are important ongoing negotiations, for example. They are also in regular electronic contact.

PSIDS meetings do not only take place at the ambassadorial level, which is an improvement on the meeting model that exists in the forum group. The PSIDS has also incorporated a working group, made up of staff from all the missions. A task of this working group is to examine the current issues at the UN, draft the PSIDS positions and make recommendations to the ambassadors for their approval.

Why the Shift from PIF to PSIDS?

There are a number of reasons why PSIDS gained impetus and superseded the PIF as the main body for Pacific Island country organising at the UN, including: differing interests with Australia and New Zealand, necessity, logic, and Fiji's suspension from the PIF.

Differing Interests

Powles (2002, p. 71) highlights the marginalisation experienced by the Pacific countries as a reason for their finding other avenues to make themselves heard. At that time, that meant organising through the forum group, however, it would seem that the Pacific Island countries and their issues were marginalised within the forum group. Joining their voices to those of Australia and New Zealand undoubtedly made their voices louder but, in practice, this actually muzzled them on issues where their interests diverged from those of their metropolitan forum colleagues. This was a point that most of the ambassadors and diplomats agreed upon. There was the general feeling that, since Australia and New Zealand were donor countries, they dealt with issues in different ways to the rest of the members of the forum group. Some were even of the view that Australia and New Zealand were using the forum group to promote their own interests, and that these interests clashed with the rest of the forum group on important issues such as climate change. For Pacific Island countries, sustainable development and climate change are the most important issues at the UN. To be marginalised within your own grouping on these issues would be grounds to find another avenue by which to make your voice heard. As one diplomat said:

PSIDS issues were never at the centre, the agenda was dictated by those that held the purse strings. If the issues were at all addressed, they were addressed sub-standardly. Within the region, the same actors and institutions are still at play, so why not form a different entity in New York at the UN to address the real challenges of the PSIDS (personal communication 2014).

Necessity

The average Pacific Island mission to the UN has three diplomats, including the ambassador, as compared to 33 diplomats at the Australian mission, and 14 diplomats at the New Zealand Mission. These numbers may seem ample for a Pacific high commission or embassy in another country, but for the sheer volume of work at the UN, these numbers can be woefully inadequate. Apart from the work of running the mission, which can range from consular and legal work to administration and finances, diplomats also have to deal with the plethora of issues and meetings that take place every day.

The United Nations General Assembly has six main committees and meetings for these committees run simultaneously. With the average of three staff per mission (in many cases less) it would be impossible for one PSIDS mission to cover all these meetings, or even all the relevant meetings. Every ambassador and diplomat spoke about the enormity of the work load and the importance of being strategic and working together. PSIDS ambassadors and other diplomats rely upon one another to cover meetings that they cannot attend and, in doing so, safeguard each other's interests. Not only do they share notes, there is genuine warmth within the grouping, and it is not unusual to have diplomatic staff from one mission calling another mission to ask for help with meeting timetables and venues or procedure.

Over the years, not much has changed in terms of manpower for the Pacific Island country missions. But recently a lot more has been achieved. Much of this can be ascribed to the collective work that is taking place amongst the PSIDS missions in New York.

Powles (2002, pp. 74–75) also talked about regional group membership as a 'daunting challenge' for the Pacific Forum Group at the United Nations, due to New Zealand and Australia being members of the Western European and Others group, and the Pacific Islands being members of the Asian group. At that time, Australia and New Zealand were pushing to bring the region together in its own UN-recognised grouping, to boost the status and influence of the region. Since then, however, the UN has reconfigured that particular status quo so that the Pacific Islands countries are part of the PSIDS group within the renamed Asia Pacific group (Tarte 2013, p. 2). It is through these groups that much of the work at the UN is done — voting, for example. It makes more sense for the Pacific Island countries to work together to raise their profile and push their interests within their own grouping.

Fiji's Suspension from the Pacific Island Forum

A few ambassadors place Fiji's suspension from the PIF in 2009 as central to the formation of, or the impetus given to the PSIDS. It was felt that Fiji's suspension lead to the reconfigured grouping as it became a necessity to ensure that Fiji was not left out after its suspension from the PIF. PSIDS was the space in which other Pacific Island countries could continue to engage with Fiji and thus the importance of the PSIDS grouping grew. The PSIDS grouping was subsequently found to be a 'comfort zone' for the Pacific Island countries, as they shared similar interests. Once they started meeting and engaging as PSIDS, recognition of the PSIDS as a separate entity from the PIF followed.

At the time Fiji was suspended from the PIF, PSIDS was already in existence and there were joint statements and actions already taking place. However, after Fiji's suspension PSIDS members began to act more in concert. This is measured by the amount of PSIDS statements that have been made and the achievements of the PSIDS at the United Nations. This gives support to the argument that Fiji's suspension from the forum was a catalyst to the PSIDS' subsequent rise at the UN. In this case, Fiji's departure from democracy can be said to have actually been a positive factor for the PSIDS in the pursuit of their goals at the UN and other global forums.

Has Organising as the PSIDS Yielded Success? How has it done this?

Success is a relative term, and it means different things in different situations. In order to get a truer picture of PSIDS' success at the UN, it is necessary to first examine what success means for the PSIDS and for individual PSIDS representatives to the UN. The underpinning definition of success for the ambassadors and diplomats was to have the ability to effect positive change for the people back in their home countries, through their work and advocacy at the UN. There also existed the notion of success as recognition, that is, being able to draw and maintain attention at the international forum despite myriad competing demands and differences. Taking into account these two main criteria — being able to effect change, and being recognised — it would not be amiss to say that the PSIDS have met with considerable success at the UN. This success has not come without serious effort; there were a series of strategic actions that the PSIDS undertook to achieve the success they are enjoying now.

In 2010, the PSIDS representatives met and decided on a plan of action to raise their profiles at the UN. The first course of action was to change the name of the Asian Group[2] to the Asia-Pacific Group. This was important to the PSIDS because they believed that how they were perceived carried a great deal of weight and to be able to achieve their ends they needed the recognition that a name change would bring. They were told that it would be impossible, but 14 months later they were able to achieve the name change. Officially, the group is now called the Group of Asia and the Pacific Small Island Developing States (Radio New Zealand 2011), however, the shortened form, the Asia-Pacific group, is in more frequent use. Achieving this level of acknowledgement made it easier and more plausible for the Pacific Island countries to put forth the PSIDS as the proper grouping to address the issues of the Pacific Island countries. This links directly to the change in focus from the PIF group to the PSIDS.

The PSIDS then started to assert themselves, insisting that the PSIDS and not the forum was the right grouping to address the issues that related to Pacific Island nations. The recognition of their group implied in the name change of the voting bloc was reflected in the PSIDS taking up the rotating monthly chair of the Asia-Pacific group when it was their turn. This laid the foundation for the next push, which entailed strategically tackling the candidature charts for elections within the UN. Changing the name of the Asian Group to the Asia-Pacific Group and becoming more involved in the running of that group was integral to the success of the PSIDS venture into the candidature charts, because the selection of candidates for elections is done through the regional grouping. The PSIDS coordinate amongst themselves and decide who should take up the seats that they find relevant to their advocacy.

A look at the Asia-Pacific Group's candidature charts for September of 2014 revealed PSIDS countries in key positions directly relevant to their development issues. Fiji sits on the United Nations Commission on International Trade (UNCITRAL) and the Governing Council of United Nations Environment Programme (UNEP). It also sits on the Executive Board of the United Nations Development Programme (UNDP), the United Nations Population Fund (UNFPA), and the United Nations Office for Project Services (UNOPS), and is currently chairing the bureau of the executive board. Fiji and Tonga are members of the Council of the International Seabed Authority. Papua New Guinea currently sits on the Executive Board of the United Nations Children's Fund (UNICEF) and the Executive Board of the United Nations Educational, Scientific and Cultural Organization (UNESCO). Solomon Islands currently sits on the Executive Board of United Nations Women and the Bureau of that executive board. Samoa currently

---

2   The Asian Group is one of the regional groupings at the United Nations, the others being the African Group, Eastern European Group, Latin American and Caribbean Group, and the Western European and Other Groups.

has an expert in the Committee on the Rights of the Child (CRC). Some of these PSIDS are serving the last leg of their tenure of these seats, but in some cases other PSIDS have been lined up to receive seats on the same boards, so that PSIDS interests are looked after. For example, Fiji's term on the Executive Board of UNDP/UNFPA/UNOPS ends in 2015 but the PSIDS have endorsed Samoa to take up a seat on that board once Fiji's term is up.

Also significant is the position of Vice President of the United Nations General Assembly (UNGA). At every UNGA, 21 vice presidents are elected and among their tasks is to sit on the general committee that scrutinises the provisional agenda at the start of the UNGA session (UNGA 2014). Since 2011 (66th session), the PSIDS have had one of their number as Vice President of the UNGA, with Kiribati currently a vice president (69th session), and Fiji taking over for the 70th session. While PSIDS countries have had vice presidency of the UNGA before (starting with Fiji in 1973: 28th session), never has there been this level of sustained representation and, consequently, recognition.

With recognition comes more leverage, and this has been the case with the PSIDS and their advocacy. Examples of this success in recent years include the passing of the first climate change resolution, French Polynesia's reinscription onto the list of non-self-governing territories and achieving stand-alone Sustainable Development Goals (SDGs) on oceans and climate change. These examples are discussed below.

On 3 June 2009, the UNGA unanimously adopted a resolution titled 'Climate Change and its possible security implications'. A few longer-serving diplomats flagged this as an important early achievement for the PSIDS, as they had to campaign hard for a long time to see it come through. This was recognised by Australia's representative at the time, who said, after the resolution was adopted, that it demonstrated regard for some of the smaller states in the international arena and that 'those states deserved congratulations for their dignified participation in the long negotiations'. If United States government cables revealed by WikiLeaks are anything to go by, it would seem that the PSIDS did make an impact. One document clearly outlines that the United States had intended that the option of negotiating the resolution was only to be used as a 'fall back'.[3] The resolution is not as strong as it could be, but the fact that it was adopted and the PSIDS were able to force the hand of the United States to adopt the fall-back position can be seen as a victory.

The second illustration of success illustrates the prominence of the Pacific Island countries at the United Nations. On 17 May 2013, French Polynesia was reinscribed onto the UN list of non-self-governing territories by a UNGA

3   See wikileaks.org/plusd/cables/08STATE82276_a.html.

resolution that was sponsored by Solomon Islands, Nauru, and Tuvalu with support from Vanuatu, Samoa, and Timor-Leste (Maclellan 2013). The Pacific Islands (acting as the forum) have had prior success getting a territory on the list. In 1978, Papua New Guinea, Solomon Islands, Fiji, and Western Samoa (now Samoa) launched a collective attack on France's continuing colonial presence in the South Pacific at the UNGA. For the next ten years, New Caledonia was a main topic at forum meetings (Fry 1994, p. 167). Between 1980 and 1986, there was a split in the forum on what to do about New Caledonia, as some countries wanted to play it safe with France and not embarrass a world power (Fry 1994, p. 167). However a centre-right change in government in that metropolitan country put the island leaders, along with Australia and New Zealand, on the same team. Vanuatu requested and gained the Non-Aligned Movement's support at the UN and the resolution for reinscription was passed, 89 votes to 24 (Fry 1994, p. 168). It is important to note here that the Pacific Island countries had to get Australia and New Zealand on side before they were able to achieve their ends.

By stark contrast, with the reinscription of French Polynesia, Australia was not supportive of the action (Maclellan 2013). Thus collective Pacific action did not come through the forum. At the forum meeting in August 2012, the call for reinscription was not endorsed, but one month later at the UN, leaders from Samoa, Solomon Islands, Fiji, and Vanuatu made the call for decolonisation at the UN and the following year in February the ambassadors for Solomon Islands, Tuvalu, and Nauru formally lodged a draft resolution at the UN which was adopted, despite strong French opposition (Maclellan 2013).

Aside from the success of helping French Polynesia work toward self-determination, for the PSIDS this represented a success in achieving autonomy from Australia and New Zealand. A long-time diplomat at the UN said that in the past (when the Pacific Islands Forum was still the main Pacific Island grouping), when the Pacific Islands wanted something, they would ask Australia and New Zealand for help, and they relied heavily on them in this way. Now, however, they meet up as PSIDS and discuss their issues and the things that they want to advocate before they inform Australia and New Zealand, and they do not depend solely on their support.

What may be the PSIDS's most important success in advocacy to date is the negotiation of climate change and oceans as stand-alone sustainable development goals. These goals will feed into the post-2015 development agenda. Virtually every ambassador and diplomat interviewed spoke at length about the importance of having these goals included and a few also talked about the renewable energy goal. There were other issues that were also important, but oceans and climate change needed to be championed in order for them to be included. There were 30 seats in the open working group for the sustainable development goals, seven of which were allocated to the Asia–Pacific Group. The PSIDS were represented by a troika of Nauru, Palau, and Papua New Guinea, who shared a seat (Sustainable Development Knowledge Platform 2014). PSIDS diplomats who were involved in the negotiation of the sustainable development goals talked about the difficulty involved in trying to negotiate comprehensive stand-alone goals for oceans and climate change. However, on 12 August 2014, the report of the Open Working Group of the General Assembly on Sustainable Development Goals was submitted to the UNGA, Amongst the 17 goals were 'Take urgent action to combat Climate Change and its effects' and 'Conserve and sustainably use the oceans, seas and marine resources for sustainable development' (UNGA 2014). It is recognised that the Pacific countries were very active in their SDGs campaign. In his address to the Pacific Islands Forum (the PSIDS is not an official grouping while the PIF is recognised) leaders on 26 September in New York, the UN Secretary General commended them on their advocacy of the stand-alone goal on oceans.

It has been over 40 years since the first Pacific Island country joined the UN; now the Pacific Islands have reached a stage where they are able to assert themselves and influence decisions in this global forum. In 2004, Pacific Island ambassadors were feeling very marginalised at the UN and they felt that their issues were not getting the attention they deserved (McNamara 2009). Ten years later, Pacific Island ambassadors and other diplomats are a lot more positive about their role at the UN. They have made great gains at the world body. Much of this can be attributed to the new Pacific diplomacy at the UN — working together and working innovatively. Pacific collective diplomacy is arguably strongest at the UN in New York, and this is fostered by shared interests, the need to work together, distance from the region, and proximity to each other in New York. The PSIDS model of cooperation is testament to the fact that 'smallness' and a lack of resources does not have to translate into helplessness. The Pacific Islands, acting together as PSIDS, have met with success at the UN, but according to one long-serving Pacific ambassador, 'success is a journey', and continued success will depend on whether or not advocacy can be continued at this level (personal communication 2014). This is the challenge for the PSIDS.

References

Fry, G., 1994, 'International Cooperation in the South Pacific: From Regional integration to collective diplomacy', in W. A. Axline (ed.), *The Political Economy of Regional Cooperation: Comparative case studies,* Pinter Publishers, London.

Maclellan, N., 2013, 'Hijacking Decolonisation: French Polynesia at the United Nations', *Inside Story*. Available at: insidestory.org.au/hijacking-decolonisation-french-polynesia-at-the-united-nations.

McNamara, K.E., 2009, 'Voices from the Margins: Pacific ambassadors and the geopolitics of marginality at the United Nations', *Asia Pacific Viewpoint* 50(1), pp. 1–12.

Powles, M., 2002, 'Making Waves in the Big Lagoon: The influence of Pacific Island Forum countries in the United Nations', *Revue Juridique Polynésienne* 2, pp. 59–76.

Radio New Zealand, 2011, 'Asian Group of Nations at the UN Changes its Name to Asia-Pacific Group'. Available at: www.radionz.co.nz/international/pacific-news/199302/asian-group-of-nations-at-un-changes-its-name-to-asia-pacific-group.

Sustainable Development Knowledge Platform, 2014, 'Open Working Group on Sustainable Development Goals'. Available at: sustainabledevelopment.un.org/owg.html.

Tarte, S., 2013, 'A New Regional Pacific Voice?: An observer's perspective on the Pacific Islands Development Forum (PIDF), inaugural summit, Denarau, Fiji, 5–7 August 2013', Pacific Island Development Program, Honolulu. Available at: www.eastwestcenter.org/sites/default/files/private/pib004.pdf.

United Nations General Assembly (UNGA), 2014. Main Committees: General Committee. Available at: www.un.org/en/ga/general/general.shtml.

Fiji's New Diplomacy

9

Fiji's Emerging Brand of Pacific Diplomacy: A Fiji government perspective

Litia Mawi

In a variety of ways, Fiji's regional presence in the Pacific has gradually yet progressively evolved since it gained independence from Great Britain in 1970. However, it is during this past decade — since the launch of the national initiative to 'Build a Better Fiji for All', through the People's Charter for Change, Peace and Progress (PCCPP) in 2007 — that Fiji's mark of true independence as a sovereign nation has intensified. The charter set in motion a national mindset that a common and equal citizenry is the only foundation upon which a modern, democratic Fiji can be sustainably developed. Vigorously but steadily nurtured, that ideal image will blossom into a Fiji that showcases the richness of its many cultures, traditions and histories.

Such a national mindset has, over this past decade, inevitably enhanced Fiji's global integration and engagement in international relations, through an asserted posture of self-determination that cautiously respects the sovereignty of others by being 'a friend to all and enemy to none' in the entire global family of nations. In retrospect, Fiji's post-2006 diplomatic isolation by traditional allies was the needed impetus for it to explore and maximise new opportunities, such as the 'look and engage north' policy, and to broker new partnerships beyond familiar spheres of interest.

It is among Fiji's silent aspirations that this bold and unwavering stance will make some imprint on the ambitions of the smaller Pacific Island developing states and territories and their relationship with Pacific development partners, to whom they are implicitly subordinated through colonial ties and obligatory mindsets.

During this blossoming period, Fiji's most notable presence at a sub-regional level was through the Melanesian Spearhead Group (MSG). During Fiji's chairmanship of the MSG, over the two years 2012–2013, culminating in the 25th silver jubilee celebration, it promoted the principles of self-determination and economic growth with equity. It also promoted inclusivity by encouraging the recognition of associate member states.

At a global level, Fiji's contribution to global peace and security has been active since 1978 in the United Nations peacekeeping activities (now evolved into peace-building) in various versions of international unrest. Such active participation has showcased to the world a breed of Fijian soldiering and policing renowned for lending their professional attitude and personality to the task of building bridges across human divides in adaptive ways.

Also at a global level, Fiji's chairmanship in 2013 of the Group of 77 plus China, the largest voting bloc in the United Nations, motivated Fiji to lead by example in advocating south–south cooperation (SSC) in the Pacific, by becoming a development partner to smaller Pacific neighbours thereby demonstrating to the international community Fiji's distinctive brand of responsible global citizenship.

What have been some of the major highlights in the last six years? Following Fiji's suspension from the Pacific Islands Forum (PIF) in 2009, Fiji has capitalised on the subsequent detachment from traditional friends to venture onto new turf through a 'look and engage north' policy; strengthening ties with Brazil, Russia, India, China and South Africa (BRICS); and new accreditations to the Association of Southeast Asian Nations (ASEAN), the Non-Aligned Movement (NAM), and other international networks, where there are no political conditionalities, but where there are shared values in the sovereign equality of states and mutual respect for domestic jurisdiction within such states.

Engaging with the Pacific

At a regional level, following Fiji's suspension from the Pacific Islands Forum in 2009, Fiji committed itself to remaining productively engaged with the Pacific by hosting three Engaging with the Pacific (EWTP) meetings in 2010–2012. It was at the third EWTP in 2012 that the Pacific leaders in attendance made a decision to establish the Pacific Islands Development Forum (PIDF). As stated by Fiji Prime Minister Frank Bainimarama when he opened the inaugural PIDF summit in 2013:

> … the 2012 EWTP Communiqué endorsed the convening of the Pacific Islands Development Forum for the purpose of engaging leaders from key sectors in implementing green economic policies in the Pacific Small Islands Developing States (or PSIDS).
>
> Why do we need a new body, a new framework of cooperation? Because the existing regional structure for the past four decades — the Pacific Islands Forum — is for governments only and has also come to be dominated only by a few. In too many instances, it no longer genuinely represents our interests and needs.
>
> We want to stand up as Pacific islanders and with one voice send a clear message to the world at large; that Pacific-SIDS are vulnerable and face unique sustainable development challenges.

Since the very first EWTP meeting in 2010, Fiji has established MOUs with seven Pacific Small Islands Developing States (PSIDS): Kiribati, Tuvalu, Solomon Islands, Nauru, Republic of the Marshall Islands, Federated States of Micronesia, and Vanuatu. These MOUs highlight the replicability of development experiences amongst PSIDS, and the need to move away from the archaic notion of aid to one of partnership and collective self-reliance. Any specificities for individual PSIDS are facilitated under separate Memorandum of Agreements, such as for the Fiji Volunteer Scheme and other emerging modes of technical assistance that capitalise on human resources capacity building. The 'perfect fit' of Fiji's skills and technologies with the needs of these PSIDS arises from the lower costs and greater appropriateness of skills and expertise available in Fiji compared to neighbouring locations. For example, a capacity building program for PSIDS officials would be far more cost effective conducted in Suva or Nadi than in Tokyo, Sydney or Auckland.

These specifically tailored Fiji–PSIDS Development Cooperation MOUs (and MOAs) are focused on nine areas of development cooperation:

- bilateral trade and investment;
- education, youth and human resources development;
- labour mobility;
- immigration;
- commerce, retail and taxation;
- fisheries cooperation;
- air and sea transportation;
- health and pharmaceuticals; and
- climate change, environment, security and energy.

These Fiji–PSIDS south–south partnerships fall neatly within the global framework for Small Island Developing States (SIDS)-specific cooperation under the Alliance of Small Island States (AOSIS). Nauru is the current AOSIS chair through its Permanent Representative to the United Nations (PRUN). The AOSIS representatives are the AOSIS PRUNs, including the PSIDS PRUNs based in New York. The global framework for SIDS cooperation also reflects the Millennium Development Goals (MDGs): 2000–2015, the Barbados Plan of Action (1994), the Mauritius Strategy (2004) and the S.A.M.O.A. Pathway (2014). In due course, they will also reflect the Sustainable Development Goals (SDGs) — post-2015 development agenda.

Within these south–south frameworks, the recurring global themes for SIDS-specific cooperation include response and resilience to natural disasters, climate change adaptation, sustainable development, maritime resources (fisheries and deep sea mining), investment and public–private partnerships, people-to-people exchanges, capacity building, the MDGs acceleration framework to 2015, and the emerging SDGs — post-2015 sustainable development agenda.

South–South Cooperation

SSC is used to describe the exchange of resources, technology, and knowledge between developing countries, and is universally promoted as an essential cross-cutting mechanism designed to deliver capacity building and technology support activities in developing countries and regions of the south. SSC can also complement north–south cooperation to enhance technical, financial, scientific and technological exchanges and innovations for development.

SSC received considerable attention as a philosophy for development during the 1960s and 1970s, when developing countries, coming out from under the yoke of colonisation, were struggling with poverty and underdevelopment. A lack of financial and technological resources and western apathy forced them to look to collective self-reliance as an engine of growth. The most significant platform for SSC is G77 plus China which was originally formed by 77 countries in 1964, and which now has 134 developing countries of the 'south'. SSC suffered a setback during the late 1980s and the 1990s, however, as a large number of developing countries faced financial crisis against the backdrop of declining resource flows.

The launch of the MDGs in early 2000 has given a new impetus to SSC. SSC is today a vital component of the international development fabric as the G77 plus China members increasingly recognise that solutions to many of the development challenges they face are better addressed through partnerships between and amongst themselves. We can only hope that, in the same manner that the MDGs provided an impetus for SSC to be invigorated post-2000, it should pick up pace again at the upcoming launch of the SDGs at the United Nations General Assembly (UNGA) in September 2015.

As implied briefly above, the binding characteristics of SSC between Fiji and PSIDS include the replicability of development experiences amongst PSIDS — partnership and solidarity for development, rather than development assistance/ aid. The appropriateness of Fiji's skills and technologies arises from a number of reasons including:

(i)   a backdrop of similar factor endowments — for example, labour abundance and relative capital scarcity;

(ii) solutions are more labour intensive rather than automated technology;

(iii) a similar state of basic infrastructure — for example, telecommunication technologies not requiring air conditioning, etc.;

(iv) expertise is attuned to similar geo-climatic tropical conditions — for example, the proficiency required for food preservation in tropical settings;

(v)   technologies and expertise are scaled down to size of markets in smaller PSIDS rather than the mass production skills in industrialised countries; and

(vi) technologies and expertise available are cost effective, having been adapted in view of low income consumers in PSIDS.

Over this past decade of such developments, Fiji now views the Pacific as distinctly different from the world's understanding of PSIDS. Fiji now asserts the position that all PSIDS are sovereign nations whose views and preferences should not be overwritten by any external lenses that are not willing to align to Pacific aspirations and self-determined priorities, and that the time has come for a distinctive and united PSIDS voice.

It is only with this view and end in mind that Fiji — or any other Pacific development partner for that matter — will be able to genuinely contribute to development initiatives and aspirations through targeted development cooperation that is customised to the felt and expressed needs of her neighbouring PSIDS.

Fiji is exploring newer modes of partnership where existing development partners of PSIDS become the triangular/trilateral partner to initial bilateral partnerships between Fiji and the smaller PSIDS. Triangular cooperation, at a very general level, involves two or more developing countries in collaboration with a third party, typically a developed country government or organisation, contributing to the exchanges with its own know-how and resources. Fiji's search for triangular development partners in the Pacific setting is particularly in the areas of human resources and institutional capacity building in the agriculture, fisheries and tourism sectors — these being the three sectors in any PSIDS that are capable of producing tradeable, exportable commodities — as well as the enabling sectors of transport (both sea and air) and energy. There is also the emerging sector of deep sea minerals, which is seen by Fiji as an area of potential collaboration with developed triangular partners.

The Way Forward: Strengthening the PIDF

So what is the way forward for Fiji's Pacific diplomacy? Following successful democratic elections in 2014, Fiji has an opportunity to further strengthen its 'hub of the Pacific' role in developing SSC through the PIDF. Inaugurated in August 2013, PIDF is the first platform in the Pacific focusing specifically on green economies and sustainable development in the series of Rio+20 Global Agenda on Sustainable Development. Fiji views the PIDF as the only forum that will truly represent the voice of the PSIDS on the sustainable development issue as the global community prepares for the implementation of the SDGs.

The inclusion of the private sector and civil society in the PIDF not only guarantees explicit commitment and civic ownership to green economic growth in PSIDS but also launches a new era of regional cooperation through genuine partnership and dialogue between governments, civil society groups, and the business community. These crucial groups had hitherto been excluded from PSIDS regional decision-making processes.

A strengthened PIDF will also validate Fiji's hub role in the Pacific and her relations with the smaller PSIDS, provided that all sincere development partners, irrespective of the length and depth of their association with individual PSIDS in whatever capacity, acknowledge their role as partners by aligning to the ownership by PSIDS of their development goals and ideals.

Fiji remains encouraged by the fact that, in addition to PIDF, there is promising potential for PSIDS triangular partners within existing Pacific regional frameworks, including the traditional Pacific partners of Australia, Japan, France, New Zealand, the USA, and the European Union; the MSG; the Council of Regional Organisations in the Pacific (CROP); the Pacific Islands Private Sector Organisation (PIPSO); the Pacific Islands Association of Non-Government Organisations (PIANGO); the UNDP Regional Program for Asia and the Pacific 2014–2017 (which is new, since Asia–Pacific became an official grouping at the UN in 2012); the UN Development Assistance Framework (UNDAF) for the Pacific, 2013–2017; the Korea–Pacific Forum; and, last but not least, Japan through the Pacific Alliance Leaders Meeting (PALM) dialogue. The state visits to Fiji in 2014 by the presidents of Indonesia and the People's Republic of China, and the prime minister of India — which also included roundtable dialogues with Pacific leaders — are clear indicators that Indonesia, China and India would be willing triangular partners to any SSC between PSIDS.

The undeniable challenge for the Pacific, like any other SSC, is financing. Like all challenges, however, it is also the greatest opportunity for exploring triangular cooperation with the above-mentioned Pacific development partners. It is also an opportunity to explore more innovative financing strategies that emphasise ownership by communities as resource owners if there are to be more sustainable social governance structures. For the immediate future, the apparent challenge is the need to shift the PSIDS mindset away from a focus on vulnerability into more positive and alternative visions for the Pacific in approaches to development, governance, environmental sustainability, security, and social cohesion which would ensure inclusiveness and self-sufficiency amongst all our PSIDS communities.

Fiji's Role as Pacific Hub

Understandably of course, there are lenses and perspectives that question Fiji's role and label as the Pacific hub in political, economic and sociocultural solidarity. Fiji sees the Pacific — not just the South Pacific — as an integrated region that is driven by the shared value of 'collective self-reliance as an engine of growth', and where Fiji has the primary role of being the hub through its geographic location and its more developed state, relative to most other PSIDS. Evidence and reassurance to validate this hub role include Fiji's successful venture into relatively unknown spheres over the past decade and in its strengthening of the economic, political and sociocultural ties that have progressively weaned Fiji off total dependence on traditional partners in a refreshed foreign and trade policy direction. Fiji can develop the capacities of smaller PSIDS who wish to take this sovereignty route.

Other evidence of reassurance and validation include Fiji's election as president of the 2014 UNDP/UNFPA/UNOPS executive board following its chairmanship of G77 plus China in 2013. Founded, as mentioned above, in 1964 by an original group of 77 countries, G77 plus China membership has since increased to 132 over the years, and during Fiji's chairmanship, it admitted Kiribati as the 133rd member nation at the UNGA in September 2013. Not only is the G77 plus China the main voice of the global south on economic and social issues in the UN system, it has boosted the bargaining strength of the south in championing the primary interests of the developing world.

As Fiji asserts her hub of the Pacific role through SSC with smaller PSIDS, it is essential that the core principles of the Paris Declaration for Development Effectiveness are consciously upheld: ownership by PSIDS of their priorities, alignment by Fiji to such priorities, harmonisation by Fiji with other development partners (including triangular partners), managing for results in both outcomes and impacts, and mutual accountability. Triangular partners, on the other hand, should be convinced to no longer ask PSIDS the question, 'what can we do for you?', but rather, 'what can we do to add value to what it is that you are already doing to help yourselves and each other?'.

With the advent of the post-2015 sustainable development goals as the broadest framework for global partnerships — be they south–south, north–south, or triangular — it has to be universally accepted by all players that these much anticipated sustainable development goals can validly build upon regional and national agendas on the one hand, yet on the other be the common denominators and underlying bases for ultimate accountability in responsible global citizenship. Amidst all this cross pollination in global integration and international cooperation, there always will be some duplication and overlap, as humanity zooms in on areas that matter most. Instead of seeing such developments as rivalry and competition, the challenge would be in converting them into complementarities for win-win solutions for all Pacific people.

Inclusion of the Pacific People

At the heart of Fiji's new regional diplomacy is the notion of 'Pacific people', embracing an inclusivity not previously acknowledged or practised in Pacific regionalism. Fiji Prime Minister Frank Bainimarama succinctly explained this notion of 'Pacific people' and its importance for future SSC in the Pacific in his remarks at the inauguration of the PIDF in August 2013. Let me conclude by reproducing his explanation of this central concept in Fiji's new regional diplomacy in full:

> Until now, ladies and gentlemen, sovereign governments have largely determined how the Pacific will respond to its many challenges. The small island territories, dependencies and protectorates haven't had a direct say. And neither have civil society groups and businesses. The people most affected by government decisions — the grassroots and their representatives — have largely been excluded from the decision-making process. Not any longer. The PIDF recognizes that governments do not have all the answers. We cannot merely prescribe solutions to the challenges we face in keeping the Pacific 'green' and 'blue'.

We need to listen more to our people and the common sense towards problem-solving that comes with grassroots participation. We need to listen more to our business communities, whose investment generates the jobs we need to raise living standards and improve the lives of our people.

So for the first time, we are bringing all these stakeholders together to discuss common solutions to our common problems in a practical and holistic way. And we will take those ideas and contribute them to the global debate in other forums — including the United Nations — the Pacific speaking with one voice based on the consensus we reach here.

The world recognises the underlying importance of this approach. In June 2012, governments and civil society groups gathered in Rio De Janeiro for the United Nations Conference on Sustainable Development. It concluded that Small Island Developing States have a special status in the debate about sustainable development because of their unique vulnerability. And it said that sustainable development 'can only be achieved with a broad alliance of people, governments, civil society and the private sector, all working together to secure the future for present and the following generations'.

So Fiji's vision is for sovereign governments, territories and dependencies, civil society groups and the business community, forming a grand coalition to protect our environment; to make sure that development is sustainable; to make sure that the common good comes before sectional interests; and that we leave the Pacific to our children and grandchildren in a better state than when we inherited it.

It is unfortunate that certain Pacific countries are not with us. They have chosen to regard the PIDF as a political event rather than grasp its true purpose — which is to address the very real threat that our people face and could be catastrophic if we don't act in a collaborative and unselfish manner. As leaders, we must always put our people first. We are one ocean, one people, seeking common solutions.

10

Fiji's Foreign Policy and the New Pacific Diplomacy

Makereta Komai

Fiji's suspension from the Pacific Islands Forum and the Commonwealth in May and September 2009 respectively was a major turning point in its relations with the international community. These two dramatic events sparked a change in Fiji's foreign policy, which has continued until today. Initially, these policies were formulated to circumvent what were seen as an Australia/New Zealand-led policy to isolate Fiji, and to counter the negative image and fallout created by the suspensions. Some radical thinking was put into the policy to ignite Fiji's standing in the international community in line with the government's 2006 Charter for Change. Pillar 11 of the charter requires Fiji to enlarge its foreign relations, extending beyond traditional allies to countries that respect Fiji's sovereignty and understand the needs and challenges the country was going through.

It is argued that this 'new diplomacy' has constituted a major departure from past Fiji foreign policies. This chapter demonstrates the sense in which there has been a fundamental change in the principles and practice of Fiji's foreign policy and what implications this has for Fiji's place in the region and the world.

Fiji's New Foreign Policies

Pacific Engagement and Leadership

Fiji's foreign policies prior to 2009 were closely aligned with its bilateral relations with Australia, New Zealand and the Commonwealth, because of its history as a colony of Great Britain. A substantial part of Fiji's trade and economic relations are linked to Australia and New Zealand, and the European Union. However, the suspension of Fiji from the Pacific Islands Forum and the Commonwealth in May and September of 2009 saw a major shift in Fiji's foreign policies. Recognising the importance of regional mechanisms in global geopolitics, the first of the five strategies applied by Fiji was to maintain its presence and leadership in the Pacific region, despite its removal from the premier political body, the Pacific Islands Forum. For Fiji, the next best option was to enlist support from within the powerful sub-regional group, the Melanesian Spearhead Group (MSG), for political reforms put in place by the Bainimarama Government to return the country to democratic rule. The endorsement of the MSG was key to reclaiming some regional legitimacy within the Pacific and proving to the world that Fiji was not a pariah state (Nayasi 2013). However, in July 2010, Vanuatu's Prime Minister Edward Natapei cancelled the biennial meeting of MSG leaders because he felt that 'the group should only be chaired by an elected leader and not someone who came to power in a military coup' (Kilman 2010). He refused to hand over chairmanship of the group to Commodore Bainimarama. Despite the cancellation, Fiji convened its own Engaging with the Pacific (EWTP) meeting to replace the MSG leaders meeting, which was deferred to another date (Balawa 2013). Vanuatu's refusal to hand over the MSG chair to Fiji caused a division among the leaders of Papua New Guinea, Solomon Islands, and Vanuatu. Former Prime Minister of Papua New Guinea Sir Michael Somare was instrumental in drawing up a compromise to show support for Fiji. Sir Michael stepped in to broker the thaw in relations between Fiji and Vanuatu, and suggested Solomon Islands as a neutral venue for the handover of chairmanship of MSG and for leaders to reconcile amongst themselves. He was the only MSG leader that stood by Fiji, asking other Pacific leaders to allow Fiji to deal with its own political situation. This support is reflected in his speech at the 25th anniversary of the MSG in Noumea on 20 June. He said Fiji needed the understanding of the MSG and recognised that the 'Melanesian values of dialogue and patience have the greatest potential to bring about the change we want in Fiji'. Bainimarama ensured that Fiji was present at the Honiara meeting, because the chairmanship of the MSG was key to Fiji asserting its presence and leadership within the region (Balawa 2013). A reconciliation ceremony was held in Honiara, hosted by Solomon Islands Prime Minister Danny Philip on 15 December, where Solomon Islands handed over the MSG leadership to Fiji.

'Look North' Policy

The second new foreign policy strategy was 'finding better partners beyond Australia and New Zealand'. As defined by Esala Nayasi, Director of Fiji's Political and Treaties Division within the Ministry of Foreign Affairs, 'these are partners who, despite the country's political situation, respected Fiji as equal and understood the policies put in place by the government to take the country back to democratic rule' (Nayasi 2013). This position was spelt out clearly by Fiji Foreign Affairs Minister Ratu Inoke Kubuabola in a speech to the Australia Fiji Business Council meeting in Brisbane in July 2013, when he said that 'Fiji no longer looks to Australia and New Zealand but to the world' (Kubuabola 2013). He said that, since 2009, Fiji had taken a 'different path' and forged new relationships with countries that understood and didn't judge the political reforms the country was going through:

> Jolted from our complacency by the doors that were slammed in our faces, we looked north — to the great powers of Asia, especially China, India and Indonesia and more recently to Russia. We looked south to the vast array of nations, big and small, that make up the developing world and we currently chair the G77, the biggest voting bloc at the United Nations. And we looked to our Melanesian neighbours, to forge closer ties with them and use our collective strength to make our voices heard in global forums and secure better trading deals for us all (Kubuabola 2013).

What Ratu Inoke expounded to the Australia Fiji Business Forum was in line with the Fijian government's strategy to enhance and deepen its 'Look North' policy. Key to this strategy was the deepening of bilateral ties with China, as reiterated by Commodore Bainimarama in his 2013 state visit to Beijing. Since 2009, Commodore Bainimarama has assured the Chinese administration that Fiji will make China a key part of its 'Look North' policy (Xiaokun 2009). Political and economic support from China has enabled Fiji's economy to stabilise and the country to make political progress with its roadmap to democratic reform and elections (Balawa 2013). Instead of giving Fiji a cold shoulder, China developed closer engagement with Fiji, stepping in to fill the gaps left by Australia and New Zealand. China's position is in line with its foreign policy, which respects sovereignty and territorial integrity, non-interference in the affairs of other states, and peaceful coexistence. In May 2009, prior to Fiji's suspension from the Pacific Islands Forum, Commodore Bainimarama said: 'The Chinese authorities are very sympathetic and understand what's happening here — the fact that we need to do things in our own way.' He was the first Pacific Island leader to meet with the new Chinese President Xi Jinping, two months after he assumed office. The deepening partnership and cooperation between the two nations has raised eyebrows in Australia and New Zealand because Australia has always regarded Fiji and the rest of the Pacific as its own backyard. While Fiji was deepening relations with China, it also deepened ties with Indonesia and South Korea, setting up diplomatic missions in these two countries in April 2011 and July 2012 respectively.

'Friends to All'

Expanding relations meant that Fiji had to look at establishing diplomatic ties with as many countries as possible — countries that understood Fiji's political situation and did not interfere with its domestic affairs (Nayasi 2013). Prior to 2009, Fiji had established diplomatic relations with 70 countries. The new strategy required beefing up Fiji's friends globally. Nayasi stated that:

> We looked at our own database and realised that we have signed diplomatic relations with only 70 countries. We saw this was something that we needed to change — first of all that we must be friends with everyone. We had to look at our comparative advantage — what we can offer rather than just depending on two countries (Australia and New Zealand).

From 2009–2013, Fiji added 63 more nations to its list of countries with diplomatic relations. According to Nayasi (2013), 'Cabinet has now given the Ministry of Foreign Affairs the go-ahead to sign diplomatic relations with the rest of the member countries of the United Nations'. Given Fiji's limited human resource capacity to set up diplomatic missions in all capitals of countries with diplomatic relations, cabinet agreed to set up diplomatic missions in all key regions of the United Nations (UN) — South Africa (Africa), Brazil (Latin America and the Caribbean), the United Arab Emirates (Middle East), and Indonesia as a key and influential nation in Southeast Asia and founding member of the Association of Southeast Asian Nations (Southeast Asia). During this process, Fiji even courted controversial friends such as Iran, North Korea, and Egypt. Nayasi said: 'As far as we are concerned, it is about respect and treating each other equally.'

At the multilateral level, Fiji actively participated in regional and international organisations, including the UN. According to Nayasi (2013):

> Since we were out of the Pacific Islands Forum, our only opportunity was to revamp our participation at sub-regional and regional organisations like the Melanesian Spearhead Group, Secretariat of the Pacific Community, the Engaging With The Pacific, which is now known as the Pacific Islands Development Forum.

In 2011, Fiji chaired the Secretariat of the Pacific Community's Governing Council, the Committee of Representatives of Governments and Administrations (CRGA) and the MSG, two key positions that lifted Fiji out of the 'political and diplomatic doldrums' it found itself in after 2006 and assured its leadership and influence in the Pacific. As assessed by Nayasi (2013), 'You can clearly see the hands of Fiji in these groups — we have become an influential member at the regional level'. At the UN in New York, Fiji continued to work within the

193-member group, securing new friends. The new strategy allows the foreign affairs office in Suva to explore benefits from being a member of an international organisation.

Fiji has actively remained engaged in the area of peacekeeping since it joined the world body. Peacekeeping is a key pillar in Fiji's foreign policies; since 1978, Fiji has derived considerable foreign revenue through remittances from soldiers on peacekeeping duties, which have provided employment to thousands of men and women. To date, UN peacekeeping has contributed over FJ$200 million in revenue per annum, earning more than traditional sectors such as sugar and garment manufacturing. Another key aspect of Fiji's peacekeeping commitment is its strategic interests in global politics. As a result of its commitments in Sinai, Iraq, and the Golan Heights, Fiji is well regarded by super powers such as the United States. At the 68th UN General Assembly in 2013, Bainimarama assured world leaders that Fiji recognises the risks involved in peacekeeping, but that it was more than ready to provide 501 troops to Syria to shore up the UN Disengagement Observer Force (UNDOF). Peacekeeping is a source of great pride for Fiji, because it allows Fiji to make a meaningful contribution to global peace (Bainimarama 2013). For the Fiji government, 'The high standard achieved by Fijian personnel in UN peacekeeping has been a focus of national pride and has earned Fiji considerable distinction in the international community' (Ministry of Foreign Affairs and International Cooperation 2009).

An attempt by Australia in 2010 to shut Fiji out of UN peacekeeping duties was foiled even before it was tabled to the security council because of a possibility of two of the five permanent members withdrawing support for the resolution against Fiji's UN peacekeeping participation (Balawa 2013). During its term as chair of G77, Fiji was actively involved in a move within the group to introduce reforms within UN peacekeeping operations. In May 2014, Fiji and the United States were tasked to negotiate an outcome on the reforms of the UN peacekeeping operations.

Significance and Implications

Global Standing

From Fiji's perspective, the new foreign policies achieved more than they set out to do. From being an international outcast in 2009, Fiji defied all the odds to emerge as chair of the powerful G77 plus China lobby group within the UN. This achievement came about in 2012 when Fiji was elected ahead of Bangladesh to lead the 133-member group, securing more than 50 per cent of the votes in the first round of votes (Nayasi 2013). Fiji and Bangladesh were the two candidates from the Asia region. Nayasi revealed that Bangladesh opted for a second round of voting, but later withdrew when it realised that it would be near impossible to surpass support for the Pacific nation. A compromise was reached and Bangladesh agreed to withdraw from the race if Fiji supported its bid to be a non-permanent member of the UN Security Council. Nayasi said chairing the G77 plus China for 2013 was the pinnacle of Fiji's achievements because it became the first Pacific Small Island Developing State (PSIDS) to lead an august lobby group of more than 130 countries at the UN.

An analysis of Fiji's G77 election by Catherine Wilson argued: 'Fiji's election will give the country's leadership a chance to reach out to the rest of the region by way of consultation in order to make sure a regional voice can be heard in the international stage.' She added that the 'Pacific will have a rare opportunity to represent itself on the global stage' (Wilson 2012). In 2012, Fiji Foreign Affairs Minister Ratu Inoke Kubuabola said that Fiji's election was a 'demonstration of the confidence of the international community in Fiji to preside over the 132 member organisation in its endeavour to advance matters that are of great importance to all developing countries' (Wilson 2012). Celebrating Fiji Day in New York on 10 October 2014, Fiji's Permanent Representative to the United Nations, Ambassador Peter Thomson, said that 2013 was a significant year because it marked the first time a small island nation from the Pacific held the chairmanship of the Group of 77 plus China, the largest intergovernmental group in the UN. Ambassador Thompson explained:

> Highlights so far for Fiji's Chairmanship have been its leadership leading up to and during the Special Event to follow up efforts towards achieving the Millennium Development Goals (MDGs), and the inaugural meeting of the High Level Political Forum. These were very significant events for UN Member states as they deliberate on setting the global post-2015 Development Agenda. In both events, Prime Minister Bainimarama was the lead speaker, as the Chair for the Group of 77 and China, signifying the critical importance of the Group's part in preparing for the post-2015 Development Agenda (Thompson 2013).

Not only was Fiji prominent in global affairs through its chairmanship of the G77 plus China group, the island nation was responsible for initiating discussion on behalf of PSIDS in New York to change the name of its regional grouping at the UN. Nayasi revealed the idea was borne out of discussion between him and Ambassador Thompson at the Fiji mission. The rationale behind the proposed name change was to give the Pacific the recognition it deserved as a member of the Asia Group. PSIDS represent a fifth of the membership of the Asia Group at the United Nations. However, its numbers are not reflected in the name of the group (Nayasi 2013). The Alliance of Small Island States (AOSIS) tried for the inclusion of Small Island Developing States (SIDS) to be a special category within the UN but this didn't succeed, said Nayasi. The AOSIS push was limited to climate change negotiations. According to Nayasi (2013), 'Fiji felt that all the issues we bring through to the UN have always been seen as a climate change and sustainable development issue. Often when it goes to the security council, it is sidelined because it lacks the politics it deserves.' Climate change and sustainable development have their own processes within the UN system. Pacific positions in these processes are represented by PSIDS, AOSIS, and G77. However, the important political manoeuvrings that moves the UN to make decisions happen at the regional grouping — where the Pacific is grouped with Asia. Nayasi reveals:

> For the Pacific to elect the President of UN General Assembly, appoint judges for the International Criminal Court or any other UN elections, these decisions are allocated or divided into regional groupings. The Africa and the Asia Group are the largest groupings at the UN with 54 members each (Nayasi 2013).

In 2010, Fiji realised that if the Pacific was to have some influence over how decisions are made at the multilateral level, it must do so within its own group, the Asia Group. The idea was conceived to lobby for its inclusion in the name of the group. Fiji prepared a concept paper which it circulated to all 54 member countries of the Asia Group, including PSIDS in New York. Discussions and negotiations took a year (2009–2010) to develop the concept before it was presented to the group. Nayasi revealed:

> We went bilaterally and basically convinced all the members except China and India. The concerns by these two countries was to do with if we are calling it the Asia–Pacific Group, it would mean that Australia and New Zealand will be part of the group because this is the demarcation in the UNESCAP regions. We had our discussion and we suggested two things — to call it the Asia and Pacific Small Island Developing States and do away with Asia-Pacific region (Nayasi 2013).

This was the compromise, and China and India agreed that the registered name of the group with the UN will be Asia-Pacific Islands Developing States but in terms of the everyday UN parlance, the group will be known as the Asia–Pacific group. 'For us to get that recognition means that the Pacific will now get a fair share of representation in the Asia Group' (Nayasi 2013). In September 2010, the Asia-Pacific group was formally endorsed unanimously by all members before the secretary general was officially notified. A Pacific diplomat based in New York told me that the name change was historical for the UN: 'There has never been any name change within any of the UN's regional grouping since the regions were divided in 1965. For the Pacific, especially Fiji to achieve this significant milestone is testament to Fiji's leading voice in New York on behalf of PSIDS.' Even though Fiji and the Pacific created history, Nayasi was disappointed with the support from the Pacific SIDS group: 'They thought that Fiji will not succeed. They were watching us and only came to support our effort at the very end and we were all credited for the outcome.' Fiji was the first PSIDS to join the Asia Group in the early 1970s. With PSIDS reflected in the group name, Federated States of Micronesia, Fiji, Marshall Islands, Nauru, Palau, Papua New Guinea, Samoa, Solomon Islands, Tonga, Tuvalu, and Vanuatu now have a prominent voice within the Asia Group.

Another boost to Fiji's global standing came in early 2012 when Brazil and India supported Commodore Bainimarama to lead the International Sugar Council (ISC) for a year. The council is the peak body for the world's largest sugar producers, representing 86 countries. Speaking after his election in London, Bainimarama said:

> The election is yet another international vote of confidence in Fiji and the Government's reform program. Our chairmanship of the ISC comes on top of the extraordinary honour of chairing the G77 and China, recently chairing the EU–ACP trade negotiations, and re-joining the Pacific ACP. Fiji's standing in the world has never been higher (Bainimarama 2012).

Regional Leadership

The establishment of the Pacific Islands Development Forum (PIDF) was a significant milestone for Fiji's new foreign policy in 2009. PIDF was formed as a result of a resolution from the EWTP initiative driven by Fiji in 2010 after it was suspended from the Pacific Islands Forum meetings. The new regional body champions the implementation of the Rio+20 sustainable development agenda, SIDS development agenda under the Barbados Plan of Action and the Mauritius Strategy for Implementation, and the post-2015 development agenda. 'PIDF's choice to champion green growth will guarantee its relevance' (Tavola 2013). The inaugural meeting of the PIDF was convened by Fiji in August 2013, attended by more than 20 Pacific Island countries and territories, as well as donors and development partners. Their attendance indicates support for Fiji's leadership of an alternative regional grouping to the Pacific Islands Forum. In an interview with *Islands Business* magazine in October this year, respected Fijian diplomat Kaliopate Tavola said the agenda of the PIDF was 'refreshing' because it responded to the growing frustrations of Fiji and other Pacific Islands towards Australia and New Zealand. Much of that unhappiness came from undue influence on the affairs of Pacific Island countries by Australia and New Zealand (Tavola 2013). Australia and New Zealand are not part of the PIDF, but were invited as observers to the inaugural meeting in Nadi.

At the sub-regional level, Fiji was able to convince all the leaders in Melanesia, except for Vanuatu, that it could lead the organisation for two years, despite the fact that it was not a democracy. In 2011 Commodore Bainimarama took over the helm of leadership from Vanuatu, although Vanuatu Prime Minister Edward Natapei had earlier refused to hand over the chairmanship. Under his chairmanship, the MSG 'grew from strength to strength'. In his handover speech given on 19 June 2013 in Noumea, Bainimarama said, 'We are turning over the chairmanship of an organisation that has grown stronger, that has carved out a firmer regional and international presence, which has a clearer vision and roadmap for the future'. Some of the achievements of the MSG during Fiji's two-year chairmanship included commitment to a single market and economic union to allow for free movement of goods, services, labour and capital; implementation of the MSG Trade Agreement with the ongoing removal of tariffs for trade between MSG; the MSG Skills Movement Scheme; regional cooperation and collaboration between law enforcement agencies to tackle transnational crimes; department of peacekeeping operations to assist an MSG peacekeeping unit for peacekeeping missions; and the Melanesian Green Climate Fund to finance regional environmental initiatives. An eminent person group led by Kaliopate Tavola also carried out a review of the MSG to mark 25 years of its existence. The review sought to chart a new way forward for the sub-regional organisation.

Conclusion

The new diplomacy was a significant and radical departure from Fiji's traditional foreign policy. The decision to build new relations with every nation willing to become friends with Fiji saw some controversial nations courted, much to the disappointment of traditional allies. Some of the milestones achieved along the way were not part of the short-term objectives set out in 2009 but have become much broader, with benefits not only to Fiji but other Pacific Island countries. Fiji has now realised that the policy changes in 2009 triggered a rhetorical response that has paved the way for fundamental foreign policy change. It is now clear that these policies have survived the 2014 return to democracy and the re-establishment of relations with traditional partners.

The experiences of 2009 to date have taught Fiji many hard lessons about diplomacy and international relations. As an independent sovereign nation, Fiji has learnt not to rely too much on its traditional partners, Australia and New Zealand, but to expand its relations to any country that respects its sovereignty and does not interfere with its domestic affairs. Fiji found out that many countries were ready and willing to engage with Fiji despite the political challenges it was going through. As a result, Fiji put in place a comprehensive foreign policy to respond to the diverse responses from the international community. The new foreign policies formulated after 2009 allowed Fiji to reclaim its position as an influential PSIDS engaging constructively with the international community both at regional and global level.

References

Ali, N.M., 2002, *The Diplomacy of Micro-states,* Netherlands Institute of International Relations, Clingendael.

Bainimarama, V., 2012, 'Fiji Elected as Chairman of the International Sugar Council', *Fiji Government Online*, 12 January. Available at: www.fiji.gov. fj/Media-Center/Press-Releases/PM-BAINIMARAMA-ELECTED-AS-CHAIRMAN-OF-THE-INTERNAT.aspx.

Bainimarama, V., 2013, 'Fiji Statement at the 68th Session of the United Nations General Assembly', *Fiji Government Online*, 25 September. Available at: www.fiji.gov.fj/Media-Center/Speeches/STATEMENT-BY-COMMODORE-JOSAlA-VOREQE-BAINIMARAMA-P.aspx.

Bainimarama, V., 2013, 'PM Bainimarama Address at the Opening of the 19th MSG Leader's Summit to Handover Chairmanship', *Fiji Government Online*, June 19. Available at: www.fiji.gov.fj/Media-Center/Speeches/PM-BAINIMARAMA---ADDRESS-AT-THE-OPENING-OF-THE-19T.aspx.

Balawa, S., 2013, 'Survival Diplomacy', interview with M. Komai, 19 September.

Davis, G., 2012, 'Australia's Humiliating Backdown Over Failed Fiji Foreign Policy', *Pacific Scoop*, 1 August. Available at: pacific.scoop.co.nz/2012/08/australias-humiliating-backdown-over-failed-foreign-policy-on-fiji/.

Fraenkel, J., 2013, 'How to respond to the impasse in Fiji?', *Devpolicy*, 15 August. Available at: devpolicy.org/how-to-respond-to-the-impasse-in-fiji-20130815/.

Kilman, S., 2010, 'Vanuatu's Kilman off to MSG Meeting in Honiara', interview with RNZI, 14 December.

Kubuabola, Ratu I., 2013, Speech at the 20th Australia Fiji Business Forum, Brisbane, 29 July.

Maclellan, N., 2006, 'Fiji, the War in Iraq, and the Privatisation of Pacific Island Security', *APSNet Policy Forum*. Available at: nautilus.org/apsnet/0611a-maclellan-html/.

McNamara, K., 2009, 'Voices from the Margins: Pacific ambassadors and the geopolitics of marginality at the United Nation', *Asia Pacific Viewpoint* 50(1), pp. 1–12.

Ministry of Foreign Affairs and International Cooperation, 2009, 'Fiji's Foreign Policy'. Available at: www.foreignaffairs.gov.fj/foreign-policy.

Nayasi, E., 2013, 'Fiji's Foreign Policies in 2009', interview with author, 17 September.

Tavola, K., 2013, 'Fiji's PIDF Here to Stay', *Islands Business* October. Available at: www.islandsbusiness.com.

Thompson, P., 2013, 'FIJI PRUN'. Available at: www.fijiprun.org/news-releases.

Watson, A., 1982, *Diplomacy: The dialogue between states*, Eyre Methuen, London.

Wilson, C., 2012, 'Fiji's Leadership of G77 a "rare opportunity" for the Pacific', *PACNEWS*, 10 October. Available at: www.pina.com.fj.

Xiaokun, L., 2009, 'Fiji to make China key focus of new policy', *China Daily*, 20 May. Available at: www.chinadaily.com.cn/kindle/2013-05/30/content_16547846.htm.

Geopolitical Context

11

The Strategic Context of the New Pacific Diplomacy

Michael O'Keefe

The new Pacific diplomacy is being shaped by politics played out in distant capitals. This chapter provides the strategic context for discussions of the new Pacific diplomacy by reflecting on the global competition that is influencing regional and national dynamics. It does not seek to devalue the issues, trends and agendas that have shaped the evolution of a new approach to diplomacy from within the region. Rather, it seeks to provide the missing piece of the puzzle with an overview of international trends that have also been integral to shaping the new Pacific diplomacy.

It highlights four broad trends. The first broad contextual trend is the geopolitical contest sparked by the rise of China, and to a lesser extent, Russia's renewed interest in the Pacific. The second is the increasing disquiet within the Pacific over the costs and benefits of regionalism. The third is Fiji's increasingly confident foreign policy and diplomatic strategy. The fourth is the impact of the first three trends on the traditional place of metropolitan powers in the region.

The Geopolitical Contest Sparked by the Rise of China and Renewed Interest of Russia

There has been a revival of global geopolitical analysis since the end of the Cold War (Brzezinski 1997). There is little doubt that global geopolitical competition is having a profound impact on Pacific affairs, but most analysis is not focused on the Pacific. The decline in military competition between the ex-imperial great powers and Cold War opponents at the end of last century should not be overestimated. Dramatic strategic change appeared to herald a new era, but as the 21st century has unfolded, old habits have resurfaced and have become more obvious, and new players have joined the game. The growing assertiveness of revisionist powers is the most notable trend that impacts on the Pacific. Revisionist powers are those that challenge the international order and the hegemon (the US). This international challenge focuses on China and Russia, although the former has much more experience and capacity to take this contest to the Pacific.

If taken to its logical conclusion, the challenge would ultimately see the Washington Consensus undermined and replaced by a hitherto undefined Beijing Consensus (WHO 2013; McKinnon 2010). However, the revisionism in this challenge may be more apparent than real. It may be more a geopolitical challenge to US dominance than an existential threat to the international system as we know it (Mead 2014).

This new geopolitics also explains the interest of the Pacific's other 'new friends' — so-called by some Pacific leaders because they don't have the long-term relationships of the metropolitan powers who dominated the region for so long. The most notable of the 'new friends' — Indonesia, India, Israel, the United Arab Emirates, and Turkey — are simply trying to increase their relative power and influence in the existing system (and in the Pacific). While the arrival of these new friends is symptomatic of increasing geopolitical competition and buttresses the new Pacific diplomacy, for the purposes of brevity, this chapter focuses on China and Russia as examples of states bringing their international geopolitical competition with the United States to the Pacific. This focus is justified by the strategic potential of the challenge from these powers whilst other new friends are not in the same geopolitical league.

The nature of global competition is the subject of much discussion and debate, which is beyond the scope of this chapter to address in full. The relevant point here is that it provides the lens through which strategy and diplomacy in the Pacific is viewed. This is why there is much debate over whether China is, in fact, challenging the US and its metropolitan power proxies in the Pacific (O'Keefe 2014; Lanteigne 2012; Hansen 2008; Yang 2011; Sen 2015).

China's rapid economic development has certainly shaped foreign and economic affairs, but a more recent trend is that it is becoming more strategically assertive. In recent years, this has included expanding its global reach through 'harmonious diplomacy' (Wang 2007; Crocombe 2007, pp. 249–67). The newly announced 'strategic partnership' with Pacific Island countries also fits this strategy (Xinhuanet 2014).

More recently, the renewal of Russia's global ambitions has added impetus to geopolitics. There is some debate over whether Russian power is expanding or declining (Ikenberry 2014), but either way Russia has been increasingly interested in exercising influence in the Pacific and has used a similar, yet much more modest, approach to China. This could be because it is a cost effective way of influencing many states and their votes in international forums and/or opening a new front in the larger geopolitical contest with the United States.

There are some signs that Russia is more interested in strategic competition involving military aid than China. For instance, Russia concluded a defence cooperation agreement with Fiji in February 2013 and has provided assistance to Fijian peacekeepers in the Golan Heights (ABC News 2013; China.org.cn 2013). This is palpably different from the largely economic focus of China's approach; it reflects the Soviet/Russian historical approach to 'influence aid' and the historical response of metropolitan powers to activities, such as the Soviet's negotiating fishing agreements in the 1980s. It may be limited in scope, but this aid is significant for Fijian peacekeeping operations, which have become a key foreign policy priority. The fact that aid was sought from a rival to the US and metropolitan powers that were Fiji's traditional defence partners is geopolitically significant.

Needless to say, any militarisation of competition has the potential to expand the scope of geopolitical competition in ways that would impact on other actors, most notably the US, but also the metropolitan powers and China. It is noteworthy from this nascent trend that, in the Pacific at least, geopolitical competition is triangular (between the US, Russia, and China). This contrasts the bilateral competition — between the US and Russia, or the US and China — that characterises other diplomatic contests. In fact, it may be that China's growing influence is an additional element that has drawn Russia into the Pacific. This potential triangular element provides greater emphasis on Russia's diplomatic activities well beyond their material involvement in Pacific security, aid or trade.

The (Incomplete) Promise of Regionalism

There has also been a growing perception that Pacific regionalism has not delivered. Pacific Island countries have viewed regionalism as a method of aggregating, increasing and sharing aid and development assistance. Regionalism was also seen as a buffer and brake on the interests of external powers and on the dominance of powerful Pacific states.

In contrast, from a critical vantage, regionalism has been shallow, uneven, incomplete and unfinished. It has imposed high costs, both in financial terms and in terms of eroded sovereignty, and has delivered small benefits relative to the costs. The financial sustainability of these activities has also been criticised.

The way that metropolitan powers have influenced development policies has also been questioned. The liberal development agenda has been viewed as too closely representing development orthodoxies developed elsewhere, or too closely tied to the interests of development partners — see, for instance, the commitments in the Waiheke Declaration on Sustainable Economic Development (PIF 2011; UNODA n.d).

Pacific government criticisms of the influence of new friends are not as pronounced as criticisms of the dominance of old friends, but criticisms are being aired in popular media. It may be that any beneficial role of new friends acting as an alternative to the metropolitan powers will also play itself out, especially if the funds dry up, preferential loans are called in, or greater conditionality is introduced.

In the security realm, agendas and agreements have focused on the orthodox security concerns of the metropolitan powers. The way that metropolitan powers have characterised the Pacific, from failed states to 'doomsday scenarios' (AusAID 2006), has also been criticised, while there is a perception that the issue of most concern to the Pacific — climate change — has not been addressed. This gives rise to statements, such as the Majuro Declaration, that place climate change at centre stage (PIF 2013).

The capacity and sustainability of many states to survive and prosper without external support has also been questioned (Reilly 2003, p. 66). Here, the Pacific that is largely aid-independent and can engage internationally and shape outcomes to support its preferences is clearly contrasted with the aid-dependent Pacific that lacks the capacity to act too far outside the interests of its influential development partners and/or donors. Larger and more economically and strategically important (to outside powers) Pacific Island countries such as Papua New Guinea and Solomon Islands have received the lion's share of development assistance, with smaller island nations receiving far less in gross terms. For all but a few states, development assistance has made up such a large proportion of government revenues as to guide and potentially distort priorities and programs. In contrast to aid-dependent Pacific Island countries, Fiji received far less external support as a per cent of GDP and has been able to shape the aid it has received to focus closely on national priorities. So the impact of external trends (whether development or geopolitical) and players (whether traditional or new sources of support) is also important to understanding the context behind the new Pacific diplomacy.

The intersection of liberal development agendas with national interests is not a new problem, but is more pronounced when new players with new rules of engagement enter the arena. Similarly, overpromising and under-delivering is not new. The regular pattern of critical self-review and reform practiced by large regional intergovernmental organisations has often been seen as 'new wine in old bottles', but this is more pronounced when there are other new players and new possibilities in relation to multilateralism in the region and beyond (Pacific Islands Development Forum, United Nations Pacific Small Island Developing States, Group of 77, etc.) (O'Keefe 2013).

The sense that there is one region is under significant strain. We may be witnessing the Pacific diplomatic identity collapsing into a hybrid of overlapping identities: the Pacific legacy, sub-regional blocs, and national interests. The ties that bind the region together are increasingly being questioned and may be unravelling. Again, this is not a new argument. Crocombe argued that 'the one region policy set by the former colonial powers is being increasingly marginalized or subordinated', and that there were overlapping regions based on the Pacific Islands Forum, Pacific Community, colonial history, and culture (Crocombe 2006, pp. 197–98, 203; Hawksley and Wolfers 2011). How important these issues and trends are depends on the outlook and geopolitical power of the state in question. What this chapter is arguing is that connections beyond the region are becoming increasingly important in how Pacific Island countries define themselves. Fiji has led the way in this regard.

The outcome has been an impetus for the development of a new Pacific diplomacy and the search for a new regional political settlement that would more closely reflect the interests of Pacific Island countries (Fry 2015). It may be that the ties that bind the region have been under sustained pressure for so long that they have stretched beyond their original scope. If so, then it is a mixture of the division between a state's external motives for engaging with the region and the internal motives for Pacific Island countries to engage with outsiders that has led to the idea of the 'Pacific' unravelling. In an era of increased geopolitical competition, we are right to question 'what is the Pacific Way?'.

Fiji's Growing Diplomatic Independence and Confidence

Fiji's place in the new Pacific diplomacy is covered elsewhere in this volume; it is the geopolitical dimension that is discussed here. The key elements of Fiji's influence could be referred to as Fiji's rise as a 'normal' state. In terms of international relations, this means that Fiji has gained the capacity and willingness to act at the international level to support its interests and shape global affairs. This capacity refers to economic, military and diplomatic capacity. Both capacity and willingness are important, and they are activated through leadership and creativity.

Fiji's 'Look North' policy began in the early 2000s as an effort to look beyond traditional relationships and traditional patterns of behaviour (such as in the Pacific Small Island Developing States grouping in the United Nations system, the Group of 77, and the Pacific Islands Development Forum). This was largely driven from the top. Successive prime ministers and ministers of foreign affairs and international cooperation have developed and expanded this approach to a policy that today appears akin to 'look north and west', but not south. The elements of this policy focus on the choice of diplomatic partners and modes of cooperation.

From the perspective of diplomatic partners, the focus has shifted to powers beyond the region. As noted earlier, relations with China have grown closer and new relationships with countries such as Russia, Indonesia and India have grown (O'Keefe 2014). More surprising was the growth in relations with Middle Eastern countries, which was unprecedented for both regions. Fiji's network of embassies expanded and the energy and dynamism of the consular corps ensured that the new relationships bore fruit. Fiji also led the way in developing new modes of cooperation that looked beyond existing forms of regionalism.

The growing confidence that came from this independence fed directly into the new Pacific diplomacy and into Fiji's position as one of the few Pacific Island countries that could be viewed as shaping the regional diplomatic environment to suit its preferences. An enabling factor in Fiji's diplomatic strategy was the sanctions regime imposed by Australia after the 2006 coup, or more accurately, the longevity and inflexibility of the sanctions and their ineffectiveness at achieving their stated goals. An unintended consequence for Australia was Fiji firming its position and looking elsewhere for new friends and new modes of multilateral cooperation. Australia may have been distracted along with its 'great and powerful friend', the US, by the long war on terror, but the outcome of maintaining the rigid sanctions regime was that Fiji moved on.

Australia's diplomatic overreach in persisting with sanctions was clear from Fiji's unwillingness to compromise. Fiji continued this policy post-sanctions and has slowly clarified its position. For instance, Australia's high commissioner took up her position in December 2014, having been announced two years earlier, while Fiji selected its high commissioner in April 2015. The proposed summit to consider the suitability of the regional architecture in the light of Fiji's concerns about the role of Australia and New Zealand in the Pacific Islands Forum, scheduled for February 2015, was abruptly cancelled without explanation. A subsequent foreign ministers meeting, focused on regional disaster management, met in Sydney in July. This allowed the Fijian foreign minister to meet with his Australian and regional counterparts but did not resolve the tensions over Fiji's position on regional governance.

On regionalism, the Fiji government has made repeated statements against involvement in the Pacific Islands Forum as currently conceived, while slowly increasing participation. In May the prime minister clarified this in a presentation to the Pacific Islands Development Forum when he noted:

> We will continue to participate in all forum activities at the public service, technical and ministerial levels … As head of government, I will not participate in any forum leader's meeting until the issue of the undue influence of Australia and New Zealand and our divergence of views is addressed (ABC News 2015).

While Australia remains by far the dominant development partner across the region, for Fiji it has been overtaken by China. Over the last decade China has provided over US$330 million while Australia provided US$252 million (Brant 2015). This was during the sanctions period in which aid was quarantined, but it did not grow in the way that Australia's aid program to other Pacific Island countries did. It will be interesting to see how the aid budget compares now that re-engagement with Fiji is firmly on the agenda.

Fiji's relationship with Australia neatly captures the sense that a new Pacific diplomacy is being formulated. However, it also highlights the additional geopolitical lens through which we need to view regional diplomacy. Fiji developed a clear understanding of its national interests in the diplomatic realm and implemented a policy to achieve its ends, independent of other Pacific Island countries (especially Pacific Island countries that supported Australia and New Zealand during the long sanctions conflict). This has major implications for the future of regionalism.

Metropolitan Powers with Pacific Interests

Another important context for understanding the influence of geopolitics on the new Pacific diplomacy is the role of metropolitan powers, specifically Australia and New Zealand (ANZ). New Zealand's role is covered elsewhere in this volume, so the focus here is on Australia.

During the Pacific colonial period the ANZ metropolitan powers were either colonies themselves, or were aligned or allied with the United Kingdom. They were colonies of choice who never left their coloniser's orbit, and this strategic culture has transferred to the present close alliance with the United States. As such, ANZ could nominally be viewed as agents/proxies of great powers in the region (Fry 2006, pp. 204–15). This was especially the case when contentious security issues arose involving geopolitical issues — from the South Pacific Nuclear Weapon Free Zone (SPNWFZ), to maintaining the regional status quo, to recent allegations of spying for the 'Five Eyes'. This in turn fed into criticisms of their undue influence over regionalism.

Australia has also been more active and more sensitive to geopolitical conflict in its backyard. Australia has its own strategic and development interests in the region, but where security is concerned Australia also acts as a proxy for the US. The US is concerned about geopolitical developments, but while the trends noted above solidified it was distracted by the war on terror and military entanglements in the Middle East. Australia was also distracted, but periodically returned to being concerned with regional affairs. However, geopolitical interests never overtook other national interests and the sanctions regime against Fiji was maintained. The subsequent regional division over sanctions clouded and shaped regional relations throughout this time. The increased Chinese interest posed a challenge to Australia's development strategy that the dictates of proximity would not allow it to retreat from, which made regional diplomacy even more complex.

China continues its pattern of 'influence aid' which developed during the height of competition with Taiwan over gaining and maintaining diplomatic recognition by Pacific Island countries. This competition is fading into history with the tacit compromise for each to keep its existing/traditional diplomatic partners (Dobell 2007). However, this 'truce' could potentially change if, in expanding its influence, China targets Taiwan's traditional partners (Lai 2007).

The point for the current situation is that China's pattern of interaction was tried and tested and is presently being expanded. Chinese aid to the Pacific has dramatically increased over the last decade, to the point where China has most probably overtaken Japan as the third largest donor, after Australia and the US (Brant 2015). Some caution is warranted, however, when viewing these figures.

There is little transparency in Chinese reporting of aid, making it difficult to measure accurately. In addition, aid from the US and France is largely focused on their Pacific dependencies so they do not have the same impact on the broader region. If this type of aid is discounted, China is probably about to displace Japan as the second largest donor, with Australia still remaining by far the largest donor —possibly at a factor of six to one (Brant 2015).

China's influence aid is a key avenue of geopolitical competition in the region. The approach of the new donors can be contrasted with the development partner approach of metropolitan powers (including Japan). For instance, preferential loans, untied aid and budget support do not fit neatly with the good governance and capacity-building agenda promoted by metropolitan powers — epitomised by the Paris Declaration on AID Effectiveness (OECD 2008). China describes itself as a friend that does not judge the values of its partners (Xinhuanet 2014), which relates to democracy and sustainable development. At this level, China and Russia could be seen as revisionist powers insofar as the liberal values of the Washington Consensus are concerned (Mead 2014).

Australia's focus on development assistance was complicated by its historical ties and increasingly complex aid diplomacy (Hawksley 2009). There was also tension between geopolitical interests — its own and a reflection of its allies — and the liberal objectives of promoting democracy and sustainable development (Firth 2013). China's increasing interest in the region was viewed in Canberra as strategic competition and competition for its largely liberal development assistance strategy, while the US saw China as a strategic rival in the South Pacific through its proxy, Australia. But as a metropolitan power, Australia has direct, enduring interests in the region, while the US is far more focused on its territories and the Western Pacific. These tensions in relation to differing strategic priorities remain unresolved.

Conclusion

China and Russia's growing assertiveness has implications for the global hegemonic state, the United States, and its interests in the Pacific. It is also having an impact on other external powers with long histories of regional engagement in the South Pacific, not least of which are the traditional metropolitan powers — Australia and New Zealand. The geopolitical interests of both groups in the Pacific makes the maintenance of relations with new friends and old friends potentially destabilising.

Despite the potential for diplomatic manoeuvring, this increased external interest also poses opportunities and challenges for Pacific states. How they are placed to manage the challenges and take advantage of the opportunities is largely based on their capacity to engage with regional and global diplomacy and their importance to new friends and old friends.

This multilayered competition will play out for some years to come, so it is worth building it into our considerations of the enabling and disenabling influence of geopolitics on the new Pacific diplomacy.

References

ABC News, 2013, 'More Fiji Peacekeepers to Support UN in Golan Heights', 10 July. Available at: www.abc.net.au/news/2013-07-10/an-fiji-announces-more-troops-to-join-un-peacekeepers-in-golan-/4810148.

ABC News, 2015, 'Fiji PM Frank Bainimarama to shun Pacific Island Forum over "undue influence" of Australia, NZ', 6 May. Available at: www.abc.net.au/news/2015-05-06/fiji-prime-minister-frank-bainimarama-slams-australia2c-new-ze/6449514.

AusAID, 2006, *Pacific 2020: Challenges and Opportunities for Growth*, AusAID, Canberra.

Brant, P., 2015, 'The Geopolitics of Chinese Aid: Mapping Beijing's funding in the Pacific, *Foreign Affairs Snapshots*, March 4. Available at: www.foreignaffairs.com/articles/143224/philippa-brant/the-geopolitics-of-chinese-aid.

Brzezinski, Z., 1997, *The Grand Chessboard: American primacy and its geostrategic imperatives*, Basic Books, New York.

China.org.cn, 2013, 'Fiji approves agreement on military cooperation with Russia', 12 February. Available at: www.china.org.cn/world/Off_the_Wire/2013-02/12/content_27944141.htm.

Crocombe, R., 2006, 'Regionalism Above and Below the Forum: The geographical/culture regions, Asia–Pacific and Others', in M. Powles (ed.), *Pacific Futures*, Pandanus Books, Canberra.

Crocombe, R., 2007, *Asia in the Pacific Islands: Replacing the west*, University of the South Pacific, Suva, pp. 249–67.

Dobell, G., 2007, 'China and Taiwan in the Pacific: Diplomatic chess versus Pacific political rugby', Lowy Institute Policy Brief, Sydney.

Firth, S., 2013, 'Australia's Policy Towards Coup-Prone and Military Regimes in the Asia-Pacific: Thailand, Fiji and Burma', *Australian Journal of International Affairs* 67(3), pp. 357–72.

Fry, G., 2006, 'Whose Oceania?: Contending visions of community in Pacific region-building', in M. Powles (ed.), *Pacific Futures*, Pandanus Books, Canberra.

Fry, G., 2015, 'Recapturing the Spirit of 1971: Towards a New Regional Political Settlement in the Pacific', SSGM Discussion Paper 2015/3, The Australian National University, Canberra.

Hansen, F., 2008, 'The Dragon in the Pacific: More opportunity than threat', Policy Brief, Lowy Institute, Sydney.

Hawksley, C., 2009, 'Australia's Aid Diplomacy and the Pacific Islands: Change and continuity in middle power foreign policy', *Global Change, Peace and Security* 21(1), pp. 115–30.

Hawksley, C. and E. Wolfers, 2011, 'Regionalism in the Pacific', in A. Cullen (ed.), *The Globalisation of World Politics: Case studies from Australia, New Zealand and the Asia Pacific*, Oxford University Press, South Melbourne.

Ikenberry, G.J., 2014, 'The Illusion of Geopolitics: The enduring power of the liberal order', *Foreign Affairs* 93(3).

Lai, I.-C., 2007, 'Taiwan's South Pacific Strategy', *Taiwan International Studies Quarterly* 3(3).

Lanteigne, M., 2012, 'Water Dragon?: China, power shifts and soft balancing in the South Pacific', *Political Science* 64(1), pp. 21–38.

McKinnon, R., 2010, 'China in Africa: The Washington Consensus versus Beijing Consensus', *International Finance* 13(3), pp. 495–506.

Mead, W., 2014, 'The Return of Geopolitics: The revenge of the revisionist powers', *Foreign Affairs* 93(3).

OECD, 2008, 'The Paris Declaration on Aid Effectiveness and the Accra Agenda for Action'. Available at: www.oecd.org/development/effectiveness/34428351.pdf.

O'Keefe, M., 2013, 'PIDF: A new era with new agendas', *Islands Business*, August.

O'Keefe, M., 2014, 'China in the Pacific: Its links with Fiji and the issues it brings', in C. Hawksley and N. Georgeou (eds), *Globalization of World Politics: Case studies from Australia, New Zealand and the Asia Pacific*, third edition, Oxford University Press, Oxford.

Pacific Islands Forum (PIF), 2011, 'The Waiheke Declaration on Sustainable Economic Development', 42nd PIF, Auckland, New Zealand 7–8 September.

Pacific Islands Forum (PIF), 2013, 'Majuro Declaration for Climate Leadership', Majuro, 5 September.

Reilly, B., 2003, 'Islands of Neglect', in R. J. May (ed.), *'Arc of Instability': Melanesia in the early 2000s*, SSGM, The Australian National University, Canberra.

Sen, Y.C., 2015, 'The Pacific Islands in Chinese Geo-Strategic Thinking', paper presented at 'China and the Pacific: The view from Oceania' conference, National University of Samoa, Apia, 25–27 February.

United Nations Office for Disarmament Affairs (UNODA), n.d., 'South Pacific Nuclear Free Zone Treaty'. Available at: disarmament.un.org/treaties/t/rarotonga.

Wang, K.-Y., 2007, 'China's "Harmonious Diplomacy" and Its Diplomatic Expansion to the South Pacific', *Taiwan International Studies Quarterly* 3(3).

World Health Organization (WHO), 2013, 'Washington Consensus'. Available at: www.who.int/trade/glossary/story094/en/.

Yang, J., 2011, 'China in Fiji: Displacing the traditional players?', *Australian Journal of International Affairs* 65(3), pp. 305–21.

Xinhuanet, 2014, 'China, Pacific Island Countries Announce Strategic Partnership', 22 November. Available at: news.xinhuanet.com/english/china/2014-11/22/c_133807415.htm.

12

New Zealand and Australia in Pacific Regionalism

Nicola Baker

Much of the current debate about the future of the Pacific regional architecture revolves around the appropriate level of engagement for Australia and New Zealand. Because they are both developed country members of the most prominent regional forum, whose presence has created some problems for their developing country counterparts, and who have contributed to the formation of other regional and sub-regional groupings, it is understandable that they are now being discussed as a single unit. They are in the same awkward position of being major aid donors to the other members of the Pacific Islands Forum, of having the resources and capacity to dominate regional meetings, and of being a hindrance to the forum's credibility and utility as a vehicle for south–south cooperation.

But is it otherwise useful to refer to 'Australia and New Zealand' as if they were umbilical twins, as analysts of regional international relations have long tended to do? Or to assume that Australia always leads and New Zealand follows, as this invariable ordering suggests? Is it simply a matter of contrasting approaches, as inferred by the common allusions to their playing 'bad cop' and 'good cop', or could it be that they have different interests in, and perspectives on, Pacific regionalism?

This chapter discusses New Zealand's role in the regionalism of the independent Pacific from the 1960s until the early 21st century. It finds that New Zealand has long had a unique sense of identification with the region, and that its interest and activity in regional matters has been enduring and intense, and that it has — usually but not always — been sensitive to Pacific Island concerns and desires. This has been based on its own calculations of what the region requires and it has tried to persuade other powers with an interest, including Australia, to behave in ways that accord with those calculations.

Perhaps the most overlooked aspect of New Zealand's engagement in the regionalism of the independent Pacific is that it has had a longer history of interest and activism than Australia. Forging ahead with the decolonisation of its territories, concerned about French nuclear testing, and impatient with the 'pottering' of the Australian initiated South Pacific Commission, New Zealand's Department of External Affairs (DEA) had by the mid-1960s begun rethinking the merits of the existing regional framework.[1] In 1961, Deputy Secretary Frank Corner had suggested that a revitalisation of the South Pacific Commission might suffice, but by 1967 he and his colleagues had begun considering the option of a completely new forum, to be composed of independent island states. They told their metropolitan counterparts (excluding France) in that year's four-power talks on the future of the Pacific that this forum 'should ideally be a grouping of indigenous governments', with Western Samoa, Tonga, and Fiji possibly forming the founding group. New Zealand warned that 'although there would be a need for metropolitan guidance, it would be best for the guidance to be inconspicuous'.[2]

The Australian delegation thought this idea a good one, but with national attention focused on Southeast Asia, and with changes in government, ministers and department heads, it appears to have slipped from the institutional memory. Australia did not begin giving serious consideration to the formation of a new regional organisation until April 1970, when Albert Henry, Premier of the Cook Islands, mentioned the idea on a visit to Department of Foreign Affairs (DFA) officials in Canberra. Australia wrongly took Henry's suggestions for change in the existing regional architecture to be tentative, and began thinking about ways in which Australia might encourage the establishment of a new regional grouping (Doran 2004). As DFA refined its thinking and its proposal wended its laborious way up to cabinet, officials grew increasingly suspicious that

---

1   New Zealand had been the only metropolitan power with territories in the South Pacific to vote in favour of the 1960 United Nations Declaration on the Granting of Independence to Colonial Countries and Peoples, had granted Samoa independence in 1962, and was working towards a change of status for the Cook Islands.
2   UK Public Records Office, FCO 32/343, 'Pacific Island Talks': Commonwealth Office notes on four-power talks in Washington, April 1967. Cited in Lal (2006).

'New Zealand thinking (and perhaps action) may be further advanced than ours'.[3] New Zealand would admit only that 'the idea for a forum had germinated slowly during the last two years'.[4]

New Zealand's early interest in the formation of a new regional organisation was driven in part by a realisation by the DEA that the country's foreign policy needed a focus that made more sense domestically and internationally. It was already imbued by a commitment to liberal internationalism, a commitment that has maintained almost uninterrupted bipartisan agreement to this day. But it had no geographic centre and was subject to the shifting interests of its allies and partners, on whom New Zealand then relied for an ultimate security guarantee and trade. The DEA official most concerned about this was Frank Corner, who had in 1951 voiced his unease in a letter about the negotiations on the formation of the Australia, New Zealand, United States Security Treaty (ANZUS) to his departmental secretary:

> My mind still finds it difficult to reconcile the arrangements we are making — An agreement for the Pacific, but commitment in reality in an area of the M[iddle] E[east] where we have no representation and no intelligence of our own; its all so untidy and I feel we are losing control of our own fate … I have the feeling that we [are] getting into a curious colonial status (cited in McGibbon 1999, pp. 78–79).

Corner went public with his proposed solution ten years later, giving a passionate speech arguing that the South Pacific should become New Zealand's primary area of foreign policy interest and activity. He began by recalling Prime Minister Richard Seddon's 19th-century attempt to bring into being a Pacific federation, claiming that in doing so he had displayed 'a solid knowledge of New Zealand's interests and a sound feeling for New Zealand's geographical position'. He went on to call for a return to a focus on the South Pacific, arguing that, 'if we do not accept the implications of our geographic and historical situation and of the dual racial origin of our people, our foreign policy can not be fully realistic, consistent or effective'.[5]

All of Corner's arguments were cited and amplified by Professor Kenneth Cumberland in a public lecture delivered later in 1961 (and attended by the future Prime Minister of Fiji, Ratu Mara). He criticised the South Pacific

---

3   National Archives of Australia, A1838, 277/1/1/PART 1, A. J. Eastman, Memo to Secretary Department of External Affairs, 'Political Forum in the South Pacific', 23 November 1970.

4   UK Public Records Office, FCO 32/795/083, 'Political Forum in the Pacific', Letter to Pacific Dependent Territories Department from British High Commission, Wellington, 31 May 1971.

5   Archives New Zealand, R22848844, folio 101, F. H. Corner, 'New Zealand and the South Pacific', Speech at the Convention of the New Zealand Institute of Public Administration, 1961.

Commission and its avoidance of 'crucial political, social and economic matters' and emphasised New Zealand's particular claim to a leading place in regional affairs by differentiating it from Australia:

> Asia may be Australia's 'Near North'. The Pacific Ocean is ours. The interests of Australia and New Zealand are by no means identical. Our environment is the 'surrounding Pacific'. In the 'surrounding Pacific' New Zealand clearly has a unique role to play (Cumberland 1962, p. 391).

In 1971, DEA officials helped island leaders persuade Prime Minister Keith Holyoake to host the first meeting of what would become the South Pacific Forum. In 1972, Frank Corner was promoted to Secretary of External Affairs (and the Prime Minister's Department) and he and the like-minded Norman Kirk, who replaced Holyoake in the same year, were able to make a concerted push to marry the different strands of what Corner saw as New Zealand's unique foreign policy identity: its place in the Pacific, its liberal internationalism, and its commitment to global disarmament. New Zealand began openly assuming its 'unique role' in regional affairs, proposing and gaining island support for the establishment of the forum secretariat, the forum declaration on the Law of the Sea, and the first attempt at a South Pacific Nuclear Weapons Free Zone (Doran 2004, p. 18; WikiLeaks 1976).

These early initiatives were not popular with Australia, with the exception of the forum declaration on the Law of the Sea. Australia did not take any sustained interest in the affairs of the forum in these years, rousing itself only to oppose New Zealand's push for a regional nuclear-free zone when the United States made its concerns known to Gough Whitlam.

The election of the Hawke Labor Government in 1983 ushered in the first period of Australian activism in Pacific regionalism since 1944. Bob Hawke proposed a modified nuclear weapons–free zone and pushed for a regional ban on drift-net fishing. His successor, Paul Keating, maintained this high profile on environmental issues and it was he and his Minister for Pacific Island Affairs, Gordon Bilney, who insisted that improved economic governance become a regional objective.[6]

During this period, New Zealand was prepared to work with Australia on initiatives that it supported, such as the ban on drift-net fishing and the revival of the nuclear-free zone concept. But it did not always cooperate or even consult. New Zealand was not initially enthusiastic about the Australian government's

---

6   Greg Fry has produced the best analyses of Australia's role in Pacific regionalism over the years. See Fry (1997) for a detailed explanation and critique of the Keating Government's focus on regional economic governance.

attempts to push island countries towards economic reform and did not keep Australia fully informed of its Bougainville conflict resolution initiatives (Brown 1997).

It was the Bougainville crisis that really gave birth to the notion of New Zealand playing 'good cop' to Australia's 'bad cop' in the region. Australia was unable to play a mediation role because of its open support for the Papua New Guinea government's position and its indirect support of the Papua New Guinea Defence Force's campaign against the rebels. As the neutral regional power, New Zealand was much more acceptable to the Bougainvilleans as a facilitator of peace negotiations and as leader of the first truce monitoring team. But the characterisation of New Zealand as 'good cop' in the Bougainville crisis implies a strategy agreed with the 'bad cop', and this was not the case as Australia's complaints about lack of consultation demonstrate.

The Bougainville experience did reveal something important about New Zealand's attitude towards cooperation with Australia and that is the significance of economic considerations, both bilateral and regional. With deepening integration into the larger Australian economy being a key New Zealand objective since the 1970s, its governments have increasingly recognised that there are 'straight commercial grounds' for getting their 'thinking clear on all issues that might affect the trans-Tasman relationship'.[7] The consequences of its unilateral diplomacy on Bougainville drove home the regional importance of cooperation with Australia. New Zealand was unable to fund or man a long-term peace monitoring presence and had to turn these duties over to a better-resourced Australia. Since then, New Zealand has adopted a more consultative approach in recognition of the fact that it needs both Australia's financial support for regional initiatives and its contributions to regional assistance missions.

Australia's interest in the region waned again after the 1996 elections. The new Liberal Party government of John Howard was not much interested in what was happening in the region or in the South Pacific Forum, which he rarely attended. Until 2003, his government's regional interests did not extend much beyond ensuring that forum communiqués on matters such as climate change did not conflict with Australia's national interests. It was left to the New Zealand governments of Bolger, Shipley, and Clark and their island counterparts to push ahead on coordination of law enforcement and on environmental and economic matters. Hawke's Defence Minister, Kim Beazley, by then on the opposition benches, was furious at Australia ceding its 'intellectual leadership' in the region (Beazley 1997).

---

7   Jim Bolger quoted in Press Release: Parliament Building, Wellington New Zealand, 17 February 1997: transcript of the Prime Minister and the Prime Minister of New Zealand, Parliament of Australia.

That 'intellectual leadership' passed to New Zealand's Helen Clark when she became prime minister in 1999, but she would make sure that the relationship with Australia was consultative. By 2000, more of the island states were having economic and political difficulties and the New Zealand government had come around to the Australian view that improved governance was a regional necessity. Despite the vast difference between their ideological outlooks, Clark and Howard were able to form a respectful, even friendly, working partnership on a range of regional issues. In a major departure from tradition, both leaders refrained from criticising each other openly, and in conversations with his major ally, the United States, Howard noted that the two governments were working well together in the region, attributing minor differences to the fact that the New Zealanders were 'soft Saxons, with a disposition to the centre-left and with fewer resources' (WikiLeaks 2006).

When 'minor differences' did occur, Clark was sometimes able to prevail, sometimes not. It was New Zealand who put the 'cooperative' into the Howard Government's regional doctrine of 'cooperative intervention', announced by Foreign Minister Alexander Downer in June 2003. When Australia suddenly decided that it was in its interests to abandon its policy of non-intervention in the Solomon Islands crisis in May 2003, it initially planned to undertake the operation unilaterally. This approach was in keeping with Howard's own realist foreign policy preferences and with those of his American counterpart at the time, President G. W. Bush. Helen Clark, who was an even more passionate liberal internationalist than most New Zealand political leaders, and chair of the Pacific Islands Forum at the time, negotiated hard with Howard and persuaded him that the intervention should have 'the approval of the Pacific Islands Forum and the involvement of as many island states as possible — not to mention the invitation of the host country' (Young 2006).

She was not so successful in trying to persuade Howard to emulate New Zealand's approach on Bougainville and take a more 'softly-softly' approach, with unarmed soldiers or police leading the intervention. Nor was she successful in persuading him that the Solomon Islands government should be closely engaged in the subsequent state strengthening process (Adams 2012).

Transforming the planned 'Australia/Solomon Islands bilateral initiative' (Trevett 2008) into the Regional Assistance Mission to the Solomon Islands (RAMSI) was not Helen Clark's first or last significant regional initiative. The Pacific Islands Forum Biketawa Declaration, under whose auspices she insisted RAMSI be undertaken, had itself been conceived and promoted by her government. In August 2000, following the ousting of elected governments in Fiji and Solomon Islands, New Zealand had organised the first meeting of Pacific Islands Forum foreign ministers. At that meeting, hosted by the Samoan Prime Minister in Apia, New Zealand's Foreign Minister, Phil Goff, had put forward a proposal that the forum build on its previous declarations on regional security and develop procedures and processes for dealing with similar situations. The Australian foreign minister did not contribute at all to the ensuing discussion (McCraw 2005, p. 220; Tavola 2014).

Helen Clark also initiated the Pacific Plan and the Eminent Persons Group review of the forum during her stint as chair from 2003–2004 (Grynberg 2013). Afterwards she continued to be active in regional affairs, acting as a valued broker between disagreeing member states, negotiating the continuation of RAMSI in 2006 and instigating a review of its performance, and then in 2008 hammering out agreement that Fiji should be suspended from the forum in the event that it did not meet a 2009 deadline for democratic elections. According to Samoa's then prime minister, Clark's negotiation skills were formidable and she could be relied on to find 'the right word to reflect the areas where compromise can be reached. She has that talent' (Trevett 2008).

Australia's 2003 about-turn on direct assistance to the Solomon Islands had marked a new phase of regional assertiveness by Canberra, which included bilateral capacity-building initiatives with Nauru and Papua New Guinea, and attempts to strengthen regionalism and enhance Australia's capacity to influence its direction. This new assertiveness had not been welcomed with unalloyed joy in Wellington, partly because some of the Howard Government's proposals such as 'pooled regional governance' would have cut across New Zealand's national interests, and partly because its approach was seen as inappropriately interventionist. Much of Helen Clark's regional diplomacy in the years after 2003 can be seen as an attempt by New Zealand to moderate Howard's new regional concerns and ambitions.

Unfortunately, New Zealand officials did not have the same tact or skill when it came to trade negotiations with the region, sorely testing relations with the forum secretariat and with island leaders. When the secretariat responded to forum declarations on trade liberalisation and the looming prospect of free trade negotiations with the European Union by putting forward plans for an islands-only free trade agreement at the end of the 1990s, New Zealand was initially unconcerned. But it did not take long before it was aligning itself with its furious trans-Tasman neighbour to demand inclusion and subject forum and regional trade officials to scorn and intimidation. One of the New Zealand academics contracted to draft alternative proposals for the Australia and New Zealand governments complained: 'The whole experience was stressful and demoralising for me, let alone for the Pacific Islands negotiators. There were times that I felt ashamed to be a New Zealander; I was just pleased that I was not an Australian' (cited in Kelsey 2004, p. 16).

As with most matters Pacific, the New Zealand and Australian positions were not identical and in the end the agreed compromise, the PICTA–PACER Agreement (Pacific Island Countries Trade Agreement–Pacific Agreement on Closer Economic Relations), was closer to that taken by New Zealand. And when negotiations for PACER Plus got under way, New Zealand proved more willing to provide the island countries with some compensation in the form of temporary access visas for a limited number of unskilled workers. But the seasonal workers scheme was not incorporated into PACER Plus and island leaders were only too aware that it could be terminated at any time. Both the negotiations and the outcome of the whole regional free trade process tarnished New Zealand's reputation for being more diplomatic and sympathetic towards their island counterparts than Australia.

This was not the first time that New Zealand had upset its island counterparts. Its honeymoon years with the forum's island members had ended abruptly with the election victory of the National Party in 1975. Prime Minister Robert Muldoon was unarguably the most realist post-war prime minister that New Zealand has had, with an abrasive and inflexible character to boot. Although he attended all the forum meetings and enjoyed doing so, he was less committed to maintaining a cordial relationship with the island governments than his predecessors — or his successors. His first priority was maintaining good relations with the United States and France, and it was this that caused the first real friction between forum island members and Australia and New Zealand. As soon as he became prime minister, Muldoon had brought the first South Pacific Nuclear Weapons Free Zone campaign to a halt, now siding with its long-time Australian government opponents and arguing down island leaders, most notably Ratu Mara, who wanted to continue the process of gaining it international acceptance (Templeton 2006, pp. 301–5). During his term, Australia and New Zealand also made an unpopular attempt to gain the United States membership in the proposed Forum Fisheries Agency.

New Zealand's dispute with the United States in the mid-1980s and its departure from the ANZUS alliance over nuclear ship access had also been unpopular with a number of the forum's island members, in particular with Ratu Mara, who had by then become more sympathetic to the United States, having been feted at the White House by President Reagan. Few in the region would have noticed that efforts to restore relations between New Zealand and the United States had begun almost immediately on both sides of the Pacific or will have appreciated the extent to which New Zealand has since sought to engage the Americans in regional affairs.

Relations between the United States and New Zealand had thawed considerably by 2003, when Helen Clark openly criticised the Bush administration's invasion of Iraq as a breach of international law. Even this proved only a temporary irritant, with New Zealand keen enough to secure a free trade agreement that it was willing to demonstrate a strong commitment to the War on Terror in other areas, namely Afghanistan and the South Pacific, albeit in the name of liberal internationalism.

New Zealand sought to strengthen American interest in the relationship by engaging it more closely in regional affairs. It persuaded the Pacific Islands Forum Secretary General, Greg Urwin, to schedule a special session for United States Assistant Secretary of State for East Asian and Pacific Affairs, Christopher Hill, after the 2006 forum meeting in Nadi, and it was Hill who suggested to Howard that Helen Clark take charge of negotiations with the Prime Minister of the Solomon Islands, Manasseh Sogavare, over his demand that RAMSI be terminated (WikiLeaks 2006). Foreign Minister Winston Peters, who had established a very cordial relationship with the US Secretary of State, Condoleezza Rice, even persuaded her to visit the region and meet Pacific Island leaders, which she did in 2009. New Zealand's efforts to sell itself as having a unique understanding of, and role in, the island Pacific met with such success in Washington that President Bush spoke of relying on 'New Zealand's leadership, with US help, to help solve the problems — and Australian help as well'.

Australia had by this time been compelled to take a less assertive role in regional affairs, partly for diplomatic reasons and partly for practical ones. On the diplomatic front, the Howard Government had managed to alienate Melanesian leaders with the aggressive cross-border pursuit of the Solomon Islands attorney general, and on the practical front, Australia's focus had swung back to its priority area of security interest, Southeast Asia. Although the Australian and New Zealand governments had by now instituted six-monthly meetings to discuss regional matters, New Zealand was left to push forward on strengthening Pacific regionalism and to provide much of the counterterrorism training and support activity in the region (WikiLeaks 2006).

By the time that Helen Clark had been replaced as prime minister by the National Party's John Key and the new Obama administration began instituting its 'pivot to Asia', New Zealand had made itself sufficiently useful to the United States that it was possible to engage in open cooperation on regional and international matters. The new Secretary of State, Hillary Clinton, visited New Zealand in 2012 and went on to the Pacific Island Forum meeting in the Cook Islands, the first in her position to do so.

The Key Government has engaged in close practical regional cooperation with the United States (and China), changed its regional aid priorities, and adopted a more informal but less tactful approach to its dealings with island leaders, but has retained an interest in strengthening the existing regional architecture. It initiated a review of the Pacific Islands Forum Secretariat in 2012 and provided support to the Polynesian Leaders Group (PLG), formed in 2011 as a response to the activism of the Melanesian Spearhead Group. The Ministry of Foreign Affairs and Trade hosted meetings of the PLG in its Auckland offices in 2013 and then flew them all to the forum meeting in Majuro with John Key. The Ministry of Foreign Affairs and Trade again played host to the PLG in 2015.

China's increasing presence in the island Pacific and Fiji's establishment of the Pacific Islands Development Forum as a region-wide but island-only organisation have both been of concern to New Zealand — as they have to Australia. They were undoubtedly factors in the hasty restoration of ties with Fiji after its 2014 elections. When Fiji then insisted that the price of its return to the Pacific Islands Forum was the relegation of Australia and New Zealand to the status of development partners, New Zealand was quick to send ministers and officials to remind their island counterparts of Australia and New Zealand's contributions to their economies. Prime Minister Key was even less diplomatic in his public pronouncements than his Australian counterpart. What, he asked, would the forum do without Australian and New Zealand funding? 'Where would they get the money to do anything? And the answer is nowhere. None of them have that' (Radio New Zealand 2015).

New Zealand's public response to Bainimarama's demands, its position on free trade, and its support for improved governance in the island countries have given many observers the impression that when it comes to regional matters, 'you probably couldn't slide a pandanus leaf between Canberra and Wellington' (Honnor 2003). And it has been assumed that it is Australia that has called the tune, because of its size and its more insistent and assertive approach. But impressions can be misleading, as this brief examination has demonstrated. New Zealand has rarely completely agreed with Australia on regional issues and has often either provided the intellectual leadership or been successful in influencing policy in Canberra. This should come as no surprise. New Zealand's identification with the fortunes of the island Pacific predates the latter's emergence as a region of independent states, while Australia has no such intense or durable interest. Small powers with limited resources such as New Zealand have an added incentive to think creatively about the pursuit of their national interests.

It is often claimed by New Zealanders that while Australia works on the region, New Zealand works in it. But in recent decades, both have given the appearance of responding to the island countries' economic and political difficulties by pushing for greater regional activism and integration. Assuming this kind of managerial role in the region and adopting a public posture of complete solidarity with Australia entails costs as well as benefits for New Zealand. New Zealand should not forget that good relations with Pacific Island governments are fundamental to the successful implementation of its efforts to improve regional prosperity, stability, and resilience, and to its foreign policy identity and international credentials. Its leaders and officials once had the imagination, creativity and tact to work with Pacific Island governments on a form of regionalism that suited everyone. It would be great pity if New Zealand were to squander the considerable regional and international capital amassed during those years by appearing more interested in defending its own interests and ideas than in listening to and engaging with the rest of its Pacific Island family.

References

Adams, P., 2012, Former Head of NZAid, Suva, interview with author, 25 November.

Beazley, K., 1997, 'Ministerial Statement: 28th South Pacific Forum, Rarotonga, Cook Islands 17–19 September 1997', House Hansard, Thursday, 2 October 1997, Parliament of Australia, p. 9100.

Brown, P., 1997, 'Document Highlights Australia–NZ Tensions', *Militant* 61(31).

Cumberland, K.B., 1962, 'The Future of Polynesia', *Journal of the Polynesian Society* 71(4).

Doran, S., 2004, *Australia and the Origins of the Pacific Islands Forum*, Australia and the World: The Foreign Affairs and Trade Files, No. 1, Commonwealth of Australia, Canberra.

Fry, G., 1997, 'Framing the Islands: Knowledge and power in changing Australian images of 'the South Pacific', *Contemporary Pacific* 9(2), pp. 305–44.

Grynberg, R., 2013, 'The Pacific Plan and Other Failures: What can be learned?', *Pacific Media Centre*, 16 January. Available at: www.pmc.aut.ac.nz/articles/ pacific-plan-and-other-failures-what-can-be-learned.

Honnor, G., 2003 'Greg Urwin I Gutpela Man Long Dispela Wok', *Club Troppo*, 17 August. Available at: clubtroppo.com.au/2003/08/17/greg-urwin-i-gutpela-man-long-dispela-wok/.

Kelsey, J., 2004, 'Big Brothers Behaving Badly: The implications for the Pacific Islands of the Pacific Agreement on Closer Economic Relations (PACER)', Interim Report Commissioned by the Pacific Network on Globalisation. Available at: www.scoop.co.nz/stories/PO0404/S00030.htm.

Lal, B.V., (ed.) 2006, *Fiji: Documents on the end of Empire,* volume 10 series B, The Stationery Office, London.

McCraw, D., 2005, 'New Zealand Foreign Policy Under the Clark Government: High tide of liberal internationalism?', *Pacific Affairs* 78(2).

McGibbon, I. (ed.), 1999, *Unofficial Channels: Letters between Alister McIntosh and Foss Shanahan, George Laking, Frank Corner 1946–1966*, Victoria University Press, Wellington, 1999.

Radio New Zealand, 2015, 'Bainimarama Mouthing off Over Forum — Key', 13 April. Available at: www.radionz.co.nz/international/pacific-news/271083/bainimarama-mouthing-off-over-forum-key.

Tavola, K., 2014, Former Foreign Minister of Fiji, interview with author, Suva, 19 November

Templeton, M., 2006, *Standing Upright Here: New Zealand in the nuclear age 1945–1990,* Victoria University Press, Wellington.

Trevett, C., 2008, 'Old Hand Bridges Pacific Divide', *New Zealand Herald*, 23 August.

WikiLeaks, 1976, 'South Pacific Forum Nations Agree on Joint Action to Counter Soviet Ambitions in South Pacific', 1 July. Available at: wikileaks.org/plusd/cables/1976WELLIN02889_b.html.

WikiLeaks, 2006, 'Pacific Islands Forum 2006, A/S Hill Underscores U.S. Engagement in Pacific', 13 November. Available at: wikileaks.org/plusd/cables/06SUVA490_a.html.

Young, A., 2006, 'Riots highlight NZ presence', *New Zealand Herald*, 22 April.

Sub-Regionalism

13

The Renaissance of the Melanesian Spearhead Group

Tess Newton Cain

Although the Melanesian Spearhead Group (MSG) has been in existence for more than 25 years, it is only recently that it has come to prominence within the sub-region and more widely. The recent renaissance of the MSG would appear to represent a blend of two things. First is the maturing diplomacy of the Melanesian states, both in terms of the increased number of relationships formed within the sub-region and the evidence of increased sophistication of those engagements, particularly in relation to trade and economic integration. Secondly, the recent prominence of this grouping is indicative of a perceived failure of pan-regional diplomacy, including (but not limited to) the isolation of Fiji in the 2006–2014 period.

This chapter presents the evolution and work of the MSG within a wider consideration of the significance of sub-regional groupings in the Pacific. It then considers what diplomatic opportunities and challenges may face the MSG with reference to the impacts of internal diplomacy on the ability of the group to act cohesively within the region and on the wider international stage.

The Background to the Recent Renaissance of the MSG

The MSG is a prominent example of a sub-regional grouping among what looks to be an increasing number of such initiatives. There are, broadly speaking, two subsets of sub-regional groups: those that are based on geographical proximity and/or cultural affinity, and those that are based on the pooling of resources to address service delivery or other policy issues.

There are three sub-regional groups that align broadly with the most widely accepted cultural demarcations in the region as a whole. The memberships of these groups comprise sovereign and non-sovereign entities. While this indicates a degree of diplomatic innovation, it can present challenges in terms of engaging in wider arenas, whether at the regional or global levels.

The Micronesian Chief Executives Summit (MCES) was convened for the first time in 2003. It brings together the political leadership of the Commonwealth of the Northern Marianas, the Territory of Guam, the Federated States of Micronesia (Yap, Kosrae, Pohnpei, and Chuuk), the Republic of Marshall Islands, and the Republic of Palau (ROP). The most significant achievement of this group to date is the establishment of the 'Micronesia Challenge', which has environmental issues and the management of natural resources as its primary areas of focus.

The Polynesian Leaders Group (PLG) was established largely in response to the growing presence of the MSG. It comprises the leaders of eight states and territories: American Samoa, Cook Islands, French Polynesia, Niue, Samoa, Tonga, Tuvalu and Tokelau. To date, it has been the least active of these groupings, with its focus being more on establishing and maintaining cultural ties than on economic or political endeavours. However, ahead of its most recent gathering in Auckland in 2015, it was announced that the group would be focusing on the enforcement of fisheries management (Radio New Zealand 2015).

The MSG is generally acknowledged to be the most established and dynamic of this set of sub-regional groupings. The MSG was established in 1988 and obtained recognition as an international organisation in 2007. Its current membership is the sovereign states of Fiji, Papua New Guinea, Solomon Islands and Vanuatu plus the *Front de Libération Nationale Kanak et Socialiste* (Kanak and Socialist National Liberation Front (FLNKS)), a pro-independence movement from New Caledonia. The FLNKS has chaired the MSG since June of 2013 and will hand over chairing responsibility to the government of Solomon Islands during 2015. It has a secretariat located in Port Vila, Vanuatu and, in recent years, has been increasingly active both politically and economically.

Pooled service delivery at the pan-regional level is fraught with challenges of varying types and there are some indications that they are easier to overcome by operating sub-regionally (Dornan and Newton Cain 2014). This form of sub-regional activity does not necessarily have to be formulated by reference to geographic proximity or cultural affinity. The most significant grouping of this type is (currently) the Parties to the Nauru Agreement (PNA). Its members are particularly concerned with management of fisheries in order to maximise economic return and promote sustainability and appear to have been more successful (at least on the former issue) than the larger Forum Fisheries Agency (ADB 2014).

It is not surprising that a grouping with the longevity of the MSG has undergone numerous changes in its lifetime. There have been changes to the membership, to the activities it has undertaken, and to its relative importance, whether to its members or within the wider region. Here, I will examine some of the milestones that have shaped the MSG as it exists today and which provide the context for the increase in prominence of the group that has been witnessed since the mid-2000s.

In 1986, the MSG convened for the first time ahead of the meeting of the South Pacific Forum. This was followed in 1988 by the adoption of the Agreed Principles for Cooperation by the leaders of Papua New Guinea, Solomon Islands, and Vanuatu. This took place in Port Vila, which has remained the home of the MSG since then. In 1989, the group's membership increased to include the FLNKS. The MSG adopted what became the precursor to the MSG Trade Agreement (MSGTA) and in 1996 Fiji became the most recent member of the group.

The current renaissance of the MSG commenced in 2007 when the membership signed the Agreement Establishing the Melanesian Spearhead Group (the MSG constitution) and deposited it with the United Nations in order to secure recognition as a sub-regional organisation. In 2008, the MSG's secretariat building (funded by the government of the People's Republic of China) was opened in Port Vila. The contemplation of further economic integration was heralded in 2012 when the leaders of the MSG countries signed an agreement for the Skilled Movement Scheme. In 2013, the MSG celebrated its silver anniversary. Also in this year, an Eminent Persons Group (EPG) undertook a strategic review of the MSG and its secretariat to inform the group's strategy and vision for the next 25 years. It was captured in the 2038 'Prosperity for All' Plan.

How has the MSG's Underpinning Philosophy Contributed to this Renaissance?

An underpinning and enduring tenet of the grouping is the commitment to independence for all peoples of Melanesia. This was articulated in the Agreed Principles for Cooperation in 1988 and further restated in the constitution in 2007. This in turn reflected the more radical activist stance of the Melanesian states in relation to continuing decolonisation issues, which set them apart from the more conservative members of the South Pacific Forum, such as Fiji and the Polynesian countries (MacQueen 1989). Until relatively recently, the focus in this regard was on independence for the Kanak people of New Caledonia. The MSG's accommodation of the FLNKS, a political movement whose purpose is to change the sociopolitical status of New Caledonia, is a defining feature of the MSG. The MSG has responsibility for oversight of the implementation of the Noumea Accords and in 2012 established a dedicated unit within its secretariat focused on progressing Kanak self-determination. The secretariat has also facilitated study visits to Timor-Leste for young Kanak professionals who will be expected to take the lead in state-building if and when New Caledonia becomes an independent country (Forau and Newton Cain 2013).

In 2013, the MSG commitment to independence for all Melanesian people was again highlighted when, at the leaders' summit in Noumea, the West Papua National Council for Liberation submitted an application for membership of the group. The process of that application (which has yet to be resolved) provides a telling insight into the complexity of relationships within the MSG and the significance of outside influences on their decision-making.

The issue of self-determination for West Papua is considered in more detail elsewhere in this volume. The issue of the membership application by the United Liberation Movement for West Papua (ULMWP) has yet to be resolved by the MSG. The MSG leaders will consider this application at their 2015 summit in Solomon Islands. The fact that the application is under consideration at all is an indicator of the ability of this group to embrace issues that have proved too diplomatically sensitive or complex for other regional organisations, most notably the Pacific Islands Forum. However, the vexed nature of this issue and the varying relationships between Indonesia and members of the MSG make it an issue that has the potential to severely test the strength of the diplomatic bonds between MSG states. For Webb-Gannon and Elmslie (2014), 'the MSG has reached a turning point and must decide whether it values West Papuan human rights over the potential economic benefits of increasing political engagement with Indonesia'.

The centrality of Melanesian culture, including tenets of reconciliation and the maintenance of cohesion, was demonstrated by the MSG in how it negotiated the difficult issue of Fiji chairing the group in 2010. Although this issue caused a significant degree of internal division and meant that the MSG was at odds with the Pacific Islands Forum, which had suspended Fiji, the MSG leaders managed to work through their differences and reach an accommodation. The period of Fiji's chairing of the MSG (2010–2013) was one of significant activity. However, it would be simplistic to say that the MSG's renaissance is wholly attributable to the influence of Fiji. As we have already seen, this resurgence commenced prior to 2010 and it is certainly the case that, since 2013, the MSG has continued to be both active and prominent despite a reduction in engagement by Fiji's political leadership. This is largely explained by the increased participation of Papua New Guinea in sub-regional and regional politics and diplomacy, under the leadership of Peter O'Neill (Hayward-Jones and Newton Cain 2014).

What has the MSG Achieved?

Perhaps the most significant thing the MSG has achieved is a measure of longevity. It celebrated its 25th anniversary in 2013 and has maintained its presence despite a number of challenges arising from internal tensions. Examples include the strained relationship between Papua New Guinea and Solomon Islands during the Bougainville crisis, and friction in 2010 around the controversial decision to allow Fiji to chair the group, even though it was (at that time) under a military dictatorship.

The MSG is the only one of the three sub-regional groups identified previously that has a dedicated secretariat housed in its own building and staffed by a team drawn from its members. Several of the secretariat staff (including the current director-general, Peter Forau) have experience of working at the pan-regional level, especially within the Pacific Islands Forum Secretariat (PIFS). So it is not surprising that some of the sub-regional 'architecture' that the secretariat has built resembles the structures and processes that the PIFS uses. So, for example, the MSG secretariat's work plan for 2015 was reviewed by a senior officials meeting and then endorsed by the foreign ministers meeting. There is also a conference of police commissioners with the potential for similar conferences for chief justices and ombudsmen from within the sub-region.

The MSGTA was signed by Papua New Guinea, Solomon Islands and Vanuatu in 1993, with Fiji acceding to it in 1997. Work on eliminating tariffs on movement of goods between the countries has progressed over time. The agreement and its value to all member countries have recently been reviewed and MSGTA3 is expected to be launched during 2015. In 2012, the group's leaders also signed the Skilled Movement Scheme, which is intended to facilitate the free movement of skilled workers between member countries, subject to an upper limit of 400 per country. To date, there has been very little take up of this, especially by the private sector (Voigt-Graf 2015) and there is expected to be more work done on promoting this scheme during 2015.

Based on the success, albeit limited, of the MSGTA, the group is now exploring opportunities for closer economic integration, which may include initiatives such as a customs union and a single currency, both of which have already been considered by officials and political leaders. The group is also looking to explore opportunities for pooled service delivery, including bulk procurement of pharmaceuticals and fuel, and increased and improved shipping services between member countries. All of these initiatives are still at the research stage and one of the characteristics of the approach taken by the MSG is to work closely with the private sector where this is appropriate and more cost-effective (Dornan and Newton Cain 2014).

Recently, the MSG secretariat has shared its experience with another of the sub-regional groupings by assisting in the establishment of the Micronesian Trade Centre and the development of a treaty to create the Micronesian Trade and Economic Community (PINA 2014).

What Does the Future Hold for the MSG?

Looking ahead, it appears that there are both opportunities and challenges for the MSG.

In the immediate to short term, the issue of most significance is the ULMWP's application for membership. Not only does this issue bring into play individual members' bilateral diplomatic relationships with Indonesia, it also has the potential to be a point of conflict within the group. If the apparent change of position on the part of Papua New Guinea is sustained, this will mark a point of departure from previous dealings where the O'Neill Government and the leadership of Fiji have sought to restrain smaller members' agitation for West Papuan self-determination.

The issue of ULMWP membership points to a related question of how much bigger the MSG is likely to become. Following the pathway established by the Noumea Accords, the French territory of New Caledonia is scheduled to hold a referendum on the transfer of remaining sovereign powers from Paris between now and 2018. In the event that New Caledonia becomes an independent country, it is expected that it will apply to join the MSG. This will not change the number of members, but it will change the nature of the composition and will have an impact on funding arrangements for the group, as FLNKS currently does not contribute to costs associated with the secretariat or meetings. Also in play is the 2015–2020 window in which the Autonomous Region of Bougainville will hold a referendum on whether it remains part of Papua New Guinea or secedes. If Bougainville were to become independent (and assuming that it does not choose to become part of Solomon Islands), it is reasonable to expect that it would join the MSG, which would increase the overall membership. It is possible, but not very likely, that the MSG would invite other Pacific Island countries, especially the smaller island states, to become members. The MSG has already made it clear that it sees itself having an important role to play in assisting small island states with solving key development challenges, such as improving transport, but it is not necessary for those countries to be members of the group to be able to benefit from accumulated expertise or new ventures that may be undertaken. If Timor-Leste were to seek to establish closer links with the Pacific Island region, it is possible that the MSG would be its preferred form for doing so. It already has a strong connection with the group, having held observer status since 2011, and the government of Timor-Leste also contributes by way of funding one of the secretariat's positions.

The MSG is expected to play an important role in the ongoing development of Pacific regionalism, including (but not limited to) the rolling out of the Framework for Pacific Regionalism, which resulted from the 2013 review of the Pacific Plan (Pacific Plan Review 2013). The rhetoric put forward at the regional level, most notably by the new Secretary-General of the Pacific Islands Forum Secretariat, is that there is much to be learned from the activities of sub-regional groups, with the work of the MSG at the forefront of that learning (Newton Cain and Taylor 2015). How this rhetoric is applied in practice remains to be seen, but Dame Meg Taylor took the opportunity to visit the MSG secretariat during a recent visit to Port Vila. This is an indication of a refreshed approach from the PIFS, based on recognition of the economic and political significance of the Melanesian sub-region. What appears certain is that the desire for more and better synergy between sub-regional and regional mechanisms forms an important part of what the MSG envisages for itself as encapsulated in its 2038 'Prosperity for All' Plan which arose from the strategic review undertaken in 2013:

> Apart from taking full advantage to develop optimally its own economies, the MSG's plan proposes to collaborate and form solidarity with other sub-regional groupings in the Pacific, with the CROP agencies and also to reach out to other PSIDS (Pacific small island developing states) by way of joint development initiatives, e.g. in climate change and fisheries, and to also share with fellow PSIDS burdened with scarcity of resources, the surpluses of its development and economic growth (Tavola 2015).

Until very recently, the MSG has been very open to approaches from numerous entities, including individual governments, sub-regional and regional organisations, think tanks, and universities. At the leaders' summit in Honiara in mid-2015, the group will adopt the Prosperity for All plan. It is expected that future relationship-building activity on the part of the group, as facilitated by its secretariat, will be more selective and strategic. This could well have significant diplomatic implications, particularly in relation to the granting of observer status. There was a certain amount of internal tension created when Indonesia was granted observer status, and this vexed relationship continues to cause discord (Webb-Gannon and Elmslie 2014). A recurrent issue of interest is what relationship Australia could or should have with the MSG. At the time that the secretariat was established, Australian diplomats came to the conclusion that, as Australia was not a member of the MSG, there was no benefit in providing financial support for the undertaking. To date, Australia has not established any formal relationship with the MSG, and has not requested observer status. Given the Australian government's position regarding the Bainimarama regime prior to the change of government in Canberra in 2013 and the 2014 Fiji elections, this is not surprising. However, it would seem sensible for Australia to establish some relationship with the MSG, given its membership includes countries that are of great economic, strategic and political significance to Canberra. There are indications from within the secretariat that the MSG would be interested in establishing a trade agreement with Australia.

The issue of funding will be an ongoing challenge for the MSG. The group has benefitted from the support of numerous donors including the government of the People's Republic of China and the European Union. However, ensuring that the member governments pay their share of ongoing costs, which are calculated by reference to relative population size, is a perennial challenge. Very recently, the group announced the creation of 'Melanesian Solutions', which is a consulting operation whose income will fund overheads and operational costs including those associated with maintenance of the secretariat.

Reference has already been made to the fact that numerous members of the secretariat (including the current director-general) have a pedigree that includes working at the pan-regional level, most notably within the PIFS. Critics of the MSG point to the apparent replication of PIFS mechanisms and methodologies. A real risk to the credibility of the MSG, therefore, is that it follows the PIFS and becomes too secretariat-centric. To maintain credibility, it needs to proactively maintain its focus on delivering real outcomes that benefit the populations of its member countries.

Conclusion

The commencement of the recent renaissance of the MSG predated the change of chairing arrangements in 2010 which saw the then interim prime minister of Fiji use this mechanism as a key plank in his assertive development of new diplomatic and political relationships as a reaction to his country's suspension from the Pacific Islands Forum. Some may have expected that MSG activity would wane once Fiji relinquished the chair of the group in 2013. This has proved not to be the case, partly because of the increased, and increasing, prominence of Papua New Guinea as a sub-regional and regional leader. The momentum around membership of West Papua has also maintained a focus on the MSG's ability and willingness to be diplomatically innovative.

The diplomatic importance of the MSG is likely to increase and alongside it there will be internal and external challenges. The group has already demonstrated a certain degree of resilience in relation to previously arisen challenges and it is to be expected that this will provide a bedrock of strength and experience to overcome future obstacles.

References

Asian Development Bank (ADB), 2014, 'Pacific Economic Monitor'. Available at: www.adb.org/sites/default/files/publication/149735/pem-december-2014.pdf.

Dornan, M. and T. Newton Cain, 2014, 'Regional Service Delivery Among Pacific Island Countries: An assessment', *Asia and the Pacific Policy Studies* 1(3), pp. 541–60.

Forau, P. and T. Newton Cain, 2014, 'Peter Forau on Why the Melanesian Spearhead Group is a Success', *Devpolicy*, 5 March. Available at: devpolicy.org/peter-forau-on-why-the-melanesian-spearhead-group-is-a-success-20130305/.

Hayward-Jones, J. and T. Newton Cain, 2014, 'Pacific Island Leadership: PNG steps up', *The* Interpreter. Available at: www.lowyinterpreter.org/post/2014/08/28/Pacific-island-leadership-PNG-steps-up.aspx?COLLCC=3972002704&.

MacQueen, N., 1989, 'Sharpening the Spearhead: Subregionalism in Melanesia', *Pacific Studies* 12(2), pp. 33–52.

Newton Cain, T. and M. Taylor, 2015, 'Regionalism, Sub-Regionalism and Women's Empowerment: An interview with Dame Meg Taylor', Devpolicy. Available at: devpolicy.org/regionalism-sub-regionalism-and-womens-empowerment-an-interview-with-dame-meg-taylor-20150308/.

Pacific Islands News Association (PINA), 2014, 'MSG Helps Micronesian States on Endeavour Towards Closer Economic Integration', 30 September. Available at: www.pina.com.fj/?p=pacnews&m=read&o=1602344024542b5789295d578f36e3.

Pacific Plan Review, 2013, 'Report to Pacific Leaders', Pacific Islands Forum Secretariat, Suva, Fiji. Available at: www.cid.org.nz/assets/Key-issues/Pacific-development/Pacific-Plan-Review-2013-Volume-1.pdf.

Radio New Zealand, 2015, 'Polynesian Leaders Meet in Auckland', 3 February. Available at: www.radionz.co.nz/international/pacific-news/265126/polynesian-leaders-meet-in-auckland.

Tavola, K., 2015, 'MSG's Opportunity to Direct Pacific Regionalism to New Heights', Pacific Institute of Public Policy, 3 March. Available at: pacificpolicy.org/2015/03/msgs-opportunity-to-direct-pacific-regionalism-to-greater-heights-2/.

Voigt-Graf, C., 2015, 'Melanesians on the move', *Devpolicy*, 2 February. Available at: devpolicy.org/melanesians-on-the-move-20150202/.

Webb-Gannon, C. and J. Elmslie, 2014, 'West Papuan Heartache?: Indonesia's Melanesian foray', *The Asia-Pacific Journal* 12(47).

14

Negotiating the Melanesia Free Trade Area

Sovaia Marawa[1]

Melanesia is gaining prominence as a powerful political and economic sub-region in the Pacific. The initial members of the Melanesian Spearhead Group (MSG) first signed the MSG Trade Agreement (MSGTA) in 1993 as the instrument to promote trade and regional integration in Melanesia. The MSGTA has been reviewed twice by its members to strengthen and improve its implementation, and in January 2013 a significant milestone was reached with the opening up of the largest regional market in the Pacific.

This chapter explores the significance of the MSG Free Trade Area (MSG-FTA) and how it has reached new heights, despite the experiences of trade wars on biscuits, kava, and beef. It also explains how it departs from the initial MSGTA and the reasons why it has been more successful than similar regional integration initiatives, such as the Pacific Island Countries Trade Agreement (PICTA). It then examines the three key factors contributing to the success of the MSG-FTA: the political will and leadership of MSG leaders to set a bold vision for closer economic integration, measures taken by members to make the

1   I would like to acknowledge Mrs Mere Falemaka, Pacific Islands Forum Ambassador to Geneva, for her editorial advice on this chapter. This is based on my research as a postgraduate student in the diplomacy program at the University of the South Pacific and should not be taken as the representing the official view of the Ministry of Foreign Affairs.

MSG more relevant and improve the implementation of the MSGTA, and the prominent role played by Fiji and Papua New Guinea (PNG) in increasing trade and investment relations within Melanesia.

Significance of the MSG-FTA

In 2013, the MSG-FTA became operational, with its members now according reciprocal tariff treatment for originating or value-added products traded within the sub-region.[2] Under the free trade area, Fiji does not have any sensitive products on its negative list; products qualify for tariff preference subject to fulfilling the Rules of Origin (ROO) criteria. PNG removed duties from the 400 products in its negative list, with the exception of three products: canned tuna mackerel, cane sugar, and salt. Although Solomon Islands deferred its tariff reduction commitments following the ethnic conflict in 2004, at least 80 per cent of its tariffs are to be reduced to zero by 2015. It is expected that all MSG parties will trade fully duty free amongst themselves by 2017.

This is a significant achievement for the MSG, which had its humble beginnings in 1981, when the founding members came together to pursue common political and economic goals that would benefit their peoples. In 1993, the first MSGTA was signed by PNG, Solomon Islands and Vanuatu as founding members of the MSG. A 'positive list approach' was taken with three products that the countries successfully exported to each other at the time: canned tuna (PNG), beef (Vanuatu), and tea (Solomon Islands). The objective of the MSGTA was to promote intra-MSG trade and strengthen economic cooperation. Fiji's desire to ratify the MSGTA in 1997 boosted the MSG to become a 'formidable entity' in the Pacific (Jayaraman 2012). Over the years, members gradually implemented reforms to reduce tariffs, accompanied by supportive economic policies to facilitate the implementation of the MSGTA. The first review of the MSGTA resulted in the expansion of the initial product list to more than 180 products through a positive list approach.

The MSG's attempts to establish a free trade area in Melanesia have faced stormy waters during the 20-odd years of the agreement. In the mid-1990s, the basic tenets of the MSGTA were put to the test as trade relations between Fiji and Vanuatu became strained following the infamous trade wars on biscuits and kava. Vanuatu placed a one-year ban on biscuits imported from Fiji, which cost the FMF Biscuit Co. Ltd more than FJ$2 million as containers were held up at the ports and entry declined into Vanuatu (ABC Radio 2012b). Vanuatu unilaterally

---

2   Products originating from MSG countries — namely Fiji, Papua New Guinea and Vanuatu — were eligible for tariff preferences under the MSGTA, subject to meeting the rules of origin.

applied the trade ban as it perceived the imported biscuits from Fiji to be undercutting its local biscuit industry. The trade ban measure contravened the basic principles of encouraging free trade within Melanesia. Through diplomatic channels, the Fijian government requested bilateral consultations with Vanuatu within 14 days to resolve the dispute. Vanuatu later revised its position by licensing importers to import only two tonnes of biscuits and imposed an additional 50 per cent import duties. However, Vanuatu's actions did not satisfy the Fijian government, who retaliated by imposing a ban on imports of Vanuatu kava. Vanuatu's kava exports to Fiji sustain the livelihood of many Ni-Vanuatu farmers who rely solely on income earned from this million dollar industry. The ban was finally removed by Vanuatu in 2005. Following the biscuit and kava dispute, PNG threatened to impose more than double import duties on Foods Pacific Ltd's canned beef in retaliation for the Fijian government refusal to allow Ox & Palm beef into Fiji. Fiji had claimed that, due to quarantine concerns, PNG could only use beef imported from Australia and New Zealand, and substantially transformed in order to qualify for tariff preferences under the MSGTA. This policy did not please PNG, since it had a thriving beef industry. Following concerns raised by the PNG government, biosecurity officials in Fiji visited PNG to inspect the canning facilities to ensure it met Hazard Analysis Critical Control Points (HACCP) standards.

The Formation of the MSG-FTA

Considering the long history of efforts made to establish free trade agreements in the broader Pacific Islands region, the success of the MSG-FTA is significant. The proposal to explore regional economic integration and a free trade area was mooted from 1971 since the establishment of the Pacific Islands Forum (PIF).[3] The PIF lacked the political will to consider the concept as the means to bring economic growth and prosperity in the region (Herr 1994). But, more importantly, the economics of trading amongst the scattered islands, and the fact that most countries produced similar goods, presented huge challenges. Even more challenging were the necessary economic reforms to achieve this objective. Regional integration was not developed further as the PIF continued to pursue regional sector initiatives such as the University of the South Pacific (USP) and the Fisheries Forum Agency (FFA).

---

3   The Pacific Islands Forum was initially called the South Pacific Forum.

In the early 1980s, the forum island countries (FICs)[4] recognised the need to secure export markets for their agriculture and fisheries resource-based products and secured the first non-reciprocal trade agreement, called the South Pacific Regional Trade and Economic Cooperation Agreement (SPARTECA). SPARTECA provided FICs duty and quota free non-reciprocal market access to Australia and New Zealand. The FICs soon realised the SPARTECA rules of origin were too restrictive for the private sector, this was particularly true for manufactured products such as Fiji garments. The exports of wholly obtained primary produce to Australia and New Zealand were increasing, although strict sanitary and phyto-sanitary requirements were applied. Although SPARTECA was beneficial for Fiji, it made it difficult for the businesses and industries in the FICs to meet the ROO. The non-reciprocal preferences accorded to FICs products through SPARTECA would automatically become redundant once the Australian government had reduced duties to zero, in line with their commitments under other regional trade agreements, such as the APEC goal of eliminating tariffs imposed by developed members by 2010. To date, the average Australian customs tariff hovers around 17 per cent. Due to these glaring realities, the FICs proceeded to develop more favourable ROO that would benefit their exporters and generate economic returns to their ailing economies.

The considerable lack of political consensus to reach new agreement within the multilateral trading system also led to countries pursuing regional integration initiatives. The FICs also faced pressure to enter into reciprocal trade agreements due to the looming deadline for the expiry of the World Trade Organization (WTO) waiver. The waiver, obtained in 2002, allowed the European Union (EU) to extend its non-reciprocal trading scheme to the African, Caribbean and Pacific (ACP) countries under the Lomé II Convention, which facilitated Fiji's sugar and tuna exports to Europe. In 2001, the EU secured an extension of the five-year WTO waiver on its Lomé preferences to allow it to negotiate Economic Partnership Agreements (EPAs) with ACP countries, which included the 14 FICs. Since the EPA would be the first agreement between the FICs and a developed partner, the agreement would be required to comply with the stricter reciprocal WTO rules on regional economic integration. The FICs agreed to negotiate a free trade agreement amongst themselves under PICTA as a stepping stone to integration with the EU through the EPA and with other major partners in the future. This would also facilitate their gradual integration into the global economy and the multilateral trading system, thereby opening up their markets to competition with the rest of the world. The Pacific Islands expansion of trading links among the FICs would bring economic and social

---

4   The FICs comprise 14 islands in the Pacific: Cook Islands, Federated States of Micronesia, Fiji, Kiribati, Nauru, Niue, Palau, Papua New Guinea, Republic of Marshall Islands, Samoa, Solomon Islands, Tonga, Tuvalu and Vanuatu. The FICs group does not include Australia and New Zealand.

benefits, and improve the living standards of all peoples. The FICs recognised the desirability of a clearly established and secure framework of rules for trade under conditions of fair competition in the Pacific region.

In its efforts to create regional integration of Pacific Island markets, the PIF leaders endorsed the PICTA. PICTA was seen as the vehicle to strengthen and enhance intra-regional trade between the FICs by eliminating trade-distorting tariffs and non-tariff barriers to trade through progressive and gradual phases in order to achieve a single regional market (PIFS 2012). This regional economic integration strategy was part of the forum leaders Pacific Plan; it was implemented by the Pacific Islands Forum Secretariat.[5] It took two years for the FICs to negotiate a PICTA trade in goods agreement. Although negotiations on the PICTA trade in goods agreement entered into force in 2003, the FICs faced significant challenges which contributed to the slow, ineffective and unsuccessful implementation of the agreement. Scollay indicated that many of the FICs lacked the capacity to undertake reforms and address inconsistencies in the PICTA and MSG schedule of commitments. Further to this, some FICs do not use automated systems for customs clearance, and some have yet to implement the harmonised system for classification for trade in goods (Scollay 2008). Even though 11 FICs ratified the PICTA, there were further complications, as only seven of the 11 FICs announced their readiness to trade (PIFS 2009).

In 2003, the FICs started negotiations on a WTO-compatible EPA to meet the looming deadline for the expiry of the Cotonou Agreement in December 2006. Since the negotiations were carried out with a developed country, this presented an opportunity for Australia and New Zealand to pursue negotiations for a free trade agreement with the FICs. Australia and New Zealand had strongly argued that they should not be disadvantaged by any trade agreement that the Pacific would negotiate with any other developed country. Noonan stated that the EPA negotiations with the EU were linked to negotiations of the Pacific Area for Closer Economic Relations (PACER) Plus in 2008 (Noonan 2011), which occurred in anticipation of the negotiations on the Interim EPA, which PNG and Fiji eventually signed and ratified in 2007 and 2009 respectively, to protect market access for its products such as canned fish, sugar and garments. PNG's commitments under the Interim EPA also triggered the removal of duties on majority of the products listed on their negative list under the MSGTA, with the exception of salt, sugar, and canned mackerel. The change in PNG's commitments in the MSG provided an opportunity for exporters to freely trade within the sub-region.

---

5   The Pacific Plan is a high-level framework designed to strengthen regional cooperation and integration in the Pacific. The framework was endorsed by forum leaders in 2005.

The conclusion of the PICTA negotiations gave the impetus for the MSG countries to review the MSGTA to ensure that the PICTA did not overtake MSG preferences and render the MSGTA irrelevant for its members. A review of the MSGTA was undertaken in 2005 which committed members to reduce tariffs to duty free on a longer positive list of goods within eight years. A new ROO, based on change in tariff heading method, which was much simpler, replaced the value-added ROO in the previous agreement. The review was critical to further promote trade and ensure that the MSG-FTA was proceeding ahead of the other free trade agreements to maintain its relevance.

The significance of the MSG-FTA is also indicated by the fact that although it initially focused on goods, there was also scope for members to create a regional market for trade in services, investment, and labour mobility. In 2012, milestones were achieved with the MSG Memorandum of Understanding (MOU) on Skilled Movement Scheme (SMS) which facilitated the movement of semiskilled personnel within the identified category of skills. Under the SMS, people with specialised skills — such as trained teachers, nurses, engineers, pilots, and doctors — are able to move freely to meet skills shortages within the MSG-FTA. The negotiations of the MSG MOU on SMS also had a profound impact for the MSG, since it only took two years to negotiate, compared to the seven years that it took the FICs in negotiating the PICTA Trade in Services (TIS) agreement. The PICTA TIS is yet to enter into force as only four out of the 14 FICs have ratified the agreement (PIFS 2014).

Political Will and Leadership

One of the critical factors contributing to the achievement of a MSG-FTA is the vision, political will and determination of the founding and current leaders to establish and advance economic integration in Melanesia. This was not easy, as most Melanesian economies faced significant challenges to creating sustainable economic growth. With increasing calls for globalisation, the MSG had foreseen the profound impact of regional integration on its members' ability to export their products and services in a competitive global environment. Since the region has an abundant supply of natural resources and a population of more than seven million people, there is huge potential for a larger sub-regional market to generate economic activities that would contribute towards employment creation, economic growth and the development of local industries.

Although MSG countries began to gradually liberalise their markets, the economies were highly protective with significant trade and investment barriers that discourage private sector development. The MSG sometimes had its own internal political differences but these were usually resolved the traditional

'Melanesian way'. In 2010, Vanuatu's Prime Minister Edward Natapei refused to hand over the chairmanship of the MSG to Fiji's Prime Minister Commodore Josaia Bainimarama on the grounds that this would undermine the MSG's democratic ideals. Some claims were made that Australia had instigated the move with the promise of aid to Vanuatu. But the chairmanship issue was resolved in the traditional Melanesian way, a first for the leaders, at a special meeting hosted by the Solomon Islands Prime Minister Danny Philip. The traditional reconciliation ceremony stamped its mark as an alternative avenue for resolving disputes within the MSG and its engagement within the wider Pacific.

In 2011, Bainimarama assumed chairmanship of the leaders' summit in Suva which set a bold vision to achieve future closer economic regional integration towards either a common market or customs union. The vision was to be achieved through a broadening of the MSGTA beyond goods to advance trade in services, investment and labour mobility. It also supported the MSG's plan to proceed at a faster pace than the rest of the FICs, given their aim to strengthen private sector development, attract investment, and create economic opportunities to grow and strengthen their economies. With the MSG members also participating in several other regional trade negotiations, it was realised that preferences accorded within the scope of the MSGTA would erode faster and become ineffective if these regional free trade negotiations superseded the MSG.

As chair of the MSG, Bainimarama also took advantage of this opportunity to share his views on the vision to ensure that the MSG would remain relevant. He was a keen advocate of greater regional cooperation in Melanesia and believed that competition would create business opportunities, and generate economic growth and a prosperous Pacific. Fiji's position as the hub of the Pacific would also support and strengthen the overall vision to achieve regional integration in Melanesia. Bainimarama not only raised the profile of the MSG by advocating issues pertinent to its people, but also enabled the institution to achieve a number of key milestones. The chairmanship was then handed over to Victor Tutugoro of the *Front de Libération Nationale Kanak et Socialiste* (Kanak and Socialist National Liberation Front (FLNKS)) in New Caledonia, who was expected to carry on the vision of the leaders.[6]

---

6   *Front de Libération Nationale Kanak et Socialiste* (Kanak and Socialist National Liberation Front (FLNKS)) is an organisation representing the interests of indigenous people in New Caledonia. Although FLNKS is a political member of the MSG, it is not yet signatory to the MSGTA.

Making MSG More Relevant

One of the many reasons attributed to the successful achievement of a MSG-FTA was its members' collective resolve to ensure that the MSGTA remains relevant in the midst of trade negotiations currently taking place in the Pacific. As part of efforts to improve the implementation of the MSGTA, Vellutini and Puech were commissioned by the MSG secretariat in 2010 to assess the implementation of the MSGTA and develop a roadmap for the creation of a common market for services and labour within a two to three year period. Vellutini and Puech found that, although the value of intra-MSG trade was small (around 3 per cent) compared to their trade with the rest of the world, intra-MSG trade was increasing and had enormous potential to increase in future, due the size of the large market of almost eight million people (Vellutini and Puech 2010). The study also found that PNG had become the largest exporter and importer in the region, surpassing Fiji. This result is not surprising considering the unprecedented growth of the PNG economy over the last eight years and its population size of almost seven million people.

One of the challenges in making the MSGTA relevant lies in addressing inconsistencies in implementation at the national level. Vellutini and Puech's study found that PNG and Vanuatu reneged on their commitments by maintaining high tariff barriers and failed to progressively reduce duties on products in their negative lists. Members were required to reduce duties immediately on products within eight years of the coming into force of the revised MSGTA. The general inconsistencies in the application of the tariff levels, the ROOs, and quarantine procedures sent out negative signals and caused a lot of uncertainty for the private sector. The findings of the report were addressed by senior trade and economic officials, who also considered a proposal to review the MSGTA legal text and architecture. Although PNG had been highly protective of its industries, a strategic shift in policy direction took place in 2011, when PNG granted duty free and quota free preferences to the EU under the Interim EPA. PNG was required under the 'Most Favoured Nation Treatment' provisions in the MSGTA to automatically extend the same preferences to other MSG members.[7] Parties to the MSGTA that enter into free trade agreements with other non-MSG members are required to extend the same tariff treatment to each other, resulting in the benefits flowing to other MSG members. With these developments, PNG duties were removed from more than 400 items listed in its negative list, except for sugar, salt, and canned mackerel. The MSG-FTA thus became operational from

---

7   The Interim EPA provides for duty-free, quota-free market access into the EU for all exports originating from Fiji and Papua New Guinea. Papua New Guinea signed the Interim EPA in July 2009, and Fiji in December 2009. European parliament approved the agreement in January 2011 and Papua New Guinea ratified it in May 2011. Fiji started to implement the Interim EPA at the end of July 2014.

1 January 2013 when at least three members (Fiji, PNG, and Vanuatu) effectively began to trade duty free. The other products exempted from zero rates under the MSGTA were alcohol, oil and fuels, tobacco, and cane sugar.

Another major driving factor that contributed to making MSG more relevant is attributed to the establishment of the MSG secretariat. A workable regional integration initiative is highly dependent on the existence of its own effective secretariat. In the early days, the work programs for the relevant committees, such as the trade and economic officials, were driven by members that assumed the chairmanship of the MSG. But the lack of capacities at the national level to facilitate and monitor the implementation of the MSGTA quite often hindered members' initiative and drive to develop work programs. In 2009, the MSG secretariat was established to facilitate the implementation of the MSGTA, identify new areas of cooperation with development partners, and provide policy and technical advice to its members on general matters relating to the MSG (Pacific Institute of Public Policy 2008). There were generous donations of financial assistance and aid in kind received from development partners to support the work program of the secretariat. The Chinese-funded secretariat building is located in Port Vila, Vanuatu.

Increasing Fiji–PNG Trade and Investment Relations

Another major contributing factor to the achievement of the MSG-FTA is the fact that both Fiji and PNG share and identify with a common vision of closer economic integration as a means of creating economic opportunities for their people. Recently, there have been continuous efforts made to strengthen commercial relations between these two largest economies in the Pacific. PNG has implemented policy changes to trade duty free on goods originating from other MSG countries in its efforts to share much of its income gained from its growth with the Pacific. This has led to PNG prioritising its obligations to pursue the MSGTA over other regional integration initiatives, such as the PACER Plus negotiations with Australia and New Zealand (Islands Business 2013). Fiji, on the other hand, recognises PACER Plus as a means to deepen regional integration with Australia and New Zealand. Fiji joined the PACER Plus negotiations in November 2014, following its successful elections held in 2004.[8]

---

8   Fiji withdrew from the PACER Plus negotiations due to the Pacific Islands Forum leaders' decision to suspend Fiji on 2 May 2009.

Historically, Fiji and PNG have enjoyed close and friendly relations ever since the arrival of Fiji's first missionaries in PNG in 1875. Political relations were only established some 100 years later and have since strengthened, with Fiji joining the MSG in 1997. As the largest economies, in the Pacific, Fiji and PNG have the potential to strengthen trade and economic cooperation in the Pacific. PNG, the fastest growing economy in the Pacific, was projected to have grown by around 8 per cent in 2012 and with a population of almost seven million people, there are increasing opportunities for job creation and investments (IMF 2013). PNG is experiencing an unprecedented economic boom driven largely by the construction of the US$19 billion liquefied natural gas project coupled with strong performance in domestic demand in the construction, transport and finance sectors. PNG has a small manufacturing sector that predominantly produces beer, soap, concrete products, fruit juices, plywood, and paint, but this is growing and diversifying.

Historically, the PNG government had been highly protective of its domestic industries, as is demonstrated by the high tariff rates it levied under the MSGTA. Under the able leadership of Prime Minister O'Neill, the PNG government fast-tracked reforms necessary to support the development of the private sector, creating employment, and promoting trade and investment opportunities. Prime Minister O'Neill shared a common vision of a unified Pacific with free movement of goods and people, but it was to be supported by strong national policies to drive economic development (Islands Business 2012). In supporting regional integration, O'Neill believed there were merits in working together to take advantage of the opportunities that would be mutually beneficial to the Pacific in resolving common issues such as climate change, food security, education, health, and potential investments. Prime Minister O'Neill stated that while PNG is experiencing an economic boom, it lacked the capacity to generate new economic activities to facilitate trade (ABC Radio 2012a). The free movement of goods and labour within the Pacific would provide opportunities in sectors of the economy where PNG lacks qualified and skilled workers, such as tourism and manufacturing.

The boom in the economy has also driven PNG investor interest in exploring other markets and entering into joint venture projects that would generate viable economic returns. In 2012, Prime Minister O'Neill led a strong private sector delegation on an investment promotion mission to Fiji. The mission coincided with the official unveiling of the Pearl South Pacific Resort and the Championship Golf Course in Pacific Harbour, following their acquisitions by PNG companies, and included visits to the PNG-owned Bank South Pacific, and the Grand Pacific Hotel (which is a joint venture project with Fiji). The PNG Mineral Resources Development Cooperation and Petroleum Resources had invested US$32 million in Pearl South Pacific at Pacific Harbour. PNG's National

Superannuation Fund and Lamana Development Ltd had invested in the Grand Pacific Hotel in Suva. Prime Minister O'Neill believed that in strengthening trade and investment ties between Fiji and PNG, the private sector could directly benefit from the huge opportunities that could flow into other MSG countries and the wider Pacific region.

O'Neill affirmed that, while Fiji was going through some challenging times, he was encouraged by the developments taking place in the country. The PNG government offered at least 50 million kina to assist Fiji prepare for the 2014 national elections and return to genuine parliamentary democracy. PNG's support for Fiji was further demonstrated in 2012 when O'Neill offered to host the special Pacific ACP Leaders Meeting in Port Moresby to resolve Fiji's concerns about its participation at all levels of the Pacific ACP forums. The PNG government also offered to host and fund an interim Pacific ACP secretariat.

Fiji, as the hub of the Pacific, and with its large manufacturing base, connectivity to the Pacific and strong infrastructure, views itself as an equal partner to explore trade and investment relations with other members, with the hope of improving the lives of every Melanesian. Fiji has a favourable trade balance with PNG, and as a competitive supplier, this trend is expected to grow in the future. Foreign direct investments also play a significant role in economic development, and already there has been a fairly good exchange of businesses operating in both countries. Some Fijian companies have invested in PNG in the areas of manufacturing, construction, hotels and restaurants. Fijian companies already operating in PNG include Punjas (PNG) Ltd, Foods Pacific Ltd, Datec (PNG) Ltd, and Hardware Haus Ltd. The growing PNG economy augurs well for Fiji's manufacturing business, and encourages more cargo, thus enhancing business for the shipping lines. There is also considerable scope to encourage investments within Melanesia, which has already materialised through cross border movements of MSG business ventures such as PNG's Bank South Pacific and Vanuatu's Bred Bank.

In his quest to strengthen trade and investment relations with PNG and take advantage of the available opportunities, Fijian Prime Minister Bainimarama led a 70-member government and private sector delegation on his inaugural state visit to Port Moresby in 2013. The objective of the mission was to promote Fijian products and services, explore trade and investment opportunities, and discuss the common vision of PNG and Fiji leading the MSG into economic union. As a result of the trade and investment mission, several Fijian companies secured orders and entered into business agreements with PNG suppliers and distributors, and two companies have registered with the PNG Investment Promotion Authority to set up businesses in PNG. Prime Minister Bainimarama also announced plans to appoint a trade commissioner to PNG, who will be responsible for promoting trade and investment, and boosting networking relationships with Fiji and PNG companies and other major stakeholders. A budget of FJ$890,000 has been allocated in 2015 to facilitate the setting up of Fiji's Trade Commission Office in PNG. The prime ministers announced that both countries will no longer require visas to facilitate the travel of citizens and business people. Further work will need to be undertaken by the respective government agencies, through a Fiji–PNG Investment Working Group, to discuss opportunities and enable government to explore ways to address bottlenecks that prevent trade and investment activities. The first Fiji and PNG senior officials meeting was convened in Suva in February 2015 to discuss plans and future engagements, with the view to strengthen existing relations between both countries. The increase in cooperation and collaboration between Fiji and PNG clearly indicates that opportunities for trade and investment can be tapped and harnessed to create mutual benefits for the countries and, in turn, stronger growth for the MSG region.

Conclusion

Since its humble beginnings in 1983, the MSG has made leaps and bounds, particularly with the creation of the free trade area from 1 January 2013. The MSG-FTA allows qualifying products to trade freely between Fiji, PNG, and Vanuatu. Solomon Islands has also progressively taken steps to remove tariff barriers and to trade freely with other members in 2017.[9] The creation of the free trade area bears testament to the political will, determination and collective efforts of the MSG leaders to make the MSG more relevant in the midst of increasing pressures to negotiate more free trade agreements within the Pacific. The MSG also places utmost importance on achieving its broad goals to provide economic opportunities and achieve sustainable economic growth.

To improve the implementation of the MSGTA, tariff barriers were reduced and inconsistencies addressed, which generated new trade and investment opportunities within Melanesia. The growing trade and investment relationship between Fiji and PNG clearly demonstrates the improvements in strengthening of business to business contacts that are mutually beneficial to both parties. The conclusion of the MSG Skills Movement Scheme will add to the success of the MSGTA. A new MSGTA that consolidates goods investment — and expands it into services investment — and labour mobility is currently under negotiation by members, making it (once concluded) the most progressive in the Pacific.

---

9   Solomon Islands have removed duties levied on 80 per cent of its products from 2013, with the remaining products to be duty free by 2017.

References

ABC Radio, 2012a, 'Fiji and PNG Trade Growth Could Affect Forum Influence', interview with Waden Narsey, 28 November. Available at: www.radioaustralia.net.au/international/radio/program/pacific-beat/fiji-and-png-trade-growth-could-affect-forum-influence/1052870.

ABC Radio, 2012b, 'Vanuatu Ban on Fiji Biscuits may Spark Trade War', interview with Hari Punja, Punjas Group Chairman, *Pacific Beat*, March.

Herr, R.A., 1994, 'Regionalism and Nationalism', in K. R. Howe, R. C. Kiste and B.V. Lal (eds), *The Tides of History*, Allen and Unwin, Sydney.

International Monetary Fund (IMF), 2013, 'IMF World Economic Outlook: October 2013: Transitions and tensions', IMF, Washington. Available at: www.imf.org/external/pubs/ft/weo/2013/02/.

Islands Business, 2012, 'Peter O'Neill's Pacific Plan: The PNG push into the region', November.

Islands Business, 2013, 'PNG's Trade Minister Keen for a Common Market in MSG Nations', interview with PNG Minister for Trade, Mr Richard Maru, May, Suva, Fiji.

Jayaraman, T.K., 2012, 'How MSG Leads the Trade Way', *Fiji Sun*, October 13. Available at: tkjayaraman.com/docs/2012/np_articles/How%20MSG%20leads%20the%20trade%20way_FIJI%20SUN_Saturday%20October%2013%202012.pdf.

Noonan, C., 2011, 'PACER Plus Progress and Promise: Regional integration challenges and opportunities in the Pacific', *Trade Negotiations Insight*. Available at: www.ictsd.org/bridges-news/trade-negotiations-insights/news.

Pacific Institute of Public Policy, 2008, 'MSG: Trading in political capital and Melanesian solidarity'. Available at: www.pacificpolicy.org/wp-content/uploads/2012/05/D02-PiPP.pdf.

Pacific Islands Forum Secretariat (PIFS), 2009, 'PICTA Status Report: 3 March, 2009'.

PIFS, 2012, 'Pacific Island Countries Trade Agreement (PICTA): Frequently asked questions'. Available at: www.forumsec.org/resources/uploads/attachments/documents/PICTA_FAQ_Jun2012.pdf.

PIFS, 2014, 'PICTA TIS Status Report: 25 March, 2014'.

Scollay, R., 2008, 'Assessment of the Extent of Trade Liberalisation in Pacific Island Countries (PICs) and Review of the Pacific island Countries Trade Agreement (PICTA)', Pacific Islands Forum Secretariat, Suva.

Vellutini, C. and F. Puech, 2010, 'Study on the Implementation of the MSG Trade Agreement and the Roadmap for Future Integration', European Consensus-Platform for Alternatives.

15

Micronesian Sub-Regional Diplomacy

Suzanne Lowe Gallen

Shifts in Pacific diplomacy, governance and development priorities are changing the context of Pacific regionalism. In these shifts, Melanesian countries are represented by the Melanesian Spearhead Group (MSG) and Polynesian countries have formed their own sub-regional response via the Polynesian Leaders Group (PLG). But what of the Micronesian sub-region? Little is known of the North Pacific's sub-regional experience, let alone its history, cultural context and governance structures. This chapter will highlight some of those experiences by pointing out the similarities and differences between the two main Micronesian sub-regional entities: the Micronesian Presidents Summit (MPS) and the Micronesian Chief Executives Summit (MCES), as well as some of the failures and successes of Micronesian sub-regionalism.

There are several prevailing misconceptions, and perhaps misrepresentations, of the north Oceanic sub-region. It is perhaps a misnomer to use the term 'North Pacific' when referring to Micronesia because Kiribati and Nauru are geographically south — the equator being the obvious divider. The terminology may sometimes also be complicated by geographic references in the United States — the 'North Pacific' or 'Pacific Northwest' refer to the US states of Washington, Oregon, and British Columbia. It is sometimes important to make this distinction because of the close Micronesian affiliations with the US. The confusion may not be so much of an issue in the South Pacific, where the US North Pacific probably is hardly ever, if at all, a topic of discussion or reference. It is undoubtedly more geographically and politically correct to refer to the sub-region as 'Northern and Central Oceania' or simply the 'Central Pacific.' Another identifying term that is used for the three northern Micronesian sovereign states is the 'Freely Associated States' (FAS), which is an entirely neo-colonial term in the sense that its primary reference is to the sub-region's relationship with the US. Another term commonly used in Micronesia for the three sovereign FAS is 'US-affiliated states', while the extension 'and territories' refers to the inclusion of the US territories of Guam and the Commonwealth of the Northern Mariana Islands (CNMI), as well as one non-Micronesian US territory — American Samoa — which is in Polynesia. Neither of these geopolitical identifiers includes the two Micronesian states south of the equator — Kiribati and Nauru — which are not US-affiliated and have more ties to Australia and other British Commonwealth countries, as former colonies of Great Britain. The focus of this chapter is the northern Pacific or northern Micronesia, terms that will be used interchangeably and are meant to describe Micronesian states north of the equator, more specifically, the Republic of the Marshall Islands (RMI), the Federated States of Micronesia (FSM) and the Republic of Palau, but also the US territories of Guam and the CNMI.

There are two main sub-regional bodies in northern Oceania. The MPS is an annual meeting among the three sovereign countries — FSM, RMI, and Palau. The MCES is a similar body, but also includes Guam and the CNMI, as well as the four states of the FSM (Pohnpei, Chuuk, Kosrae, and Yap). The issues discussed at each conference are often very similar, sometimes even the same, but their approaches are entirely different, given that one entity comprises sovereign states, while the other also includes non-sovereign states.

Political Background of Micronesia

Micronesia is made up of over 2,000 islands, with a land area of 2,700 square kilometres and an ocean area of 7.4 million square kilometres. Historically, there are four main island groups: the Gilberts and Nauru; the Carolines (which comprises Palau, Yap, Chuuk, Pohnpei, and Kosrae); the Marianas (comprising Guam and CNMI); and the Marshall Islands. This chapter mostly discusses the latter three, or those that make up what is often referred to as the northern Pacific, as discussed above: the three sovereign states of the RMI, FSM and Palau and two territories under the US — Guam and the CNMI. As a side note, one of the three independent states, the FSM, is made up of five separate governments (the four state governments and the national government); this is why there are often references to more governments than there are countries.

Northern Micronesia was colonised by Spain, Germany and Japan, before falling under United Nations (UN) trusteeship, administered by the US. This mandate was called the Trust Territory of the Pacific Islands (TTPI), which was initially under control of the US Navy, before being handed over to the US Department of the Interior in the early 1950s.

Overview of Government Structures

In the mid-1970s, efforts toward sovereignty finally made headway and a political futures committee was commissioned. The committee produced several political options from which the islands could choose, this is how the sub-region ended up with a variety of government structures. Guam opted to remain a US territory; CNMI opted for commonwealth status (which holds an entirely different meaning here than is referred to in the British/Australian system); the four states of Yap, Chuuk, Kosrae,[1] and Pohnpei became the FSM[2] and opted for a federation in free association with the US, as did RMI. Palau was the last TTPI district to become independent in 1994, also opting for free association.

The referenda of the 1970s laid out the governments that exist today in northern Micronesia. The three sovereign FAS, in keeping with the terminology introduced earlier, are all constitutional democracies in free association with the US. However, in terms of government structures, this is where the similarities end. The FSM has a highly decentralised national government with four states, each with its own separate government, and a unicameral congress from which the president and vice president are elected. The RMI operates as a mixed parliamentary–presidential government, with the president elected by the Nitijela (parliament). The Republic of Palau (ROP) has a bicameral congress called the Olbiil Era Kelulau with the president and vice president elected by popular vote.

Challenges

The challenges the sub-region faces are similar to challenges faced in other parts of the Pacific and other small island developing states: climate change, food security, high transportation costs, unreliable shipping services, geographical limitations, limited resources, and high emigration rates. There are other

---

1   Kosrae was initially an outer island of Pohnpei, but became a state when the FSM was formed.
2   While constitutions were adopted in 1979, US administration formally ended in RMI and FSM in 1986 with the signing of the Compacts of Free Association. The UNSC formally ended their trusteeship status in 1990, the same year they both became UN members.

challenges that are more unique to certain Micronesian islands, such as an air service monopoly (in the FSM), and uncertainties regarding the future of economic provisions under Compacts of Free Association with the US.

Micronesian Sub-Regionalism

As a response to the many challenges faced by the sub-region, bilateral and multilateral cooperation through sub-regional bodies has increased in the past two decades, particularly since the late 1990s and early 2000s. It was around this time that significant changes in Pacific regionalism were also taking shape, signalling broader inclusivity. In 1997, the South Pacific Commission changed its name to the Secretariat of the Pacific Community to better reflect its wider Pacific membership (SPC 2011). Following suit, discussions at the 29th South Pacific Forum (SPF) hosted by the FSM in 1998 included the issue of changing the name of the forum to be more inclusive of northern Pacific members. The name was formally changed to the Pacific Islands Forum at the 2000 Annual Forum Meeting, hosted by Kiribati (PIFS 2015). In early 2000, the Secretariat of the Pacific Community (SPC) welcomed its first Micronesian head, Chamorro Lourdes T. Pangelinan (SPC 2011). Pangelinan served six years as SPC's head, leaving behind other legacies — being the first female head of SPC and with the opening of a North Pacific Regional Office in Pohnpei, FSM, in January 2006, the same month she left the organisation. The South Pacific Regional Environmental Programme also appointed a Micronesian, H.E. Asterio Takesy, to serve as its executive director in late 2002. Takesy served two consecutive three-year terms, from 2003 until 2009.

Despite these attempts at greater representation from the northern Pacific, and the changes in Pacific regionalism to incorporate Micronesia more explicitly in South Pacific regionalism, more often than not northern Micronesia has been sidelined in Pacific regional issues, owing largely to geographical distance (and related transportation limitations), but mostly due to historical and political dissimilarities as a result of being colonised by the US (compared to the South Pacific's affiliations with European colonisers). Up until very recently, while the South Pacific may sometimes go to great lengths to include them, northern Micronesian participation in Pacific regional matters has largely been characterised by a sense of detachment.

The relegation of Micronesia may sometimes be self-perpetuated, as in the case of the FSM Department of Foreign Affairs receiving executive instructions from President Emanuel Mori in 2007 to close down its embassy in Suva. While the FSM embassy closure never materialised, it suggested that the newly appointed FSM president was dismissing Pacific relationships as inconsequential to his country's priorities. This could not have been farther from the truth, particularly when it comes to issues such as climate change, which the FSM leadership would have quickly come to realise had it not been for other leaders in the northern Pacific pushing the issues through already established sub-regional entities — the MPS and the MCES.[3]

Micronesian Presidents' Summit

In May 2001, leaders from the three northern Pacific sovereign countries, Leo A. Falcam from the FSM, Tommy Remengesau Jr from the Republic of Palau, and Kessai Note from the Republic of the Marshall Islands, met in Pohnpei to discuss issues of 'working together to improve communication and planning on areas of common interest to their nations and to the region' (FSM Information Services 2001). The meeting was called by President Falcam as a way of forging a common ground to establish closer ties, and to communicate on national and regional issues of mutual concern and importance to the three nations (FSM Information Services 2001). Of particular urgency at the time were issues of maritime surveillance and opportunities for information technology upgrades, but also high on the list of priority issues was the matter of US withdrawal from the Kyoto Protocol (FSM Information Services 2001). These and other issues discussed at the first meeting laid a foundation for future meetings.

At a second presidential meeting in 2002, recognising the fact that each of the three nations was becoming more involved in regional and international forums, it was agreed to begin negotiating with one another to establish an official North Pacific regional alliance. This official alliance would provide a single voice on appropriate sub-regional and broader Pacific regional issues. One of the stated aims of the forum was to collaborate on issues related to US association. The FSM and RMI at the time were renegotiating their respective Compacts of Free Association with the US, and Palau had a vested interest in monitoring the outcomes as a precedent for their future renegotiations. The MPS has been an annual, sometimes biannual, meeting since then, and the acronym MPS now more generally refers to the political entity, rather than to the meeting itself.

In the early days of MPS, invitations had also been extended to Nauru and Kiribati, and in 2009 a formal joint invitation was extended in the form of a resolution that made a statement of 'Micronesian Solidarity' (MPS 2009). The three northern Micronesian presidents acknowledged the significance

---

3   There is also an FSM-only sub-regional entity called the FSM State and National Leadership Conference (SNLC), comprised of the FSM president and vice president, four FSM state governors and heads of legislatures — speakers from Pohnpei, Kosrae, Yap and Chuuk, plus the President of the Chuuk State Senate.

of consolidating Micronesian support in order to strengthen their position in broader Pacific regional settings, in international settings, and with development partners (MPS 2009). To date, however, Kiribati and Nauru have not joined MPS and are not likely to join anytime soon. The reasons for this are the same as those underlying northern Micronesia's sense of detachment from the rest of the Pacific — their different colonial history and difference in primary development partners, combined with geographical distance compounded by transportation limitations, which create differences in priorities during discussion.

High-priority regional and sub-regional issues have generally dominated the MPS agenda. Those issues may be, but are not necessarily always, centred on relations with the US. The respective foreign affairs office in each of the nations[4] is typically charged with servicing the meetings — scheduling, drafting and compiling the agenda, background and briefing documents, taking of minutes, and finalising outcome documents — with the host nation customarily tasked with on-the-ground planning and logistical arrangements. Many of the issues seem to be permanently ingrained in the agenda (for example, immigration, climate change, and security). Others may emerge as needed for some type of action, then die out either over time or once completed to the satisfaction of the leaders. Examples of short-lived action items at the MPS include the FSM's bid to host the Western and Central Pacific Fisheries Commission ('Tuna Commission'), extension of the University of the South Pacific campus in the RMI, and US appropriation-related items such as prior service, US postal services, and other issues that may or may not be referred from the other sub-regional body, MCES.

Micronesia Chief Executives' Summit

In 2003, the chief executives of four western Micronesia island governments (the Republic of Palau, the US Territory of Guam, CNMI, and the State of Yap within the FSM) formed a unified sub-regional multilateral body for cooperative governance known as the Western Micronesia Chief Executives' Summit (WMCES). Similar to the MPS, this summit was created in order to initiate and advance sub-regional issues among leaders in western Micronesia, the key difference being that the WMCES membership includes non-sovereign states (Guam and the CNMI). While the meeting itself was the product of separate informal bilateral discussions between Palau's President Tommy Remengesau Jr and then Governors Felix P. Camacho of Guam, Benigno R. Fitial of the CNMI, and Robert Ruecho of Yap, it was Governor Camacho who pushed for the entity's creation after Palau, the FSM and RMI refused access to the MPS for non-sovereign entities. However, the credit for convening the first meeting belongs

---

4   FSM Department of Foreign Affairs, RMI Ministry of Foreign Affairs, and Palau Ministry of State.

to President Remengesau, who, in true Micronesian brotherly solidarity, invited Governors Camacho and Fitial as leaders of non-sovereign entities to Palau to meet separately on the margins of the third MPS. Robert Ruecho, the Governor of Yap (another non-sovereign entity), was also invited at the last minute. So within less than two years after the MPS was created, the separate WMCES was initiated, both as a response to the MPS rejection of non-sovereign state membership and based on several key attributes shared by the four entities: geographical proximity in western Micronesia (hence the name of the sub-regional body), cultural affiliations, and historical connections that date back to pre-foreign contact days. Since the first meeting was called by President Remengesau in 2003, the WMCES has typically met twice a year. As with the first meeting, held in Palau in 2003, WMCES meetings have usually been held in tandem with the MPS to minimise logistical problems and scheduling conflicts, and to save on costs.

In March 2007, CNMI hosted the seventh WMCES summit in Saipan. Then Governor Benigno Fitial summed up the sentiments of chief executives with regard to the importance of the meetings:

> This summit is successful because it facilitates information sharing on so many levels: from the chief executive level to the staff level and from the public sector to the private sector and vice versa. We have vertical and lateral information exchanges, within each government as well as between the governments and the private business sectors ... by working together as sub-regional governments and by partnering up with private industry, we put ourselves in a far better position to collectively address these regional challenges (Donato 2007).

That particular summit would have been newly elected Yap Governor Sebastian Anefal's first meeting. However, his background as FSM Secretary of Foreign Affairs probably influenced his decision to seek endorsement from the FSM national government prior to sitting in on a WMCES meeting. Ensuing discussions between Governor Anefal and President Mori in early 2007 solidified the FSM's subsequent move to join the WMCES, further paving the way for other FSM states to become members.

In 2007, after two presidencies and four years of formal and informal invitations, the FSM national government, through then President Emanuel Mori, joined the WMCES. At the next meeting in Palau in 2008, RMI, Kosrae, and Pohnpei also joined, and the 'Western' portion of the name was dropped, becoming the MCES. The subsequent meeting in Pohnpei, co-hosted by FSM President Emanuel Mori and Pohnpei Governor John Ehsa, seated Chuuk's then Governor Johnson Elimo as the final member.

There have been informal, and rather unconvincing, discussions of further extending membership to American Samoa. While American Samoa would culturally be better suited to join the PLG, the territory's close affiliation with the US makes membership in the MCES more enticing, given the US relations–dominated agenda, but more so, because of their non-sovereign status similar to that of fellow US territories, Guam and the CNMI.

The issues discussed at the MCES, while similar to the MPS, are approached quite differently given that the entity comprises sovereign and non-sovereign states. For example, it would be pointless to hold in-depth trade discussions at the MCES (as the US controls areas such as customs and immigration for Guam). Similarly, it is not unknown for Guam and CNMI to bring along a Washington-based US fisheries official to an MCES meeting. This would be regarded as a diplomatic blunder, not to mention highly discourteous, to any of the three sovereign Micronesian entities were it to occur in an MPS meeting.

There are currently nine committees within the MCES, each with its own structure, oversight and management: Regional Workforce Development Council, Micronesia Regional Invasive Species Council, Micronesia Challenge, Renewable Energy Committee, Pacific Island Regional Recycling Initiative Committee, Regional Transportation Committee, Regional Tourism Council, Regional Health Committee, and Communications Committee. Some committees are funded by governments themselves, while others partner with NGOs or bilateral donors, depending on the issue. The committees meet outside of the MCES, typically prior to the final preparatory or pre-summit meetings, to finalise what is to be put before chief executives at the plenary. Full-length presentations are requested during pre-summit meetings and are further filtered for plenary meetings. The high-priority issues highlight accomplishments, challenges and recommendations. Unlike the MPS, the MCES has a more structured secretariat, the Center for Micronesian Sustainable Futures.

Sub-Regional Achievements

There are several success stories of activities that would not have been possible without the Micronesian sub-regional dimension either forefronting or advancing the issues. While these are examples of Micronesian solidarity on issues of great importance to the region, not all stories are as successful. In fact, despite the terms that established the sub-regional bodies to better align members, it is not uncommon for differences within the sub-region to sometimes surface, as in the case of RMI offering open immigration and customs, while the FSM and Republic of Palau have consistently and contentiously failed to reciprocate. Some examples of sub-regional successes and failures are outlined below.

Climate Change

The issue that stands out for Micronesia is that of climate change. The significance of this critical issue is reverberated at every opportunity, in virtually every leadership statement. Just as important as the issue of climate change, and in many cases more important, is the face or voice that represents it.

Palau's President H. E. Tommy Remengesau Jr has long been a strong advocate for the environment. He has won numerous environmental awards, and was featured as one of *Time* magazine's Heroes of the Environment for his Micronesia Challenge initiative (Shuster 2009). He was also the co-winner of the 2014 Laureate Policy Leadership award. After serving the constitutional limit of two consecutive terms in office, Remengesau shifted to parliament after winning a seat in the 2008 Palau general election. This meant he could no longer be the face of conservation efforts in Micronesia, which was considered a setback by the environmental community. Environmentalists and conservationists in the sub-region clamoured to find a voice that could take over, ending up with FSM's then President Manny Mori, who had just under a year as chief executive under his belt.

In 2008, The Nature Conservancy (TNC), a worldwide environmental non-government organisation with a chapter in the FSM, tried to get President Mori more interested in environmental issues by inviting him to head an FSM delegation to a convention on biological diversity in Rome.[5] President Mori gave a resounding speech at the Convention on Biological Diversity. However, if there was any success associated with the trip, it ended there. As a staunch Catholic, Mori made it a priority to visit the Pope while in Rome, which immensely detracted from the primary purpose of the trip, much to the dismay of his TNC trip sponsors. While many of his subsequent speeches included issues of climate change and its importance in the sub-region, President Mori never quite captured the essence of the matter in a way that conveyed its fundamental significance. Suffice to say, environmentalists soon found that it would not be easy to live up to Remengesau's legacy, let alone simply have someone else pick up where he left off.

---

5   Convention on Biological Diversity Second Meeting of the Ad Hoc Open-Ended Workshop on Protected Areas.

In November 2012, Tommy Remengesau Jr again won the Palau presidential election, sparking renewed fervour in the Micronesian environmental community and re-igniting the flame that had gradually dimmed since his temporary departure from the political limelight: 'Palau may be small, but with President Remengesau at the helm, it has a big voice' (UNEP 2015). Barely a year after the Liberal–National Coalition took power in Australia, with Prime Minister Tony Abbott announcing that climate change was not a priority for the country (Phillips 2014), Remengesau sent waves of encouragement around the Pacific with his Oceans Declaration during Palau's hosting of the 45th Pacific Islands Forum. The Oceans Declaration calls on the international community to commit to genuine partnerships to protect and manage the region's marine resources sustainably for future generations, culminating in the advocacy of a stand-alone Oceans Sustainable Development Goal. The declaration did not originate in the sub-regional bodies, however, Palau has gone on record in the MPS promoting the initiative and seeking full support from its northern Micronesian neighbours (MPS 2014).

The Micronesia Challenge

Micronesian leaders have jointly committed to the Micronesia Challenge, an initiative to effectively conserve at least 30 per cent of the near-shore and 20 per cent of terrestrial resources across Micronesia by 2020. Leaders have agreed to further advocate and promote the Micronesia Challenge at regional and international meetings, and the need to review the various work programmes (national and regional), for implementation with a view to integrate and streamline functions.

Every conservation activity in Micronesia's five jurisdictions is now linked to the Micronesia Challenge, including national plans, government strategic action plans and NGO plans. The Micronesia Challenge has also spawned several other regional environmentally related challenges around the world, such the Caribbean Challenge Initiative and the Coral Triangle Challenge.

Micronesian Conservation Trust

The environment and conservation fields have garnered worldwide financial support for adaptation and mitigation efforts. The Micronesian sub-region has established a financial mechanism for the Micronesian Challenge and other conservation efforts. The Micronesian Conservation Trust (MCT) is headquartered in Pohnpei, capital of the FSM, with an objective to build an endowment to provide sustainable financial support for conservation and natural resource management across Micronesia. MCT was chosen by the UN Office of Project Services to host the Micronesia Global Environment Facility and Pacific Environment Fund Small Grants Programme. In April 2015, MCT became the first national implementing entity accredited by the Adaptation Fund, allowing it to now apply for projects up to US$1 million to support climate adaptation work in Micronesia.

Rock Island Airlines

There had been talk of Palau establishing a sub-regional airline for several years and in September 2002 that dream finally became a reality. Start-up costs were estimated at US$5 million, contributed by both private and public donors, including the FSM (US$1 million from Yap, US$500,000 from the FSM national government) and Japan (US$1 million). Operations started in August 2004 under an Air New Zealand air operators' certificate, with experienced pilots from Australia and New Zealand, and a leased 128-seat Boeing 737–33A airplane from a Swedish company. Lease costs for the aircraft were extremely low, since the company was established soon after 9/11 and the SARS epidemic.

Nevertheless, operations were suspended in December 2004, after only four months, due to high costs and under-performing sales. The under-performing sales were very discouraging because most air travellers in the region preferred to travel with the sub-region's then principal airline, Continental, on account of receiving frequent flyer benefits.

If anything beneficial resulted from the Rock Island Air debacle, it was that it realised some untapped potential and prompted Continental (now United Airlines) and other airlines to increase services to Palau. As of 2013, Palau was seeing over 40 flights a week from United and other airline carriers, which has contributed significantly to tourism in the country.

Sub-Regional Opportunities

In spite of the many challenges for the sub-region, there are also many opportunities. From trade and diplomatic representation to international and regional programme access, the prospects for further Micronesian sub-regionalism are immeasurable. To harness this immense potential, however, will require leadership towards a common identity for the sub-region.

During the seventh MPS in 2007, leaders directed ministers and staff to look into the possibilities of establishing a Micronesian trading bloc. After several years of negotiations, the Micronesian Trade Committee Treaty was signed in September 2014 in Samoa on the margins of the Small Island Developing States Conference. While the treaty signing was hailed as a big step forward, there is still a long way to go in terms of creating a Micronesian Trade and Economic Community (MTEC). The treaty allows for the committee to openly and actively pursue financial and other resources in order to further pursue steps toward the MTEC. The following steps have been proposed: phase one — setting the rules, institutions and infrastructure for preferential trade and investment; phase two — towards free trade and investment; phase three — harmonisation of trade and investment policies towards a customs union; phase four — realisation of a common market leading to an economic union.

There are also opportunities that have been formally or informally raised, such as Micronesian joint diplomatic representation in Europe (as a result of increasing European Union presence in the region) and tapping into the potential of high numbers of retiring Micronesian US military service members. Other possible opportunities that are more focused on the South Pacific include membership in the new Pacific Islands Development Forum and the long established University of the South Pacific. There is also a joint Micronesian effort to gain improved access to international and regional programmes, such as the United Nations Development Programme Pacific Centre, Pacific Islands Forum Secretariat, Secretariat of the Pacific Community,[6] other CROP Agencies, and the Development Cooperation Scheme between Fiji and the Pacific Island countries, in which only RMI, Nauru and Kiribati have thus far participated since its inception in 2013.

It can be said that personalities in northern Micronesian sub-regionalism are just as important as the issues themselves. One critical sub-regional opportunity that is currently unfolding is that of the new FSM leadership. The FSM congress has recently installed President Peter Christian, former chair of the FSM's compact renegotiation team and a career politician known for his no-nonsense attitude with US policy-makers. In 2011, Senator Christian introduced a resolution in the 17th FSM congress to prematurely terminate the Amended Compact of Free Association with the US. FSM Congress Resolution Number 17–61 submitted, among many other allegations, that the US had abused its power under the Amended Compact with the FSM and made decisions that are contrary to the interests of the country. At a time when all three northern Micronesian nations are fighting an uphill battle of prioritising development interests both independently and under their respective Compacts of Free

---

6   Despite FSM's hosting of a regional SPC office in Pohnpei.

Association, a categorical yet guarded cynicism is an indispensable quality to have in current leaders. President Christian, a veteran statesmen, may be just the right person needed to bring those long overdue qualities to the forefront of the sub-regional agenda.

Conclusion

Sub-regionalism has established a secure foundation in northern Micronesia. However, two questions remain to be answered: who is sub-regionalism for, and what characterises Micronesian identity? Perhaps a coordinated response can answer both questions and, given the many opportunities that exist, these questions will be answered sooner than one may think. In the meantime, while regional experience, knowledge and information-sharing are the wind needed in the sails of Micronesian sub-regionalism, leaders of the FSM, RMI, and Palau, as well as Guam and the CNMI, must recognise that the 'Micronesian Way' of looking north is coming to an end. It is time to look south, where true solidarity rests with fellow Pacific Islands.

References

Donato, A.E., 2007, 'Micronesian Summit Ends Successfully', *Saipan Tribune*, 22 March. Available at: pidp.eastwestcenter.org/pireport/2007/March/03-23-01.htm.

Federated States of Micronesia (FSM) Information Services, 2001, 'Historic Meeting of Heads of Government', press release, May, FSM Office of the President. Available at: www.fsmgov.org/press/pr05000c.htm.

Micronesian Presidents' Summit (MPS), 2009, 'Eneko Communique: Ninth Micronesian Presidents Summit', Majuro, Republic of the Marshall Islands, 16–17 July, FSM Information Services, Public Information Office, FSM Office of the President, Palikir, Pohnpei.

Micronesian Presidents Summit, 2014, 'Pasa Island Communique: 14th Micronesian Presidents Summit', Pohnpei, Federated States of Micronesia, 17–18 July, FSM Information Services, Public Information Office, FSM Office of the President. Palikir, Pohnpei.

Pacific Islands Forum Secretariat (PIFS), 2015, 'About Us: The Pacific Islands Forum'. Available at: www.forumsec.org/pages.cfm/about-us/.

Phillips, A., 2014, 'Anger Mounts after Australian PM calls Climate Concerns 'clutter,' Refuses to Mention Them', *thinkprogress.org*, 3 April. Available at: thinkprogress.org/climate/2014/04/03/3422480/australian-g20-climate-neglect/.

Secretariat of the Pacific Community (SPC), 2011, 'About SPC: History'. Available at: www.spc.int/en/about-spc/history.html.

Shuster, D.R., 2009, 'Micronesia in Review: issues and events, 1 July 2007 to 30 June 2008: Republic of Palau', *The Contemporary Pacific* 21(1), pp. 136–43.

United Nations Environment Programme (UNEP), 2015, '2014 Laureate Policy Leadership (co-winner)'. Available at: www.unep.org/champions/laureates/2014/remengesau.asp#sthash.eX2IlBSH.NYqd5WsT.dpbs.

Climate Diplomacy

16

Marshalling a Pacific Response to Climate Change

Nicollette Goulding

This chapter seeks to address the question: 'Are Pacific states marshalling a collective and cohesive Pacific response to climate change?' In doing so, it will examine how the expansion of the United Nations Framework Convention on Climate Change (UNFCCC) to include more interest areas, actors and alliances, has had an impact on Pacific cohesion. Firstly, it will examine how the splitting and subsequent division of Pacific states into various issue areas has led them to engage in new affiliations known as climate clubs, alternative forums and alliances; secondly, it will assess the efforts of regional institutions in facilitating a more coordinated Pacific response to climate change at the international level.

Fragmentation in the Climate Change Regime and Pacific Cohesion

The shift in the global climate change regime from policy-making to actual implementation of actions has resulted in the creation of new areas which are causing a 'spreading out' of interests of Pacific states. From the establishment of the Kyoto Protocol in 1997, the agenda of the UNFCCC has shifted from one of policy formation to that of implementation (Shibuya 2004), and as such there is an emerging trend for the establishment of state clubs whose members are drawn together by commonalities. Engberg-Pedersen (2011) argues that sector-based groupings are more conducive to reaching agreements, as the number of actors is reduced and the issue areas more focused. This shift towards implementation has also seen a shift in the influence of traditional institutions, such as the Alliance of Small Island States (AOSIS) (Shibuya 2004) as countries begin to focus on the implementation of actions to best suit their national needs.

Faced with conflicting national priorities, Pacific states are increasingly choosing to speak and make individual submissions and interventions within the UNFCCC negotiation process. This trend is shown in Figure 16.1 for the period, 2006–2011, with Fiji, Republic of the Marshall Islands (RMI), Federated States of Micronesia (FSM), Papua New Guinea (PNG), Samoa, Solomon Islands, Tuvalu, and Vanuatu choosing to make separate submissions outside of their AOSIS coalition. This shift in the actions of Pacific nations coincides with the shift in the UNFCCC process from discussions and negotiations to implementation and actions — a more 'sectoral approach' to dealing with climate change issues. This clearly shows that the shift in the UNFCCC process affects the movement or shift in how Pacific Island Countries (PICs) engage in climate change negotiations.

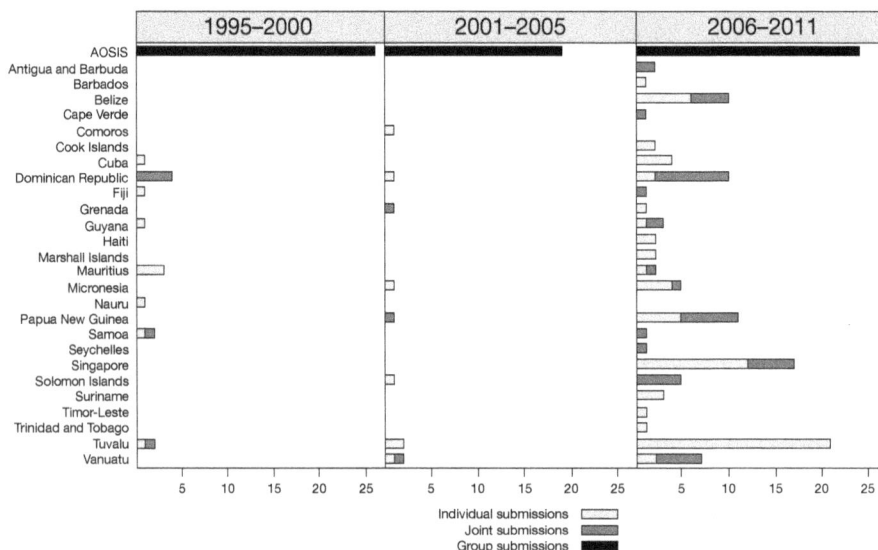

Figure 16.1: Count of AOSIS and AOSIS members submissions, 2006–2011

Source: Author's research.

Coalitions are formed on the basis of mutual interest and compromise, however, when individual members can no longer see their interests adequately reflected in the common position, they may choose to leave the coalition

(Betzold et al. 2011) or seek other coalitions to fill the gaps and better address their needs. As processes in the UNFCCC shift towards implementation and a sector-based approach, Pacific cohesion is becoming tested as PICs become increasingly more active in areas that appeal to their own national agenda as opposed to a common regional agenda. Despite being established as the core institution for climate change, the UNFCCC has increasingly been deemed a mechanism for goal setting and not implementation. This has led to the proliferation of sector-based clubs (Widerberg and Stenson 2013), which leads to further fragmentation. This fragmentation has had a rippling effect, causing fragmentation to Pacific cohesion, and creating uncertainty and panic as PICs look to the horizon for new partnerships as the deadline to an agreement to succeed the Kyoto Protocol looms nearer in 2015.

A particularly contentious subject on which PICs have not reached consensus is the mechanism of REDD+ (Reducing Emissions from Deforestation and Forest Degradation) an incentive that provides payment for actions that prevent the loss and destruction of forested areas. AOSIS and Pacific solidarity on this issue was first tested in the mid-1990s, when the negotiating bloc of JUSCANZ (Japan, United States, Canada, Australia and New Zealand), led by New Zealand and Australia, attempted to obtain the support of Melanesian States (Fiji, PNG, Vanuatu, and Solomon Islands) on the issues of land use, land use change and forestry (Barnett and Campbell 2010). Although this would have had benefits for the Melanesian states, they instead chose to maintain their solidarity on this occasion with their fellow PICs and the AOSIS coalition (Barnett and Campbell 2010). This stance could be attributed to the 'Pacific Way' — a term that was coined by Fiji's first Prime Minister, Ratu Sir Kamisese Mara, which is synonymous with consensus, and usually refers to shared ideas about solidarity and reciprocity, and the fostering and maintenance of kinship networks.

However, with growing recognition and interest in REDD+ within the UNFCCC process, the interest of PICs who can benefit from this mechanism has also increased. Only the large volcanic islands with vast forest cover — PNG, Solomon Islands, and Fiji — stand to gain, as opposed to low lying atolls, such as Kiribati, Tuvalu and RMI, who have no forest cover and therefore nothing to gain from this initiative (Boydell 2008). The Melanesian countries' decision to sign up to the REDD+ Partnership is a step that goes against the grain of Pacific solidarity and the 'Pacific Way', where consensus is usually the order of the day. Tuvalu and PNG have been the most vocal, locking horns over this issue. This was quite visible at UNFCCC COP (UNFCCC Conference of the Parties, the annual global conference to negotiate climate change policy and targets) in Copenhagen in 2009, where tensions over REDD+ led to PNG breaking ranks with AOSIS (Ryan 2010). Both Fiji and Tuvalu have invested a great deal of time and resources on this issue, making 18 and 16 interventions respectively on the topic of REDD+ between 2007 and 2009 (see Figure 16.2). Given the long list of issues on the agenda at UNFCCC conferences, and taking into account PICs' limited resources and capacity, even when pooled together, it is particularly interesting to note that certain countries are investing much of their limited resources and capacities on issues such as REDD+ where there are contrasting views between certain Pacific states. This points to the fact that the coalition of AOSIS cannot be used as a vehicle to drive this issue and, as a result, some states are opting to pursue the issue individually or with a select few in the group that have similar vested interests. Given the capacity constraints, these resources could be better used in lobbying for other substantive shared issues, such as adaptation, mitigation, and climate financing.

Country	Adaptation, vulnerability	Migration, compliance	Kyoto flexibility mechanisms	Sectoral mechanisms	Monitoring, reporting and verification	LULUCF	REDD	Finance	Capacity building, technology transfer, R&D	Consequences of climate politics	Shared vision
AOSIS	51	76	26	1	12	3	1	65	32	8	14
Tuvalu	7	40	27	7	2	20	16	16	0	4	3
Singapore	1	23	5	3	1	0	0	0	0	3	1
Micronesia	4	17	8	4	4	1	1	1	0	0	1
PNG	0	5	3	0	0	10	3	3	1	0	0
Guyana	1	3	0	0	0	1	2	2	2	0	1
Barbados	2	3	0	1	0	0	4	4	2	4	2

Note:PNG stands for Papua New Guinea. Source Earth Negotiation Bulletins (IIS, 2007-2009), own coding

Figure 16.2: Topics of interventions by AOSIS countries between 2007–2009

Source: Betzold et al. (2011).

Growing dissatisfaction with the sub-optimal progress in the overall UNFCCC negotiations has seen a swing towards the forming of new alliances (both formal and informal). Several Pacific Island states have joined climate change forums that run parallel to the established UNFCCC process. Described as the 'thousand flowers blooming' (Maybe et al. 2013), the increase in the numbers and types of climate clubs has created paths for states to pursue their interests (see Figure 16.3). A majority of these clubs' objectives work in tandem with the objectives of the UNFCCC (Bailer 2012), and thereby provide a means for Pacific Island states to caucus strategically in order to better serve their national interests. Overall, these clubs fill the governance gaps and allow like-minded states to garner support and use available opportunities to advocate their national climate change needs. As Bo Kjellen, former chief UNFCCC negotiator for Sweden, said regarding such clubs: 'Only when national conditions are favourable for an agreement, can an international agreement be met' (Eritsland 2013). Some of the Pacific Island states are actively forming new alliances and engaging in forums such as Cartagena Dialogue, Global Bio-Energy Partnership, Coalition of Forested Nations, REDD+ Partnership, Renewable Energy and Energy Efficiency Partnership, and the MRV and International Partnership.

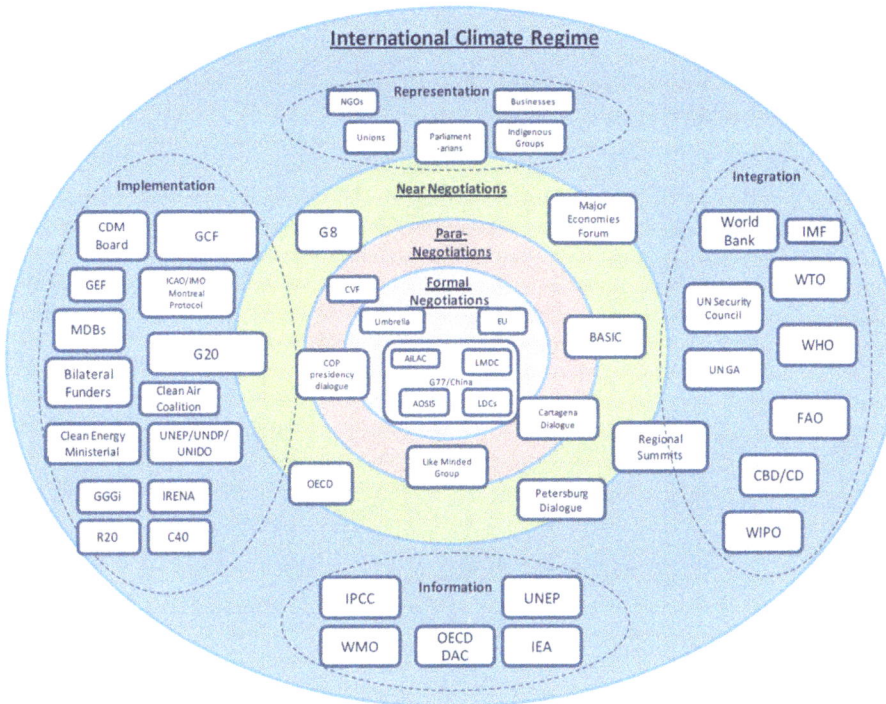

Figure 16.3: A near-comprehensive illustration of the many climate clubs, groupings and actors in the climate change regime, described as the 'thousand flowers blooming'

Source: Maybe et al. (2013).

With the growing frustration over the deadlock in UNFCCC negotiations on mitigation targets, countries are increasingly finding alternative forums through which they can articulate their priorities with other like-minded states. The Climate Vulnerable Forum, initiated in 2009, is such a forum, consisting of a partnership of states that are considered the most vulnerable to climate change impacts. The members of this forum are not only vulnerable states, but also developed nations from Africa, Asia, the Americas and PICs — Kiribati, Tuvalu, and Vanuatu. When Kiribati hosted the forum in 2010, Solomon Islands, Tonga, and the Marshall Islands also participated.

The Cartagena Dialogue for Progressive Action — described as a progressive dialogue for furthering the climate change debate — is another new alliance that has developed as an alternative forum. The forum, which consists of developing and developed states from across the traditional negotiating alliances, allows members to openly express and discuss their national interests in a safe space (Maybe et al. 2013). Seizing the opportunity to move beyond the deadlock in the UNFCCC, Samoa and Marshall Islands are the lone Pacific countries participating in the dialogue. Though this dialogue group does not negotiate together within the UNFCCC, they do develop a joint position. (Maybe et al. 2011). Motivation to join such an alternative alliance is best articulated by Marshall Islands Foreign Affairs Minister, Tony de Brum, who said: 'We don't restrict our climate change efforts to the UNFCCC, and we think that's good practice because you never know what might happen' (Tong 2013). As national interests and uncertainty become the dominant narratives of the climate change discussions, Pacific states are increasingly having to engage in these new forums and clubs as individuals or smaller subsets, limiting their links with each other, as is shown in Figure 16.4.

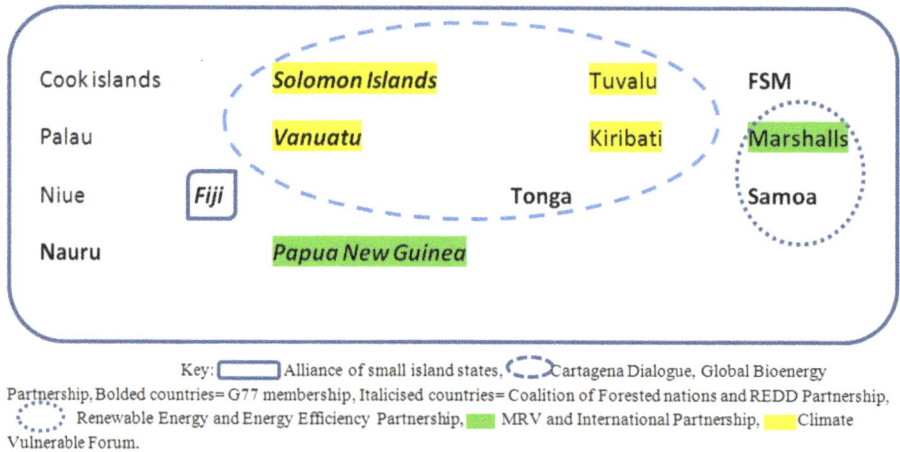

Key: ▭ Alliance of small island states, ⟨‿‿⟩ Cartagena Dialogue, Global Bioenergy Partnership, Bolded countries= G77 membership, Italicised countries= Coalition of Forested nations and REDD Partnership, ⋰⋱ Renewable Energy and Energy Efficiency Partnership, ▨ MRV and International Partnership, ▨ Climate Vulnerable Forum.

Figure 16.4: The alliances, climate clubs and outside forums in which PICs participate

Source: Author's research.

Apart from participating in these informal spaces, Pacific states are also trying to engage in debates on climate change outside of the UNFCCC, and in certain cases this has led to greater cohesion. According to Keohane and Victor (2011), because of diversity and uncertainty in the problems of climate change, states have difficulty in seeing linkages between different alliances and areas within the UNFCCC process. Within the United Nations, PIC cohesion has been revitalised by the creation of the Pacific Small Island Developing States (PSIDS) grouping which caucuses over issues pertaining to sustainable development and climate change (Tarte 2014). As a result of this grouping, the united voice has been more audible in COP events in Cancun, Durban and Doha. It is also the case that since the formation of this grouping there has been better coordination between the various traditional alliances to which each of these PICs are party. Given the important roles that PICs are playing in major alliances, such as Fiji role as chair of the G77 plus China, Nauru as the chair of AOSIS, and Tuvalu playing a significant role within the Least Developed Country (LDC) grouping, it would appear that PICs are increasingly working cohesively and finding common ground within these alliances. However, the very fact that coordination resulted outside of the UNFCCC suggests that Pacific states find it difficult to come together within the UNFCCC. As RMI Foreign Affairs Minister Tony de Brum stated: 'Small Pacific states sometimes find other avenues much easier to engage with, because of the practical and psychological barriers to accessing the United Nations talks' (ABC News 2014).

In the pursuit of achieving their individual country agendas, PICs are forging new alliances and their active participation in these climate clubs, aside from affecting Pacific cohesion, could have other serious implications. One such implication is that of 'forum shopping'. As defined by Eritsland (2012), forum shopping is 'the strategic selection of favourable venues from a menu of alternative governance arrangements, but also withdrawal from old and creation of new arrangements'. As these forums and alliances are relatively new, they rarely contain established rules of conduct. This could lead to uneven power dynamics, resulting in larger states negatively influencing and unfairly dominating priorities and diluting the focus interest of the smaller states. This was evident, for example, when Australia pulled out of the Cartagena Dialogue in 2013 as a change in government resulted in a change in its climate policy.

These new developments could also endanger the central role that the UNFCCC plays in establishing a legally binding agreement that includes all developed and developing nations, as countries may choose to continue working within alternative groups that better suit their interests. This may lead to less ambitious emission targets than would have otherwise been achieved had the UNFCCC remained the central forum for debate. There is a need to not only draw links between these new extensions, but to recognise the increasing role that these structures may have in furthering or detracting from the main debate. Amongst other possible solutions, this may involve states reporting developments in these forums to the UNFCCC. However, with all states, particularly small Pacific states, already overwhelmed with reporting to the UNFCCC on existing issues, this process may need a regional solution.

Coordinating a Pacific Response

As the PSIDS make attempts to bridge their relations at the international level, regional efforts to feed into this process are equally important for Pacific cohesion on the climate change agenda. As stated by President Anote Tong (2012): 'As we focus our attention on our relations beyond our region, we need also to look at how we relate with each other within our region. There can be no doubt that there is greater strength in regional solidarity.' Since the introduction of the climate change issue to the Pacific region at the Pacific Forum leaders meeting held in Rarotonga in 1991, the Pacific Islands Forum (PIF) was charged with regional coordination of efforts to help PICs to find solutions to combat and cope with the negative effects of climate change. Under the theme 'Environmental Issues', and in later years under 'Climate Change', this has been an agenda item in the annual leaders' communiqué.

In 2005, at the Pacific Islands Forum in PNG, the Pacific leaders agreed on developing the Pacific Plan as a framework for strengthening regional cooperation and integration. The Pacific Plan has since undergone a major review and been replaced by the Framework for Pacific Regionalism. The framework is intended to support focused political conversations and settlements that address key strategic issues, including shared sovereignty, pooling of resources, and delegation of decision-making. Rather than providing a list of regional priorities, it seeks to set out a robust process through which regional priorities will be identified and implemented.

The annual leaders' communiqué is essentially a to-do list for the region to implement. The communiqué drives the actions, and the vehicles for the implementation of these actions are the Council of Regional Organisations in the Pacific (CROP) organisations, which have their own governing councils, and the Pacific Islands states themselves, through their national plans and strategies. Since 2010, these actions have largely focused on strengthening access to, and management of, climate change financial resources for member countries. The emphasis has been on accessing international climate change financing and facilitating improved management of these resources at the national level.

The issue of climate change has gained deep and wide traction within Pacific societies. National governments, non-state actors, regional and inter-regional bodies, schools, and businesses have ramped up the rhetoric for advocacy. The rhetoric has touched the hearts of the leaders and this is reflected in their adoption of the Majuro Declaration for Climate Leadership on 5 September 2013. In a concise and focused way, the declaration captures the Pacific's political commitment to be a region of climate leaders and to spark a 'new wave of climate leadership' that can deliver a safe climate future for all. In this declaration, Pacific leaders (with the exception of Fiji, which was suspended from the forum in 2009 and has not yet rejoined, despite it meeting the criteria for doing so) are committed to take on the role of climate leaders for Pacific Island Forum states in a bid to set targets for the reduction of greenhouse gas emissions. However, as has been seen in previous forum communiqués, there can sometimes be a disconnect in the messages coming from the forum leaders at a regional level and their actions at the international level. For example, in the lead up to the development of the Kyoto Protocol in 1997, the Pacific lobbied at an international level for targets to reduce emissions. However, in the same year, the Pacific Islands Forum leaders statement was toned down to non-committal language — 'recognition of climate change impacts' — and urged participants to be forthcoming on emissions targets.

The watering down of the communiqué text on climate change points to the immense influence that Australia and New Zealand have on forum outcomes, diluting the Pacific's message on climate change. Regional efforts on climate have been greatly hampered by Australia's insensitivity to Pacific concerns. At the 2009 Pacific Islands Forum leaders meeting, the following comments were made by Seni Nabou, a leading Fijian advocate for climate change:

> The Forum Communiqué comes as a slap in the face for the Pacific leaders who went into the PIF calling for 45 per cent cuts in greenhouse pollution by 2020. Today they leave agreeing to 50 per cent cuts by 2050. They went in with a strong position that global warming needs to be kept below 1.5 degrees, and finished up agreeing to 2 degrees (Rowell 2009).

This occurred because of the leaders buckling to pressure by Australia. Speaking at the RMI's mission in New York in September 2014, Foreign Affairs Minister Tony de Brum said that he and leaders of other PICs were bewildered by 'backsliding' on climate change by Australia, whom the region considers as a 'big brother down south'. This was a response to the Abbott Government's abolition of the carbon tax, and defunding of scientific and advisory bodies for climate change research. Minister de Brum said that PICs felt abandoned in light of this back-pedalling, especially after they had all come together and supported Australia's successful bid for a seat on the Security Council.

The process detailed below shows that the forum leaders' communiqué reflects the regional climate change position that was arrived at after extensive discussions. The Secretary General of the Pacific Islands Forum Secretariat holds the permanent chair of CROP, as mandated by leaders in 1995 and reaffirmed in 2004. The CROP executives meeting, which is attended by the CEOs and heads of CROP organisations, occurs annually, biannually, or when the need arises to discuss pertinent regional issues — climate change is one such issue. The outcomes from these meetings are gathered with the outcomes of other regional ministerial meetings, councils, committees and working groups and are consolidated at the Forum Officials Committee meeting (the governing council of the Pacific Islands Forum Secretariat, which is made up of representatives from member governments who are tasked with oversight of the secretariat's activities) where recommendations on climate change matters are submitted as an agenda item for consideration by the leaders. A climate change position or directions on further climate policy development, implementation or reporting could form part of the leaders' communiqué which reports on the decisions at the leaders retreat. However, with growing criticism rising over the interference of Australia and New Zealand, it is questionable whether the PIF will still be regarded as a forum representing the interests of the Pacific on the climate change issue.

While the PIF is the pre-eminent authority in coordinating the climate change issue, the Secretariat of the South Pacific Regional Environmental Programme (SPREP) is mandated to take the lead on environmental issues. Established as an independent intergovernmental organisation in 1992, SPREP is the Pacific's central agency responsible for regional climate change policy, programmes and projects. SPREP's role in coordinating a Pacific response to climate change is broad-ranging. Apart from providing assistance to its 20 member states, including representation at international meetings and coordinating the Pacific Climate Change Roundtable (PCCR), it also serves as a conduit for disbursement of climate change funding to PICs, disseminates information on climate change, and implements climate change projects in the region (Barnett and Campbell 2010).

There is however, some criticism of SPREP's preoccupation with implementing adaptation actions in the region at the expense of creating Pacific cohesion in global negotiations (Barnett and Campbell 2010). The need for the Pacific to work together towards common goals within AOSIS in COP processes is fundamental, as is overcoming limited capacity and skills to effectively negotiate against developed nations. This is a point stressed by the Director General of SPREP, David Sheppard, at the SPREP preparatory meeting in the lead up to the COP in Durban. In reality, SPREP's role extends only as far as the provision of advisory services and limited capacity development for UNFCCC negotiations, and responding to the needs of countries on a request basis. It does not extend to aiding Pacific states to find a joint negotiation position.

Being an issue of regional concern, climate change seems to find its way onto the agendas of most regional and sub-regional forums. For example, as diplomacy between Melanesian Spearhead Group (MSG) member states intensifies, so too have discussions of climate change, to the point that, in 2012, the MSG met to develop its own position on global climate change negotiations (Tarte 2014). This was done in part to acknowledge that they needed to hash out differences that could cause divisions between them. This points to an alternative important step towards building a coherent and cohesive Pacific position to the UNFCCC. MSG actions may have shown the way a broader Pacific might arrive at a unified stance on climate change — by thrashing out sub-regional differences and ultimately coming to an amicable decision.

The Pacific Islands Development Forum (PIDF) has been touted as the institution that will further enhance the development of cohesion in Pacific joint positions on issues regarding sustainable development and climate change. The notable absence of Australia and New Zealand from PIDF is said to better encourage the traditional 'Pacific Way' of consultation and discussion (Tarte 2014). With its agenda focusing on areas such as green growth, its impact may primarily be on implementation within the region. Its inclusiveness of governments, civil society, CROP agencies, development partners, and the private sector provides the potential for Pacific states to enhance linkages between themselves.

As the climate change issue evolves, understanding the implications of overlapping alliances will be central if Pacific states want to continue the momentum from PSIDS efforts. This may require further engagement with non-governmental and civil society groups, and the networks that they can provide. For example, Tuvalu's links with the organisation 350.org demonstrates how engagement with such organisations can bring positive attention to a country's cause. Such affiliations can allow for the formation of partnerships that could allow Pacific states to better engage with each other at various levels and in different forms — such as youth groups, private sector, NGOs, etc.

Conclusion

'Consultation and consensus' (Tarte 2014) is the epitome of the 'Pacific Way' of diplomacy. When threatened by the impacts of climate change, Pacific states responded in a similar way to previous times of crisis — they banded together and formed alliances with similarly vulnerable states in order to increase their ability to appeal to global states' sense of morality against the common challenge of 'climate change'.

Climate change is not a single problem, but rather a plethora of intertwined challenges with unique 'attributes, administrative challenges and distinctive political constituencies' mingled with a host of diverse interests from various states and non-state actors (Keohane and Victor 2011).

Perhaps the bottom line for tackling the climate change problem is aptly described by Tony de Brum: 'Climate Diplomacy is most effective when you are able to speak to someone else about his or her political and national interests.' (de Brum 2014). Such effectiveness however may come at the cost of Pacific cohesion. With the impact of climate change beginning to batter their island homes, it is not surprising that Pacific states should want to take advantage of every possible opportunity, even if it means doing so without their traditional Pacific allies.

The climate change debate, however, is not limited to the UNFCCC. When PICs are not contesting the debate within the UNFCCC, they are finding themselves on the frontline of other battles in informal and formal spaces outside the UNFCCC.

Stalemates within the UNFCCC, such as occurred with the highly controversial Copenhagen Accord, are becoming too common an occurrence. Dissatisfaction with the UNFCCC process is leading states to pull away or join parallel forums. These new arenas are becoming potentially better alternatives for furthering the climate change debate in a manner which is less divisive, more open to actors' self-interests, and progressive enough to allow for experimentation in alternative solutions (Fuhr et al. 2011). Desperate for a globally binding agreement by 2015, PICs are engaging in these alternative forums and forging new alliances to help build momentum toward this goal.

Enhanced Pacific coordination in forums such as PSIDS in the UN underscores the inability of Pacific states to achieve the same within the UNFCCC via AOSIS. Regional efforts to improve Pacific coordination within the UNFCCC process appear to be limited by several factors. The interference of New Zealand and Australia, and the focus on capacity development and regional implementation actions in the PIF and SPREP, prevent adequate opportunities to coordinate a Pacific response to climate change. However, with recent leadership and initiative shown by the MSG in attempting to discuss differences between themselves, and the development of the PIDF, there are indicators that there is some recognition of the need to develop a better coordinated Pacific response. It is glaringly apparent, however, that at present there is no means to develop a Pacific position in climate change negotiations leading up to Paris 2015.

Climate change vulnerability is high on the agenda of all Pacific states. It cannot, however, be ignored that the complexity and fragmentation of the UNFCCC is having obvious implications for PIC cohesion as PICs break out into various clubs in a desperate attempt to tackle different aspects of the climate change issue. With the growing literature on the impact of UNFCCC fragmentation pointing out that this may lead to more effective climate change actions, including better avenues for achieving long term emissions reduction, the question that needs to be answered is: 'Is Pacific cohesion really necessary to achieve a global commitment to climate change action that addresses Pacific interests and priorities?'

References

ABC News, 2014, 'Marshall Islands Minister Unsure of Australia's Stance on Climate Change'. Available at: www.abc.net.au/news/2014-04-01/an-marshall-islands-urges-urges-australia-to-take-22leadership/5360510.

Bailer, S., 2012, *Bargaining Resources and Strategies in Climate Change Negotiations,* Swiss Network of International Studies, Zurich. Available at: www.snis.ch/system/files/4_bailer_-_bargaining_resources_and_strategies_in_climate_ch_0.pdf.

Barnett, J. and J. Campbell, 2010, *Climate Change and Small Island States: Power, knowledge and the South Pacific,* Earthscan, London.

Betzold, C., P. Castro and F. Weiler, 2011, *AOSIS in the UNFCCC Negotiations: From unity to fragmentation,* Centre for Comparative and International Studies, Zurich.

Boydell, E., 2008, 'A Different Divide?: Pacific Island countries and north–south agendas in the evolution of global climate policy', *Cross-sections: The Bruce Hall Academic Journal* 4.

de Brum, T., 2014, 'Climate Diplomacy: A perspective from the Marshall Islands', *Climate Diplomacy*, 29 September. Available at: www.climate-diplomacy.org/news/climate-diplomacy-–-perspective-marshall-islands.

Engburg-Pedersen, L., 2011. 'Climate Change Negotiations and their Implications for International Development Cooperation', Danish Institute for International Studies. Available at: um.dk/en/~/media/UM/English-site/Documents/Danida/Partners/Research-Org/Research-studies/Climate%20change%20negotiations%20and%20their%20implications%20for%20international%20development%20cooperation%202011.pdf.

Eritsland, S., 2012, 'Fragmented Systems for Collective Action: Can the institutional architecture in East Asia carry the challenge of climate change?', unpublished MA thesis, Universitetet i Oslo, Oslo.

Fuhr, L., B. UnmuBig, H.J.H. Verlome and F. Yamin, 2011. *A Future for International Climate Politics: Durban and beyond,* Heinrich Böll Foundation, Berlin.

Keohane, R.O. and D.G. Victor, 2011, 'The Regime Complex for Climate Change', The Harvard Project on International Climate Agreements Discussion Paper 10-33. Available at: belfercenter.ksg.harvard.edu/files/Keohane_Victor_Final_2.pdf.

Maybe, N., L . Gallagher and C. Born, 2013, *Understanding Climate Diplomacy: Building diplomatic capacity and systems to avoid dangerous climate change,* Third Generation Environmentalism, London.

Rowell, A., 2009, 'Copenhagen: Australia accused of selling-out Pacific Islands', *Oil Change International*, 7 August. Available at: priceofoil.org/2009/08/07/copenhagen-australia-accused-of-selling-out-pacific-islands/.

Ryan, Y., 2010, 'COP 15 and Pacific Island States: A collective voice on climate change', *Pacific Journalism Review* 16(1), pp. 192–203.

Shibuya, E., 2004, 'The Problems and Potential of the Pacific Islands Forum', in J. Rolfe (ed.) *The Asia–Pacific: A region in transition*, Asia-Pacific Center for Security Studies, Honolulu, pp. 102–15.

Tarte, S., 2014, 'Regionalism and Changing Regional Order in the Pacific Islands', *Asia and the Pacific Policy Studies* 1(2), pp. 312–24.

Tong, B.A., 2012, 'Keynote Address', launch of the Pacific International Relations Forum of the School of Government, Development and International Affairs of the University of the South Pacific, 9 October. Available at: pidp.eastwestcenter.org/pireport/2012/October/10-11-sp.htm.

Tong, D., 2013, 'The Man Behind Majuro: Minister Tony de Brum', *Climate Tracker*. Available at: adoptanegotiator.org/the-man-behind-majuro-minister-tony-de-brum/.

Widerberg, O. and D.E. Stenson, 2013, 'Climate Clubs and the UNFCCC', FORES Study 2013:3, Fores, Stockholm.

Establishing a Pacific Voice in the Climate Change Negotiations

George Carter

When asked about the greatest challenge to global climate change negotiations at the United Nations Third Small Islands Developing States Conference in 2014, the leaders of three Pacific Island states expressed similar sentiments. Enele Sopoaga, Prime Minister of Tuvalu, said that 'Pacific negotiators need to be in sync at the UNFCCC'; Tony de Brum, Minister of Foreign Affairs of Marshall Islands, asserted that 'there has been a failure of traditional diplomacy at the UN … we need a new brand of diplomacy … one voice diplomacy'; and President Anote Tong of Kiribati argued 'we need to establish alliances that are non-traditional, that serve our best interest'. These responses echo the frustration of Pacific leaders at the state of current negotiations as they prepare for the Conference of the Parties (COPs) in Paris, 2015. The COPs 2015 is especially significant as it attempts to produce a new global climate change action agreement for post-2020.

For almost 25 years, the global climate change regime has been an arena of complex and multifaceted diplomacy involving seemingly endless negotiations on a wide range of issues with a plethora of actors (state, civil society and private businesses).[1] The climate regime is based on the 1992 United Nations Framework Convention on Climate Change (UNFCCC), which commits its 196 state parties to reduce greenhouse gas emissions under the mechanisms of the Kyoto Protocol. Despite the various negotiation impasses, the constant contact of negotiators has allowed for innovative forms of climate diplomacy. An important aspect of climate diplomacy, and a complementary bargaining tool to a state's climate policy position, are the political groupings or interstate coalitions to which they belong. As reflected in the above responses, Pacific leaders are increasingly placing a strong emphasis on Pacific coalitions or political groupings as a means to accentuate a Pacific voice in the climate change regime at the global level.

This chapter explores the work of Pacific Island states in establishing a Pacific voice at global climate change negotiations. It seeks to draw out several trends in the academic literature relevant to Pacific states' participation in the UNFCCC, through interstate coalitions. For the student of Pacific diplomatic studies and international relations, the general literature is disappointing in its lack of attention to the Pacific Islands experience. To paraphrase Carsten Holbraad, the Pacific Islands have always been objects of international relations theory building, and never the subjects of analysis (Holbraad 1971, p. 78). In piecing together the trends and behaviour of Pacific state participation through coalitions, a student of diplomatic studies finds not only the employment of innovative tools of diplomacy, but also exciting avenues of future empirical research.

There are many coalitions with which the 14 Pacific Island states that are party to the convention are associated.[2] While it is the prerogative of a state to be associated with any grouping, this raises two important questions. Firstly, why is it important for Pacific states to join coalitions? Secondly, what is the advantage gained from joining multiple coalitions in the regime? This paper will address these questions in three parts. The first part of this paper will outline why coalition blocs are an integral part of the climate change regime. The second part will provide an overview of the various blocs with which Pacific states are associated. Finally, the paper will focus on the benefits of joining multiple coalition blocs for Pacific Island states.

---

1   On average, over 7,000 country delegates and 4,000 media representatives attend the COPs. In smaller negotiations during the year there are on average 2,000 participants. These figures do not include the various UN agencies staff. Over 1,500 observer organisations have been registered for accreditation in the negotiations.
2   The 14 Pacific Islands states that are party to the UNFCCC are: Cook Islands, Fiji, Federated States of Micronesia, Kiribati, Marshall Islands, Nauru, Niue, Palau, Papua New Guinea, Samoa, Solomon Islands, Tonga, Tuvalu, and Vanuatu.

Coalition Diplomacy in the Climate Change Regime

Coalition Diplomacy Literature

The study of coalitions has high theoretical and practical significance for the discipline of international relations. Its theoretical contributions have critical impact on the stability (or otherwise) of the international system (Narlikar 2003, p. 12). There already exists a vast amount of scholarship devoted to analysing the implications of multipolar versus bipolar alliance structures and coalitions of the willing, of war and peace.[3] More importantly, the policy significance of interstate coalitions lies in the fact that they provide opportunities for member countries. As Christophe DuPont argues, there are two core functions of coalitions. Firstly, coalitions function as a means for maximising bargaining power for its members (Dupont 1996, p. 49). Secondly, coalitions function as a means for managing complexity of processes and issues within a regime where a common platform that incorporates the minimal demands of each coalition member is easier to handle and negotiate than the sum of individual items (Dupont 1996, p. 49). These two core functions are especially important for small countries with limited negotiation resources and political clout in climate negotiations, such as Pacific Island countries.

Although considered to be a significant part of the UNFCCC regime, coalitions are relatively understudied. Coalitions are mentioned briefly in the neoliberal regime literature by academic negotiators such as a Yamin and Depledge (2004) and Depledge (2005). Within the burgeoning area of global environmental politics, the focus of research has mainly been on individual state bargaining, asymmetrical power relations of states (polluters), and non-Annex I states (Bailer 2012), especially theorising conditions for a global climate change agreement. At best, the limited literature available compares the strategies of climate coalitions with those in the areas of trade, the international criminal court (Wallbott and Deitelhoff 2012), or coalitions of epistemic communities and non-government organisations (NGOs) (Gough and Shackley 2001). Recent studies on the issue of climate justice (Audet 2013) and the emergence of post-Kyoto coalition blocs (Blaxekjær and Nielsen 2014) emphasise a complex landscape of political coalitions within the regime.

Only a handful of studies highlight the work of Pacific state participation in coalitions of the UNFCCC, but these studies are primarily focused on the broader Alliance of Small Island States (AOSIS). Ashe et al. (1999), Chasek (2005) and Betzold (2010), for example, have analysed the influence of AOSIS, especially

---

3   See the work in alliance and coalition theories by Waltz (1979), Walt (1987), Morgenthau (2003), Snyder (1997), and Sheehan (1996).

regarding agenda setting in the early days of the regime. A more recent paper by Betzold, which highlights intra-bloc diplomacy, finds that although AOSIS continues to function as a group, incidents of internal disagreements have prompted a questioning of its cohesiveness (Betzold et al. 2012). While this body of work on AOSIS is useful in producing some insights into the work of Pacific Island states in negotiations, it does not fully uncover the internal politics of the group. Most importantly for our purposes here, the perspectives of Pacific negotiators are hidden by the strong leadership voice of Caribbean countries.

Coalitions in UNFCCC

Coalitions are an integral part of the climate change regime, as it would be logistically impossible to conduct negotiations among the 196 individual country delegations. The existence of coalitions, some of which speak with a common voice, helps to streamline the negotiation process and transaction costs (Gupta 2000, p. 34). Their very presence leads to a dual structure in the climate change regime: issues are negotiated at the coalition level first, before common positions are presented in a COPs and Subsidiary Bodies (SBs) meeting. These coalitions inadvertently become clearinghouses or filters for key positions and rallying support for major submissions.

Despite the prominence accorded to the work of the coalitions by the parties themselves, there are no hard and fast rules or formal processes for establishing a negotiation coalition. States may simply decide to do so, and then usually notify the COPs bureau, SBs, or secretariat of their actions (Gupta 2000, p. 35). Without a registry of blocs, the precarious ad hoc nature of these arrangements makes the tracking of coalitions difficult. The well-known coalitions document their existence through plenary statements, submissions, media releases and engagement in public debate. Those coalitions that are not well documented, on the other hand, are often involved in secret side-door or back-room negotiations. Although such coalitions are widely known and can be useful, they can also be detrimental, as evidenced by the Copenhagen COP 15, where secret dealings changed and derailed negotiations.[4]

Coalition blocs are intrinsic to the climate change regime, with UNFCCC article 3 dividing the 195 Parties into two major camps: Annex I countries (developed countries) and non-Annex I countries (developing countries). In recognising that developed countries are principally responsible for the current high levels of greenhouse gas emissions in the atmosphere as a result of more than 150 years of industrial activity, the protocol places a heavier burden on developed nations under the principle of common but differentiated responsibilities (UNFCCC n.d.). This north–south divide, also referred to as 'the firewall', becomes the basis upon which political groupings are formed.

---

4   See the work on new political groupings in UNFCCC since Copenhagen 2009 in Blaxekjær and Nielsen (2004).

Pacific States in UNFCCC Coalitions

There are 21 coalition blocs that have actively participated in the climate change regime. The membership of states within these blocs is varied. Some blocs comprise only Annex I countries or non-Annex I countries, while others include both. Of the 21 coalition blocs, there are six blocs associated with one or more Pacific parties. As climate change negotiations progress with little action improving the situation for Pacific states, Pacific leaders are responding by creating new Pacific blocs in an attempt to create a united Pacific voice in the hope of affecting real change in global climate change negotiations. This section will provide a brief outline of the six traditional coalition blocs of which Pacific states are currently members before discussing the emergence of new Pacific blocs.

Table 17.1: Coalition Blocs in UNFCCC Negotiations

Annex I	non-Annex I	Both Annex I and non-Annex I
Economies In Transition (EIG)	African Group (AG)	Environmental Integrity Group (EIG)
European Union (EU)	Alliance of Small Island States (AOSIS)	Cartagena Dialogue for Progressive Action (CD)
Umbrella Group (UG)	Bolivarian Alliance for the Peoples of our America (ALBA)	Durban Alliance (DA)
	Central American Integration System (SICA)	
	Central Asia, Caucasus and Moldova (CACAM)	
	Coalition of Rainforest Nations (CfRN)	
	League of Arab States (LAS)	
	Least Developed Countries (LDC)	
	G77 and China (G77)	
	Organisation of Petroleum Exporting Countries (OPEC)	
	Brazil, China, South Africa, India (BASIC)	
	Climate Vulnerable Forum (CVF)	
	Mountains Landlocked Developing Countries (MLDC)	
	Like Minded Developing Countries (LMDC)	
	Association of Independent Latin American and Caribbean Countries (AILAC)	

Note: The coalitions which some or all of the 14 Pacific states are involved with appear as underlined.

Source: The list is attributed to research by Blaxekjær and Nielsen (2004) which focuses on coalitions that arose after COPs Copenhagen 2009.

G77 and China

Founded in 1964, in the context of the UN Conference on Trade and Development, G77 and China has been active since the early days of the convention. Of the 134 members in the group, 10 are from the Pacific: Fiji, Federated States of Micronesia, Kiribati, Marshall Islands, Nauru, Papua New Guinea, Samoa, Solomon Islands, Tonga, and Vanuatu.

The membership dynamics of the group are diverse, ranging from vulnerable small island states, least developing countries, and oil exporting countries, to large and middle income nations, each with differing interests on climate change issues. Despite this, the G77 remains the most important and powerful coalition. The group develops common positions on substantive issues by consensus: if there is no consensus, there is no position. The chair of the group is the first to take the floor in the main negotiations and presents the common positions.

The role of chair rotates annually and although it is a highly respected position, not all countries feel able or willing to take it on due to the economic and institutional resources required, the difficulty of bringing members to a common position, and the fact that the G77 chair may have to stand against some powerful countries, which could trigger wider political repercussions (Gupta 2000, p. 36). While countries such as Papua New Guinea and Samoa chaired G77 subsidiary bodies, the landmark year for Pacific leadership in the group came in the form of Fiji's chairmanship of the whole G77 in 2013.

Least Developed Countries

The Least Developed Countries (LDC) bloc was formed in 1971 as an offshoot from a UN categorisation of countries. Of the 48 countries in this group, only Tuvalu, Solomon Islands, Kiribati and Vanuatu are from the Pacific. (Samoa left the group following its LDC graduation in 2014).

The bloc has become increasingly active in the climate change process, often working to defend its particular interests — with regard to vulnerability and adaptation to climate change, for example (UNFCCC n.d.). The bloc works together at the intergovernmental negotiations under the UN Framework Convention on Climate Change with two aims. The first is to demand that wealthier nations act in accordance with their responsibility for creating the problem and their capability for addressing it. The second aim is to play a leadership role in global efforts to prevent dangerous climate change (Least Developing Countries Group n.d.).

Alliance of Small Island States

Established in 1990, the Alliance of Small Island States (AOSIS) has and continues to be the premier bloc in the formal negotiations with close resonance to Pacific Island needs. It comprises 44 small island states and low-lying coastal states that are highly vulnerable to climate change. All 14 Pacific Island countries are part of the coalition, with American Samoa and Guam having observer status. Although the diverse membership of AOSIS derives from the Pacific, Caribbean and Indian Oceans, they are united by the common immediate threat posed to their survival by climate change.

The bloc proved instrumental in shaping the regime when it prepared the original draft of the Kyoto Protocol, advocating for 20 per cent cuts in carbon dioxide emissions from 1990 levels by 2005. Famously quoted as the 'moral conscience' of the negotiations, the ad hoc lobby group gives voice to the Small Island Developing States (SIDS) on environmental matters and climate change threats. The bloc is the main focal point for many Pacific negotiators in terms of technical resource and capacity support. Its ambassadors in New York meet periodically throughout the year to be apprised on positions, but key discussions occur in the weeks prior to and during the negotiations. One of the most notable contributions of the bloc has been successful lobbying for SIDS as special case in the Rio Summit of 1992 that led to the establishment of the SIDS conferences.

Coalition of Rainforest Nations

The Coalition of Rainforest Nations (CfRN) was founded in 2004 and brings together tropical rainforest developing countries to collaboratively reconcile forest stewardship with economic development. Of the 41 members, Fiji, Samoa, Solomon Islands, Vanuatu and Papua New Guinea are drawn from the Pacific.

The coalition operates as a forum to facilitate consensus among participating countries on issues related to the domestic and international frameworks for rainforest management, biodiversity conservation, and climate stability. The work of the bloc has been instrumental in the establishment of the Reducing Emissions from Deforestation and Forest Degradation (REDD) program, which was vigorously negotiated as the Bali Action Plan. The success of the REDD program owes much to the tactical plea of Papua New Guinea Prime Minister Michael Somare and Papua New Guinea Special Envoy Kevin Conrad in the Bali COPs of 2007. The breakthrough moment when Kevin Conrad called out to the United States, 'If you're not willing to lead, then get out of the way', has been described as 'the mice that roared' incident (von videoarchitekt 2007).

Climate Vulnerable Forum

The Climate Vulnerable Forum (CVF), founded a month before COPs Copenhagen in 2009, is an international partnership of countries highly vulnerable to a warming planet. The forum is premised on the idea of a south–south cooperation platform for participating governments to act together to deal with global climate change (Climate Vulnerable Forum n.d.). Kiribati, Tuvalu and Vanuatu are within its 20-member country grouping.

The forum of highly vulnerable developing countries argues that they are already experiencing the negative effects of climate change. In 2010, Kiribati was the chair of the CVF and hosted the Tarawa Climate Change Conference, which was instrumental in bringing together Pacific states and their major development partners to sign the Ambo Declaration. The 12 signatories to this declaration were Kiribati, the Solomon Islands, Tonga, the Republic of the Maldives, Cuba, Brazil, Fiji, Japan, China, the Marshall Islands, New Zealand and Australia (Packard 2010).

Cartagena Dialogue for Progressive Action

Established in 2010, the Cartagena Dialogue for Progressive Action (Cartagena Dialogue) was formed after the breakdown of the Copenhagen COPs, recognising the need to rebuild trust between developed and developing countries. The group continues to meet outside formal UNFCCC negotiations. While its members claim that it is not a political bloc, the dialogue provides a platform for delegates from developed and developing countries to have frank discussion to better understand each other's positions and find areas of possible middle ground. This fluid membership is useful, as developing countries apparently find it difficult to be too closely associated with developed countries in negotiations due to formal group memberships and a sense of loyalty to G77 (Blaxekjær and Nielsen 2014, p. 4). Of the countries involved in the dialogue, only Samoa and Marshall Islands have been actively involved. The 2014 Cartagena Dialogue was held in Marshall Islands and focused on opportunities to break the international deadlock and find common position for a 2015 binding agreement (Islands Business 2014).

The Emergence of 'Pacific' Coalitions

In the past five years, there have been new developments in the political landscape of coalition blocs in relation to the Pacific Island countries. While the six groups described above appear to remain cohesive and functioning, new groupings have emerged due to intra-bloc disagreements. As one lead negotiator states, the traditional blocs 'have not been sufficient in addressing our Pacific needs … the particular issues of coral islands nations are drowned amongst the bigger tropical rainforest, harbour and oil-producing nations' (Pacific negotiator 2014). These groupings exist on the fringes of the six traditional blocs, and strive to provide a more powerful voice for the Pacific in negotiations. The two new Pacific climate change blocs are Pacific SIDS and the Coalition of Atoll Nations.

Pacific SIDS

The advent of the Pacific SIDS (PSIDS) group in the climate regime is arguably a natural progression. PSIDS is a consortium of ambassadors of the 12 Pacific embassies based in New York, whose work encompasses the major thematic areas of the UN. The group was once the Pacific Islands Forum contact group in New York, however, in a show of solidarity towards Fiji, it continued its work with less Australian and New Zealand influence. Since 2007, PSIDS has grown organically to be the main Pacific grouping whose work encompasses the major thematic areas of the UN. While it is not clear when the group officially became involved in the climate debate, the first submission by the group to a Subsidiary Body meeting came in 2009 (just before Copenhagen). Since then, the PSIDS has been a clearing house for key joint positions of the Pacific states for AOSIS and subsequently for G77. According to one negotiator, there is an increasing feeling amongst Pacific leaders that PSIDS should become more vocal as a bloc in the regime (Pacific negotiator 2014).

Coalition of Atoll Nations on the issue of Climate Change

In July 2014, a new grouping was formed by 'front-line states' out of further frustration with the results of negotiations. The Coalition of Atoll Nations on the issue of Climate Change (CANCC) was the initiative of President Anote Tong. It comprises four atoll nations: Kiribati, Tuvalu, Marshall Islands, and the Maldives from the Indian Ocean. Their positions revolve around the rhetoric of atoll nations being in the frontline of the impacts of climate change and who consider themselves as the early warning system for the rest of the world. As one negotiator argued: 'Time after time, coral atoll nations have supported the work of the blocs, [but] because of our small populations (and bureaucratic incapacities) we are continually left out of climate financing initiatives and have to be content with only small pilot projects' (Pacific negotiator 2014). The group remains committed to pushing legally binding agreements and ambitious targets at the global level, and for easier access to resources for the 'smallest of small island nations'. The ultimate goal of the group is for UN special recognition in the convention for coral atoll nations (as in the case of AOSIS pursuing SIDS as a special case).

Benefits from Coalition Diplomacy

The continued involvement of Pacific states in various coalition blocs and the growth of new groupings is testament to growing Pacific agency within the regime. Notwithstanding the work of individual country delegations, association with the blocs has not only empowered their positions, but has developed their diplomatic finesse. The many diplomacy lessons and benefits that can be derived include access to a wide network of negotiators, development in climate leadership, and engagement in climate public diplomacy.

Negotiators Network/Service

Through associations with these groupings in a year-long calendar of negotiations, it is only natural that a network of negotiators is established. The typical Pacific negotiator is no longer someone from the Ministry of Foreign Affairs. Coalitions are able to bring together a plethora of interested and needed actors from country delegations (including prime ministers, ambassadors, ministries of foreign affairs, environment and other national agency officials), scientists, regional organisation officials (such as Secretariat of the Pacific Regional Environment Programme, Secretariat of the Pacific Community, and Pacific Islands Forum Secretariat), environmental NGOS, international lawyers (such as the Foundation for International Environmental Law and Development), academics, and media. As a result, Pacific delegates are able to talk 'climate speak' fluently in the big negotiations (Betzold 2010, p. 141).

This constant contact of members can easily be mistaken for a global foreign service of negotiators. Armed with countless emails of text drafts and issue papers, they travel from the Pacific Islands to Bonn (for the SBs) and then to some metropolitan city (for the COPs), while their base remains at the UN headquarters in New York. The daily dialogue, bargaining, and instructions on procedural matters are delivered from ambassadors in New York. It is now common practice for each country to have at least one or two permanent negotiators (other than the ambassador) focused on climate change. Institutional knowledge is key, and rotation of personnel is thus not only a step back for a country, but also for coalitions.

To enhance the capacity of country and lead coalition negotiators, the groups have funded private firms that specialise in multilateral negotiations. The G77, LDC, CfRN and AOSIS groupings have all facilitated research, assembled advisory capacity, undertaken policy development, coordinated economic and technical regulatory frameworks, and overseen implementation. While the annual work of negotiators may be entrenched in what Chasek and Rajamani (2003, p. 257) call 'text diplomacy', they are unconsciously creating both a diplomatic culture and a network of Pacific negotiators.

Climate (Diplomatic) Leadership

A defining theme that resonates through the blocs is the attention to climate leadership. The concept of climate leadership evokes a call to immediate action to address the complex issues surrounding climate change by charting a course through global agreement. To paraphrase a top UNFCCC official, climate change is a challenge for all peoples and generations, and it calls on leaders to lead by example and leave a legacy for future generations (Figueres 2014).

While the concept has been a fundamental message in the rhetoric of Pacific leaders since the convention was established, their participation in the blocs has enabled them to influence global consciousness. Pacific statesmen and ambassadors have been chairs of various blocs — such as Vanuatu's Robert van Lierop, Samoa's Tuiloma Neroni Slade, Tuvalu's Enele Sopoaga, Nauru's Marlene Moses (for AOSIS), Papua New Guinea's Michael Somare, Kevin Conrad and Robert Aisi for the CfRN, and most recently Fiji's Ratu Inoke Kubuabola and Peter Thomson for the G77 Plus China. Although individual chairs have brought a unique style of leadership to the coalitions, it is undeniable that the increased participation of Pacific leaders in the coveted role of chair has instilled in the groupings, and the regime as a whole, more attention to the vulnerability of the Pacific Island states.

In line with recent developments of Pacific-only negotiating blocs, there has been a flurry of shuttle diplomacy within the region. With the impending demand for a new agreement in Paris in 2015, Pacific leaders have sought to increase regional and global awareness by lobbying in, and through, multiple arenas. Pacific leaders had no hesitation in raising climate change as a key issue in dialogues with President Francois Hollande of France, Prime Minister Narendra Modi of India, and Chinese President Xi Jinping, during their visits to the Pacific in 2014. At the UN Third SIDS 2014 meeting, Pacific leaders made sure that they negotiated to have the issue enshrined in the S.A.M.O.A Pathway outcome document (UN 2014), and urged the 4,500 participating representatives — from government, business, NGO, and epistemic organisations — to contribute to a legally binding agreement in Paris.

The Marshall Islands hosted the Cartagena Dialogue in 2014 and the PIF leaders summit in 2013, both important forums that brought leaders, negotiators and scientists to witness the impact of climate change first hand in the 'frontline states'. 'It was my first time on an atoll', stated Swedish Climate Change Ambassador, Anna Lindstedt. 'It was an eye-opener. It's not until you see it for yourself that you understand the situation (of islands)' (Johnson 2014). The Majuro Declaration of Climate Leadership, the first document of its type, which attempts to encourage Pacific forum leaders and post-dialogue partners to list specific commitments on greenhouse gas emissions, was a key document in both the Forum Leaders Summit and the Cartagena meeting. Called the 'Pacific gift' to the world by Marshall Islands Foreign Minister Tony de Brum, the declaration is a draft of the Pacific region's commitments that is intended to be a platform for an upward spiral of action to urgently address reduction of greenhouse gases.

Climate Public Diplomacy

Beyond the lobbying in multilateral meetings, dialogues, and, in some cases, in airport and hotel lounges, the coalitions have acknowledged the need to reach out to citizens. With the advent of new information technology allowing mass communication, many individuals and interested groups have become more connected than ever to the progress of the negotiations. Rather than relying on traditional media to communicate their messages, the blocs have utilised public diplomacy tools to better inform a global audience.

E-diplomacy tools have allowed Pacific parties to become more innovative in their diplomacy. The six main blocs each have comprehensive and lively websites that publicise current news, meetings, partnership information, podcasts, and negotiating positions on particular issues. They hold a wealth of information, with archival documents from speeches, position papers, and country reports. Social media, through Facebook, YouTube and Twitter accounts, has facilitated dialogue with a global audience. The Twitter accounts of Marlene Moses (the Nauruan ambassador and former chair of AOSIS), Tony De Brum, the LDC chair, and G77 chair have a combined following in excess of 15,000. The tools of e-diplomacy have also been used to support the civil society climate activism of such organisations as 350.org, Pacific 350, and Peoples Climate March (Visenten 2014). And who can forget Kathy Jetnil-Kijine, the Marshallese poet who brought world leaders to tears at the UN Climate Summit, who now has more than 500,000 views on YouTube?

A further development in the role of e-diplomacy is the use of contracted professional negotiation and public relation firms. Experts in public relations have trained coalition members, and some have been placed as short-term contracted spokespersons, to ensure coalition members are able to communicate effectively to the global media. Public relations firms have ensured that various coalition key positions are communicated in both traditional and social media forms in a timely and effective manner. A notable firm within the negotiator circles is the Independent Diplomat, used by the Republic of Marshall Islands, AOSIS, and the Cartagena Group. This group of independent former diplomats, international lawyers, and international relations experts has been associated with the blocs since 2009, providing diplomatic support, advice and technical assistance on the 'legal form' for the post-2012 climate regime, including the future of the Kyoto Protocol.

Conclusion

Despite the importance of coalitions in climate change negotiations, there remains a lacuna in the literature on coalition-building and coalition diplomacy in the regime more broadly. More importantly, there is little empirical research on the diplomacy of Pacific states in these coalitions and the regime, despite their being among the states that are the most vulnerable, sensitive, and susceptible to the effects of climate change. While this chapter is purely conceptual in highlighting the literature and trends of Pacific state participation in UNFCCC coalitions thus far, it emphasises the potential, and the need, for students of diplomatic studies to research the phenomenon. One such area for future empirical work is exploring the intra-coalition politics of Pacific states and their coalition allies.

It is undeniable that the global political landscape of coalition blocs is complex, adding to an already complex climate change regime. The two decade-long regime has evolved and become more complex, with more actors and issues. In respect of the diplomacy of interstate coalitions, this chapter argues that, as climate change negotiations have evolved and processes matured, so too have the diplomatic capabilities of Pacific states.

According to Dupont, coalition blocs function to allow states to manage the complex regime and to maximise their power. They function as a clearinghouse for common positions with parties with similar economic development concerns, and provide a space for dialogue with developed countries, and, more importantly, to highlight small islands development needs. By joining coalitions, Pacific states have become better equipped to navigate the regime, giving them a louder voice to affirm their vulnerabilities, and build resilience to climate change. The coalitions have empowered Pacific states and their leaders in their diplomatic finesse by providing access to a wide network of negotiators, the capability to employ climate leadership, and the utility of public diplomacy tools to inform their citizens and a wider global audience on climate issues.

However, frustrations remain, and the increasing rhetoric has been that the regime and blocs have not delivered on Pacific-specific and coral atoll nation needs. This in turn has motivated Pacific leaders to create new vehicles, such as the PSIDS, to bring a united Pacific voice to the fore in climate change negotiations. The emergence of Pacific blocs can therefore be seen as a natural progression in the global dialogue on climate change, as Pacific states develop their capacity and capability as agents of change. The participation of Pacific states in wider coalitions, and the formation of their own, is striking evidence of the new Pacific diplomacy, driven in this case by the urgency of the issue in the Pacific Islands — where it is one of survival — and by the wide divergence between the climate change positions of the forum island states and those of Australia and New Zealand. Although the emergence of the PSIDS and CANCC is at the fringes of UNFCCC attempts to address these concerns, only time will tell if these blocs become a force to be reckoned with in climate negotiations.

References

Ashe, J.W., R. Van Lierop and A. Cherian, 1999, 'The Role of the Alliance of Small Island States (AOSIS) in the Negotiation of the United Nations Framework Convention on Climate Change (UNFCCC)', *Natural Resources Forum* 23(3), pp. 209–20.

Audet, R., 2013, 'Climate Justice and Bargaining Coalitions: A discourse analysis', *International Environmental Agreements: Politics, law and economics* 13(3), pp. 369–86.

Bailer, S., 2012, 'Strategy in the Climate Change Negotiations: Do democracies negotiate differently?', *Climate Policy* 12(5), pp. 534–51.

Betzold, C., 2010, '"Borrowing" Power to Influence International Negotiations: AOSIS in the climate change regime, 1990–1997', *Politics* 30(3), pp. 131–48.

Betzold, C., P. Castro and F. Weiler, 2012, 'AOSIS in the UNFCCC Negotiations: From unity to fragmentation?', *Climate policy* 12(5), pp. 591–613.

Blaxekjær, L.Ø. and T.D. Nielsen, 2014, 'Mapping the Narrative Positions of New Political Groups under the UNFCCC,' *Climate Policy* 14, pp. 1–16.

Chasek, P.S., 2005, 'Margins of Power: Coalition building and coalition maintenance of the South Pacific Island States and the Alliance of Small Island States', *Review of European Community and International Environmental Law* 14(2), pp. 125–37.

Chasek, P.S. and L. Rajamani, 2003, 'Steps toward Enhanced Parity: Negotiating capacity and strategies of developing countries', in I. Kaul (ed.), *Providing Global Public Goods: Managing Globalization*, United Nations Development Project, Oxford University Press, New York.

Climate Vulnerable Forum, n.d., 'About the Climate Vulnerable Forum'. Available at: www.thecvf.org/web/climate-vulnerable-forum/.

Depledge, J., 2005, *The Organization of Global Negotiations: Constructing the climate change regime*, Earthscan, Sterling.

Dupont, C., 1996, 'Negotiation as Coalition Building', *International Negotiation* 1(1), pp. 47–64.

Figueres, C., 2014, 'Christiana Figueres Addresses 2014 Climate Leadership Conference'. Available at: www.youtube.com/watch?v=6loTK3FI_fQ.

Gough, C. and S. Shackley, 2001, 'The Respectable Politics of Climate Change: The epistemic communities and NGOs', *International Affairs* 77(2), pp. 329–46.

Gupta, J., 2000, *On Behalf of My Delegation: A survival guide for developing country climate negotiators*, Center for Sustainable Development of the Americas International Institute for Sustainable Development, Washington, D. C.

Holbraad, C., 1971, 'The Role of Middle Powers', *Cooperation and Conflict* 6(1), pp. 77–90.

Islands Business, 2014, 'Cartagena Group Expresses Climate Action Optimism: Marshall Islands Foreign Minister', Suva, Fiji.

Johnson, G., 2014, 'Majuro Cartagena Dialogue Wraps Up, Optimism Expressed,' *Pacific Islands Report*, April 7. Available at: pidp.org/pireport/2014/April/04-07-06.htm.

Least Developing Countries Group, n.d., 'LDC Group at UN Climate Change Negotiations'. Available at: ldcclimate.wordpress.com/about-the-ldc-group/.

Morgenthau, H.J., 2003, *Politics Among Nations: The struggle for power and peace*, McGraw-Hill Education, New York.

Narlikar, A., 2003, *International Trade and Developing Countries: Bargaining and coalitions in the GATT and WTO*, Routledge, New York.

Pacific negotiator, 2014, personal communication with Pacific Negotiator, 2 September.

Packard, A., 2010, 'Kiribati Climate Change Conference Calls for Urgent Cash and Action', *Guardian*, November 6.

Sheehan, M., 1996, *The Balance of Power: History and theory*, Routledge, London.

Snyder, G.H., 1997, *Alliance Politics*, Cornell University Press, Ithaca.

United Nations (UN), 2014, 'SIDS Accelerated Modalities of Action [S.A.M.O.A.] Pathway: Outcome of the Third International Conference on Small Island Developing States, 1–4 September 2014, Samoa'. Available at: www.sids2014. org/index.php?menu=1537.

United Nations Framework Convention on Climate Change (UNFCCC), n.d. 'Party Groupings'. Available at: unfccc.int/parties_and_observers/parties/ negotiating_groups/items/2714.php.

UNFCCC, n.d., 'UNFCCC Basic Facts and Figures'. Available at: unfccc.int/ essential_background/basic_facts_figures/items/6246.php.

von videoarchitekt, K., 2007, 'Moment of the "Bali Break Through"'. Available at: www.youtube.com/watch?v=F-G1v--DONM.

Visentin, L., 2014, 'Poet Brings World Leaders to Tears at UN Climate Summit', *Sydney Morning Herald, 25* September.

Wallbott, L. and N. Deitelhoff, 2012, 'Beyond Soft Balancing: Small states and coalition-building in the ICC and climate negotiations', *Cambridge Review of International Affairs* 25(3), pp. 345–66.

Walt, S.M., 1987, *The Origins of Alliance*, Cornell University Press, New York.

Waltz, K.N., 1979, *Theory of International Politics*, Addison-Wesley, Reading, Massachusetts.

Yamin, F. and J. Depledge, 2004, The International Climate Change Regime: A guide to rules, institutions and procedures, Cambridge University Press, New York.

Tuna Diplomacy

18

How Tuna is Shaping Regional Diplomacy

Transform Aqorau

Introduction

This chapter examines how tuna has shaped regional politics and influenced the relationship between the Pacific Island states and two of the world's largest trading blocs, the United States and the European Union (EU). This relationship has come under stress in recent years because of the development of arrangements such as the purse seine Vessel Day Scheme (VDS),[1] the emergence of regional alliances such as the Parties to the Nauru Agreement (PNA) grouping of countries, and because of the strong desire of the Pacific Island states to control their tuna fisheries and maximise their share of the economic benefits flowing from the exploitation of their tuna resources.

The geopolitical underpinnings of the region's tuna management provide an interesting backdrop to this analysis. All of the world's major trading states are involved in this fishery — Japan, Korea, the United States, the EU, and China. Japan has the longest presence in the region's tuna fishery. More recently, China has become a major force in the longline fishery. The region's tuna

---

1   The VDS is a management measure that sets a limit on the number of days purse seine vessels are allowed to fish in the waters of the Parties to the Nauru Agreement (PNA) group of countries and Tokelau. The days are allocated to each party, who then charge fishing companies/vessels for each day they fish.

resources have become a key focal point for the prosecution of the strategic geopolitical interests of these powers. Access to the region's tuna resources allows them a physical presence over a large geographic area of the Pacific, from which they can pursue their strategic interests. The analysis presented here, however, focuses on fisheries relations between the Pacific Island states, the United States and the EU.

This chapter argues that there is a multiplicity of strategic interests that underlie the management of the region's tuna resources. These are often inimical to the interests of the Pacific Island states who want secured rights to their tuna resources. However, it is often assumed that this leads to the Pacific Island states having a shared interest, and that a regional framework fits the strategic and political aspirations of individual states. This is not necessarily the case. It is argued that the regional configuration and architecture has changed, and that Pacific Island states have a diverse range of strategic interests that are not often amenable to a common approach to their relations with external fishing interests.

These differences are manifested not only in Pacific Island states' relations with external fishing states but also their relations with each other. They also explain the difficulties in accommodating the interests of Pacific Island states in current negotiations to extend the Treaty on Fisheries with the United States and conclude a Comprehensive Economic Partnership Agreement (CEPA) with the EU. The conclusion is drawn that regional fisheries interests are not homogenous; these interests are not necessarily shared, and these differences have informed the evolution of a new Pacific regional tuna architecture that has impacted on the shaping of the relations between the Pacific Island states, the United States, and the EU.

The Heterogeneous Tuna Fishery: Skipjack, albacore, yellowfin, and bigeye

In order to appreciate the impulses that inform the evolution of fisheries management arrangements in the region, it is necessary to understand the structure and dynamics of the region's tuna fishery.

Tuna is a highly migratory resource. It is found in the Exclusive Economic Zones (EEZs) of all the Pacific Island states. However, the abundance and distribution of the different tuna species is not shared equally amongst the Pacific Islands. The major species of tuna are skipjack (*Katsuwonus pelamis*), albacore (*Thunnus alalunga*), yellowfin (*Thunnus albacares*), and bigeye tuna (*Thunnus obsesus*). The distribution and abundance of these four species have helped shape the cooperative arrangements that have been developed over the past 30 years. Skipjack, for instance, is found mainly in the equatorial waters of the Federated States of Micronesia, Kiribati, Marshall Islands, Nauru, Palau, Papua New Guinea (PNG), Solomon Islands, Tuvalu, and Tokelau. These countries are colloquially known as the Nauru Group. They have used their common interest in skipjack, which is targeted by purse seiners, to establish their own regional arrangements. Albacore tuna tend to be caught further south in subtropical and temperate waters. This fishery is confined to the waters of countries such as the Cook Islands, French Polynesia, Samoa, Tonga, Fiji, Vanuatu, New Caledonia, New Zealand, and Niue. There is also a sizable albacore fishery in Solomon Islands, PNG, Tuvalu and the Southern Gilberts, who are members of the Nauru Group.

The countries where albacore dominates their fishery have formed the Tokelau Arrangement — a coalition to advocate limits for albacore fishing and to maximise economic returns from albacore tuna. There is cross membership within these different groups by countries such as Tuvalu and Solomon Islands, who are members of both the Nauru Group and the Tokelau Arrangement, reflecting the different fisheries in their waters. Albacore tuna also provides the backdrop for another species aligned coalition, the Te Vaka Moana Group, which consists of Samoa, Tonga, Niue, Tokelau, Cook Islands, New Zealand, and Tokelau. This is a New Zealand inspired and funded Polynesian group formed around shared interests in albacore tuna; but it is also motivated by a shared desire among these countries to cushion the growing influence of the Nauru Group. That leaves bigeye and yellowfin tuna, which is a bycatch in the skipjack fisheries within the Nauru Group of countries, and to a lesser extent in the albacore fishery in the southern Pacific Islands countries, but which is also a core target species in the tropical longline fishery which occurs mainly in the high seas areas, often adjacent to the EEZs of the Nauru Group

There is also the Melanesian Spearhead Group (MSG) Fisheries Committee. This is not a species-focused group, but is aligned around the common trade interests of the Melanesia countries of PNG, Solomon Islands, Fiji, Vanuatu, and the Kanak Independence Movement of New Caledonia. In the main, the MSG have explored issues in which they can maximise their involvement in the value chain in the various fisheries, including coastal fisheries. This transcends both the longline and purse seine fishery. These sub-regional coalitions and alliances have been built around a variety of factors, including the geographic range of different stocks, the fishery that targets these stocks, and cultural ethnicity (in the case of Te Vaka Moana and MSG Fisheries Committee). The effectiveness and success of these various groups have varied. While the MSG represents the largest demographic group in the region, its fisheries committee is yet to make any impact, perhaps reflecting the fact that alliances are better drawn around fishing interests. Similarly, the Te Vaka Moana's influence has been minimal.

Some of these alliances are based around policy coordination, advice generation, and a forum whereby allocations are set. The efficacy and effectiveness of these alliances are dependent on their architecture. Unlike the skipjack Nauru Group–affiliated arrangements, the other alliances do not have legally binding decision-making regimes, and to some extent this has influenced their efficacy in shaping regional tuna politics, in particular, the extent to which they can leverage influence.

It is instructive to note that these alliances work within two overarching political frameworks, namely the Pacific Islands Forum Fisheries Agency (FFA) and the Western and Central Pacific Fisheries Commission (WCPFC). The FFA is a coalition embodying all the Pacific Island states but its core functions are to coordinate policy advice and provide technical support to the Pacific Island countries. It does not manage tuna. The WCPFC is a body initiated by Pacific Island Forum leaders to bring compatible governance into high seas areas through the establishment of conservation and management measures for tuna inside and outside the EEZ, although EEZ measures are applied and adopted by the Pacific Island countries pursuant to their sovereign rights. Its membership includes the FFA member countries and the major fishing states: France, the EU, China, Japan, Taiwan, Indonesia, Philippines, Korea, Canada, and the United States. It is probably best described as a coalition of the unwilling, as it provides a forum whereby stakeholders unwillingly cooperate with one another. Both organisations provide an effective forum for discussions.

There are serious limits to the effectiveness of the WCPFC. While it has been successful in adopting conservation measures for seabirds and sharks, it has been less successful in adopting effective measures for bigeye tuna, which is currently subject to overfishing. This is attributable to different interests in the organisation which make it difficult to arrive at mutually acceptable outcomes. The tuna measures adopted by the WCFC have evolved from PNA initiatives, underscoring the role that sub-regional arrangements play in ensuring the WCPFC discharges its obligations.

The vacuum that has been created by the WCPFC's failure to provide an effective forum for management of the target tuna species is being filled by PNA countries. The influence of the powerful PNA bloc hinges on the leverage that it is able to apply through access to member country EEZs. This may be explained in part by the catch statistics illustrated in Figure 18.1, which shows the catches of four key species. In 2013, 2.62 million metric tonnes (mt) of tuna was caught in the Western and Central Pacific Ocean (WCPO). Of this, the purse seine catch accounted for 1.9 million mt, of which skipjack tuna was 1.8 million mt, bigeye tuna 150,000 mt, yellowfin 524,000 mt, and albacore tuna 143,000 mt. About 68 per cent of the skipjack catch is taken from the waters of the PNA waters. This is important, because the proportion and size of the skipjack tuna that is taken from the PNA gives them influence, which they have been able to leverage against fishing states and the other Pacific Island countries.

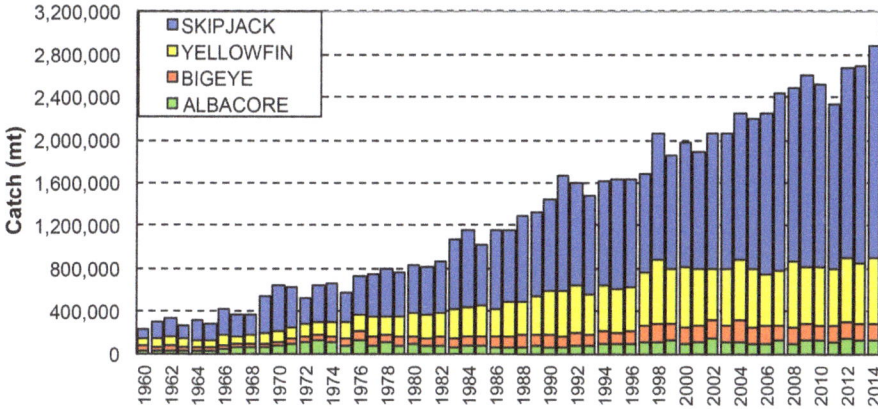

Figure 18.1: Total tuna catch WCPO

Source: SPC, Noumea, 2015.

Figure 18.2 illustrates the proportion of catch by gear type. As discussed above, some of the alliances formed in the region are related primarily to the predominance of gear. Catch by gear is thus dominated by purse seine vessels, which are the largest fishery in terms of value and volume of catch, followed by longline, pole and line, and others, such as trolling and handlines. It should be noted that this data also includes Indonesia and the Philippines.

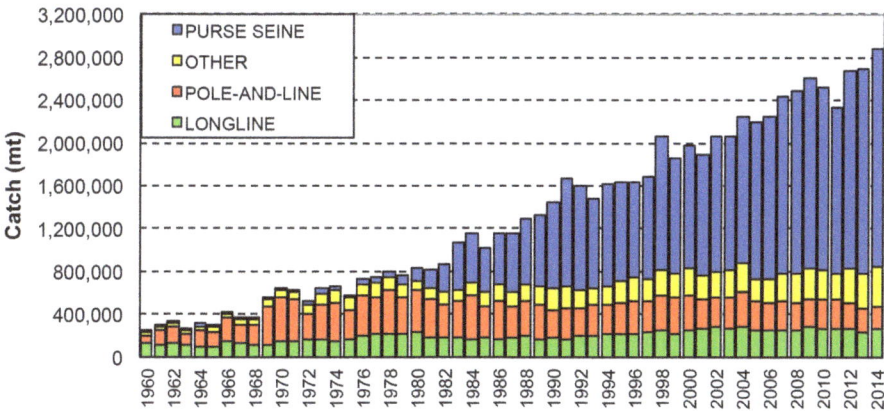

Figure 18.2: Total tuna catch by gear

Source: SPC, Noumea, 2015.

The differences that have emerged in regional tuna diplomacy since the 1976 forum declaration on the Law of the Sea are a function of a variation in commercial interests, and do not necessarily reflect a lack of desire for common action. In the mid-to-late 1970s, when the Pacific Island states were gaining independence, they had a collective and shared interest in the EEZ regime, as extended maritime jurisdiction intertwined with the idea of self-determination. In the 1980s, when the US fleet fished illegally in the region, the Pacific Island states had a common cause: to control US vessels, and support the US in preventing the region's exposure to overtures from the Soviet Union. Thus the Treaty on Fisheries was negotiated. With time, changes in dynamics, the development of fisheries, and more clearly defined fishing rights, the interests of Pacific Island states have diverged and become more narrowly aligned along economic goals based on the different fisheries that occur in their EEZs.

References to a common interest in the tuna fishery by the Pacific Islands states are not entirely accurate. It is argued that those who advocate a common approach to the management of tuna in the Pacific Islands region misunderstand the dynamics at play and the different arrangements that underpin the management of the different stocks. Nowhere are these differences more pronounced than in the negotiations of two regional instruments, the Economic Partnership Agreement (EPA) with the EU and the negotiations to extend the Treaty on Fisheries with the United States.

The Treaty on Fisheries between the Governments of Certain Pacific Island States and the United States

Differences over the form and shape of the 1987 treaty have emerged in recent years because of its rigid structure, subsidisation from the US government, the failure of US vessels/industry to pay commercial rates for access, and the difficulty of shaping an arrangement that meets all of the stakeholders' interests. These differences have caused friction between the PNA and non-PNA members within the FFA, and between the Pacific Island states and the US government. The treaty was designed to address a major problem with the US position in the 1970s. During the negotiations of the 1982 United Nations Convention on the Law of the Sea, the US did not accept that highly migratory fish stocks such as tuna could fall within the sovereign rights of coastal states. They argued that tuna stocks could only be managed internationally. They enforced this interpretation of the law of the sea through Magnuson Act embargoes, which they applied to any state that arrested US vessels for tuna fishing illegally in their EEZ. Papua New Guinea and Solomon Islands were at the receiving end of US sanctions, which caused friction between the US and the Pacific Island states in the 1980s.

In order to resolve this issue, the Treaty on Fisheries was concluded in 1987, giving US vessels the right to roam freely throughout the Pacific Islands region and catch tuna in return for a fee. Initially, the licences were valid for a period of five years. The second and third licensing terms were for 10 years, locking in access at a fixed price for 10-year periods. While this provided the US with a stable environment for their vessels to operate in the region, it did not give the Pacific Island states much flexibility. Tensions began to arise when the PNA VDS became fully operational and US fleets were not being subjected to the VDS. These tensions were also exacerbated by the way in which the treaty constrained the ability of the Pacific Island states to amend their national laws. The treaty prohibited the Pacific Island states from adopting national measures if these were in conflict with the treaty. There were various tensions at play. There was tension between the Pacific Island states and the US because of the Pacific Island states' lack of flexibility to apply national laws in their EEZs without US consent if the matter fell within the purview of the treaty. There was tension between the Pacific Island states, with the PNA wanting to see the treaty come under the VDS. The PNA also wanted US industry to pay commercial market rates for their fishing days. The non-PNA countries supported the status quo, as they received a proportion of the share of the treaty funds — which the US government paid for access for its flagged vessels — and did not want to see their share reduced. These issues emerged because the VDS had seen an increase in the value of access from other fleets, but there have not been enough funds from the treaty to ensure that US industry paid a premium for their multiple zone days. This became a source of tension between the PNA and non-PNA countries. These tensions largely reflected the different disparate interest groups discussed above. The treaty is essentially a purse seine arrangement targeting skipjack tuna. Almost all of the efforts of the US fleet occurred in PNA waters, where US industry were in effect paying just ten per cent of the regional benchmark for regional, as opposed to bilateral, access.

The Treaty on Fisheries, once a symbol of regional cooperative success, has become politically divisive, impacting on relations between the US and the Pacific Island states, the PNA and non-PNA members, and within the PNA group itself. The rigid form and shape of the treaty has made it incompatible with a market-based instrument such as VDS, especially where parties are compelled to contribute days to allow US vessels to operate in the region. Although the treaty's design was suitable at the time of its signing in 1987, it has begun to impact on the effectiveness and efficacy of the VDS. It was inevitable that there would be a conflict between stakeholders because of the different interests at stake. These difficulties have been somewhat ameliorated as a result of the willingness of parties to set aside their differences. Whether they have been fully resolved remains to be seen. By June 2013, the treaty had been assimilated under the VDS, but under arrangements in which the PNA were compelled to allocate days to the treaty, rather than voluntarily contribute days based on the value of those days. This is a matter of ongoing negotiations with the United States, and is the cause of some friction amongst the Pacific Island states. The PNA have also been interested in reshaping the treaty to deal directly with the US tuna industry, but have been frustrated because the treaty does not allow for access to be individually negotiated as commercial arrangements between the Pacific Island states and US boat owners.

The Treaty on Fisheries has defined the relations between the US and the Pacific Island states, as underscored by Secretary of State Hillary Clinton in her letter to Pacific Island leaders in November 2011:

> Over the past quarter century, the treaty has been the cornerstone of the economic and political relationship between our countries. In particular, the treaty has:
>
> - Provided a foundation for active cooperation for the conservation and management of the region's valuable fisheries resources and related issues, including cooperation on fisheries monitoring, surveillance, and enforcement;
> - Supported a vital economic and commercial relationship involving the US fishing industry;
> - and provided economic benefits to the Pacific Island parties of approximately $450 million over the past 25 years.

The importance of this relationship and the framework that the treaty provides for it is not lost on the PNA members and the rest of the Pacific Island states. The weight which they give to this broad political and economic relationship, however, varies. PNA members view fisheries access as commercial arrangements and therefore delink the aid component of the treaty, which is contributed by the US State Department as economic assistance and is the subject of a separate agreement between the US and the FFA, known as the Economic Assistance Agreement. PNA members view US aid and its political and strategic ramifications as being separate from the commercial access that US vessels enjoy in their EEZs. However, it is clear that there will have to be more flexible arrangements for the US industry if there is to be an ongoing relationship between the Pacific Island states and the United States. This will have to be defined around the principles articulated by the PNA members at their meeting with the United States in March 2014. These include:

- PNA and Tokelau recognise the regional and political importance of the treaty and will thus continue to cooperate among themselves in the provision of access for US vessels, which is conditional on meeting the needs of their domestic fleets and maximising benefits from fishing in their waters.

- There is a range of interests, needs and opportunities among Pacific Island states which must be recognised in any future arrangements for the provision of access for US vessels, including, as appropriate, through bilateral and sub-regional arrangements.

- The value and competition for access to waters where the VDS applies is continuing to increase. Fees for US vessels will need to meet the market conditions for vessel days in these increasing competitive processes. US vessel owners may have to bid for days.

- Participation in the provision of access for US vessels must be on a voluntary basis, and no party should be pressured to provide access.

The non-PNA members have not agreed to these principles. They have disagreed on the contribution of fishing days to the treaty and the distribution formulae for funds received from the treaty. Even within the PNA, there have been disagreements over the distribution formulae for days that are to be contributed to the treaty. There have been disagreements between the United States and the Pacific Island states over the structure of the treaty. Getting a regional arrangement to fit neatly within the different interests at play has not been easy. Pacific Island states, the PNA in particular, want greater flexibility. This is simply to reflect the range of interests, needs and opportunities among the Pacific Island states. While there are a range of regional and sub-regional interests, the general approach of the Pacific Island states to management of the purse seine fishery is a rights-based approach. These approaches only work when the rights holders are able to use or discharge their rights in an unrestricted way according to their circumstances. As such, their interests, pushed by the PNA, are to provide access opportunities to US vessels in a greater range of forms than in the past.

The Economic Partnership Agreement with the EU

The negotiation of the CEPA with the EU has brought out differences within the region, which have had implications for the negotiation of a regional trade agreement between the Pacific Island states and the European Union. Developing a regional comprehensive trade arrangement that reflects all the interests of the Pacific Island states has been difficult, especially negotiating an instrument as a single region. While the imbalance in the trade interests between countries such as PNG and Fiji on the one hand, and Niue, Tuvalu, and Kiribati on the other, are obvious, it is the difference in fisheries interests between the PNA, non-PNA, and the EU that have impacted most on negotiations, reflecting the central role of fisheries in the external and internal relations of the Pacific Island states.

The CEPA purports to establish a trade agreement between the EU and the Pacific Island states in place of the development arrangement known as the Cotonou Agreement. This supersedes the better known Lomé Convention. Negotiation of the new trading arrangements commenced in September 2002 and CEPAs were supposed to enter into force by 1 January 2008. Negotiating as a single region ignores the differences that divide the Pacific Island states. The differences in the fishing and trading interests of the Pacific Island states culminated in a 2007 split by PNG and Fiji, when they initialled the Interim EPA to avoid disruption to market access for their canned tuna and sugar. The Interim EPA was negotiated by the Pacific–African, Caribbean and Pacific (PACP) group but the other Pacific Island states did not initial the Interim EPA on the grounds that it did not address their development needs, insisting instead that all Pacific Island states continue to negotiate a development-friendly CEPA that included tuna.

After the initialling of the Interim EPA, the Pacific Island states and the EU decided to explore opportunities to further develop an agreement leading towards a comprehensive free trade agreement that would contain provisions for investments, services, and intellectual properties.

Differences over the fisheries component of the EPA reflect the different interests of the PNA and the non-PNA countries, and processing and non-processing countries. PNG had secured global sourcing for HS 1604 and HS 1605 fisheries products — cooked and processed products which were of particular interest to the PNA members — in the Interim EPA. However, during CEPA negotiations, some of the Pacific Island states expressed interest in the export of fish pieces in their natural state (HS 0304-0305) and demanded global sourcing opportunities for fresh fish products. In return for this access, the EU expressed interest in re-securing guaranteed access of five per cent of the total fishing effort under the management of the Pacific Island states. Just what five per cent meant and where it might be processed has never been explained, but no investment has been proposed on account of these proposals.

After the Interim EPA was initialled and ratified, the EU Spanish fishing interests started lobbying against the global sourcing given to PNG and Fiji in the Interim EPA. This resulted in the EU parliament setting up a committee on fisheries to evaluate and research the negotiations and preferences offered to the EU under various trade agreements. Reports given to the EU parliament, such as the 2013 Fraga Report, were blatantly misinformed and misguided, and intended to portray a negative slant on the management of the tuna fisheries by the PNA member countries.

The non-PNA members wanted the PNA members to sacrifice their fisheries development and management interests in return for a trade agreement with the EU at any cost. The EU further demanded oversight of PNA governance and endorsement of rejected EU proposals at WCPFC level. Additionally, the EU demanded the reopening of the global sourcing provisions of the Interim EPA.

The PNA were concerned about sacrificing fishing opportunities for surface fisheries in exchange for global access for fresh fisheries — products that studies have suggested may only provide seasonal opportunity at best and are not accessible because only three PACP countries currently have EU recognised competent authorities, which, even if fully domestic, would be eligible under rules of origin without global sourcing. The PNA members were concerned about the EU's approach to tuna fisheries in the region not only because of their poor track record of conservation in other oceans, but they were now seen to be using the CEPA negotiations to manage the region's tuna resources.

The differences between those that want access to the EU market at any costs and those, such as the PNA, who do not want to sacrifice market access by acceding some of their tuna management and conservation rights to the EU, have exacerbated the complexity of negotiations. Arguably, this merely reflects different national interests that belie the various fisheries that exist within the region. During the negotiations, the EU have openly challenged the Pacific Island state-inspired regional fishery partnership agreements and sovereign rights to manage their EEZs, in favour of a wider accord, 'where any fisheries agreement between the EU and Pacific States shall be concluded taking into account the conservation and management measures of the WCPFC'. In other words, the EU wants to decide how the Pacific Island states should manage their fisheries resources. The PNA viewed the EU as being divisive and cutting a wedge amongst PNA, and between the PNA and the rest of the Pacific Island states. In its Fisheries Partnership Agreement (FPA) with Kiribati, the EU actively sought to undermine the regional management measures advocated by the Pacific Island states, including abuse of the VDS and pursuing a negative conservation agenda of anti-selective fishing against mesh size increases, pro-Fish Aggregating Devices (FADs), and opposition to closed areas.[2]

The introduction of the PNA purse seine VDS represents a global threat to the EU's FPAs. The changing structure of fishing access arrangements, with the VDS creating a seller's market, represents a threat to the EU FPAs. The average

---

2   The mesh size restrictions relate to the size of mesh in the purse seine nets. The minimum mesh size is intended to ensure that smaller size fish are able to escape after being caught in the nets. FADs are floating objectives that tend to attract other species. Vessels target these because it is easier for them. The problem is that there is a higher proportion of juvenile bigeye tuna, which is already overfished, caught with FADs. The EU have opposed closures of high seas areas in the eastern Pacific areas where the proportion of their catch of bigeye tuna is about 18 per cent, whereas bigeye tuna bycatch on other areas is about 5 per cent.

returns from the VDS have been about US$400 per metric tonnes on catch, which is generally above the EU FPAs. Arguably, the boot is no longer on the foot of the EU as a competitive market for access arrangements. Support for the VDS has meant that the EU has been put on the back foot, consequently it has had to resort to other tactics, such as using the CEPAs to enforce its global domination. Throughout the negotiations of the CEPA, the EU has been seeking to increase its control of the tuna fisheries in the Pacific by putting pressure on the Pacific Island states to allow it to have a say in the way they manage their tuna resources.

Obtaining a regional consensus on this has not been easy. The PNA members believe that the benefits generated from access to the European fresh fish product market are insignificant compared to other markets, and will probably fail to materialise because of the high cost of trade. The price for this small gain in accepting EU fishing access to the Pacific would be the sustainability of the tuna resource and loss of higher rentals, which can be achieved through agreements with friendlier fishing and trading partners.

The difficulties with achieving consensus on these issues reflects the different fisheries that exist in the region, together with the varying levels of development and interests. What is clear is that if the heavy handed approach of the EU extends to all sectors under a CEPA, the Pacific Island states could have less independence than a French territory in the region.

Conclusion

This chapter examined the emergence of regional arrangements aligned along different tuna stocks, the fishery that targets them, and the influence that these arrangements have had on two key regional negotiations: the renegotiations of the Treaty on Fisheries with the United States and the CEPA with the EU. Some commentators have derided the emergence of sub-regional groups. However, in the context of fisheries, sub-regional groups such as the PNA have had a major influence on regional tuna negotiations and fulfilment of national development goals. Since most of the fishing takes place in their waters, they can dictate the terms and conditions under which access is negotiated. Having a single region arrangement is useful for some purposes, but not for others. It is clear though that single region arrangements are normally determined by the lowest common denominator. This is known as the Niue factor. In single region arrangements where decisions must be made by consensus, a small country such as Niue — with no US fishing in its waters and no trade with the EU — can prevent the best outcomes because their interests also have to be taken into account. The increase in treaty funds from the Treaty on Fisheries —

from US$18 million to US$21 million — was delayed for some years because Niue wanted an increase in shares apportioned as project development funds. Conversely, the increase in treaty payments — from US$21 million in 2012, to US$63 million in 2013, and US$90 million in 2015 — was driven by the PNA and demonstrates the power of the VDS. It is doubtful that this would have been possible through a single region approach because of the Niue factor. Similarly, if the PNA members were not opposed to global sourcing for fresh fish in return for allowing the European Union a say in how their fisheries are managed, the region would have a trade arrangement in which only the EU could have a direct say in what Pacific Island states do in their own waters.

The complexity of the dynamics in fisheries and the relationships between the Pacific Island states and their external partners is creating new challenges to the way these issues are addressed. The diplomacy of the past, the 'Pacific Way', and doing things by consensus is not going to work because of the complexities of the issues that the Pacific Island states now confront. These challenges raise questions about the efficacy of existing regional architectures, the role of nation states, and the need to explore models of integration that can best deliver outcomes for the various fisheries. The PNA arrangements, in which measures are legally binding and where a common currency is shared amongst VDS membership, might be a model that could be considered by other Pacific Island states. It is imperfect, but it has strengthened the negotiation hands of its members.

19

The New Pacific Diplomacy and the South Pacific Tuna Treaty

Jope Tarai

The shift to a new Pacific diplomacy, where the Pacific's agenda is no longer externally driven, but is to an extent led from within the Pacific, can be seen in the case of the negotiation of the South Pacific Tuna Treaty.[1] To demonstrate this shift, this chapter will highlight the factors shaping the inception of the treaty, and those influencing the current negotiations. These include the regional agenda, the Pacific's leveraging capability, and the influence and roles of the regional institutions. It will highlight the role of the Forum Fisheries Agency (FFA) at the time the initial treaty was signed in 1987, and the role of the islands-only Parties to the Nauru Agreement (PNA) in the contemporary era. This will demonstrate how the new Pacific diplomacy has been instrumental in elevating the Pacific's negotiating position.

---

1   The South Pacific Tuna Treaty is officially known as the Treaty on Fisheries between Governments of certain Pacific Island States and the Government of the United States of America.

Negotiating the Original South Pacific Tuna Treaty

The South Pacific Tuna Treaty was signed in 1987 and came into force in June 1988 (Chang 2007). The treaty is a multilateral agreement that brings together a total of 16 Pacific countries with the United States of America.[2] It allows for a maximum of 50 purse seine vessels to be licensed. Initially, it had guaranteed a total of US$12 million per year, for a total of five years, spanning an initial period of 1988–1993 (Glebbeek 1990). This payment combined a majority of US government funding with a smaller portion paid by industry. Of the agreed financial package of US$60 million over the first five-year period, 85 per cent was allocated to countries according to catch volume within the various Exclusive Economic Zones (EEZs) of participating countries. The remaining 15 per cent was apportioned equally among all parties, irrespective of catch, in the form of project aid and technical assistance.

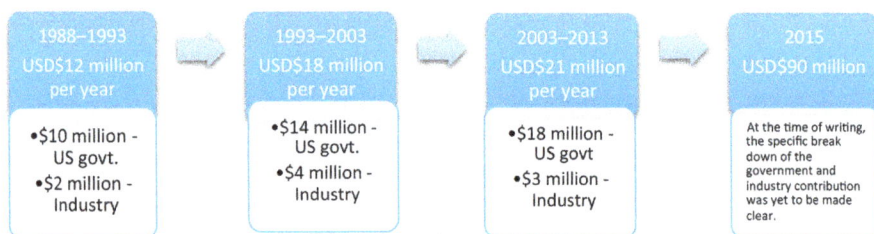

Figure 19.1: The South Pacific Tuna Treaty
Source: Author's research.

The original settlement of the treaty had not been without controversy. In the early 1980s, this was mainly attributed to the conflicting interpretations of the United Nations Convention on the Law of the Sea (UNCLOS)[3] of 1982 (Maw 1983; Lugar 2004; Kengalu 1988). The US refused to recognise coastal state claims to tuna stocks as highly migratory species within their EEZs (Malone 1983). This led to the Pacific's so-called 'Tuna Wars', which saw a number of US vessels confiscated by Pacific states, leading to retaliatory US trade embargoes, including the infamous *Jeanette Diana* and *Danica* debacles (Kengalu 1988; Gubon 1987).[4]

---

2   The 16 countries include: Australia, Cook Islands, Federated States of Micronesia, Fiji, Kiribati, Marshall Islands, Nauru, New Zealand, Niue, Palau, Papua New Guinea, Samoa, Solomon Islands, Tonga, Tuvalu, and Vanuatu.

3   The coastal states took Article 61 and Article 64 of the UNCLOS to claim jurisdiction over highly migratory species (tuna), while the US disregarded this claim, which fuelled much of the contentious interpretation between the two sides.

4   The Solomon Islands government seized the US vessel *Jeanette Diana* in June 1984 after it was caught illegally fishing within the Solomon Island's Exclusive Economic Zone (EEZ). The US fishing vessel *Danica* was confiscated by the government of Papua New Guinea in February 1982 for illegally fishing within PNG's EEZ.

Despite these tensions and differences, when the treaty was concluded, the Pacific was able to secure significant financial returns, through access fees, and a degree of recognition of ownership over migratory species within its EEZs. The treaty was outstanding at the time because it was able to accrue a 10 per cent rate of return compared to the 3 per cent average for bilateral access agreements, while providing the FFA comprehensive effort and catch data (Tarte 1998).

The difference in the interpretation of the UNCLOS, and the Pacific's push for the US to recognise their claim to highly migratory species within their EEZs, was the main agenda for the Pacific at this time. Pacific Island states, like other coastal states, were adamant in their claim over highly migratory resources. Ultimately, this claim would allow the Pacific states to derive financial returns from access fees and benefits through cooperative engagements with distant water fishing nations (Gubon 1987).

However, it is instructive to note that this agenda was externally motivated, rather than internally initiated. The agenda was more a response to the US policy of non-recognition, which indicated that the *modus operandi* of Pacific diplomacy at the time was more reactive to external influences. It developed as an attempt to mediate the uncompromising position of the US. While the UNCLOS did provide a basis for the assertion of jurisdictional claim for the Pacific, it was in essence an external leverage.

The looming presence of the Soviet Union, at least in the mind of western powers, provided an additional leverage for the Pacific during the diplomatic tensions with the US in the 1980s. Kiribati seized their opportunity and secured a fishing agreement with the Soviet Union in 1985, with keen interest shown by Vanuatu and varying other Pacific states (Dora 1985). This engagement with the Soviet Union motivated the US to negotiate a multilateral agreement that, to an extent, conceded to the Pacific's demands (Dora 1985; Gubon 1987; Doulman 1986). The security and power balancing concerns brought on by the Soviet presence were too great for the US to ignore (Lugar 2004). This creatively produced the 'Pacific's Leverage' which enabled the Pacific to bargain with unprecedented effect. The Pacific was well aware of how much power and impact the Soviet engagement had on the US. Proof of this was seen in the early 1980s. In a blunt response to the United States, at the height of its diplomatic tensions, the Solomon Islands threatened to engage the Soviet Union directly (Gubon 1987). Such diplomatic *démarche* can be termed the 'Alternate Leverage Strategy' to asserting Article 64 of the UNCLOS, and the universality of international law. The Tuna Wars proved the latter to be a weak bargaining point for the Pacific, leading to substantive losses from sanctions and embargoes imposed by the US. Playing off the strategic interests of the US and the Soviet Union provided more effective leverage for the Pacific, which not only pressured the US into concessions but also elevated the power of the Pacific.

There is no denying that the Pacific successfully utilised this leverage to its best possible extent, however it was still subject to the continued competition between the US and the Soviet Union. As a result, basing the bargaining power of the Pacific on this strategic competition was only useful until the Soviet Union's demise in the late 1980s. This also indicated that Pacific diplomacy at the time was more reactive to external influences. Such reactive approaches provided insufficient space for the Pacific to take full ownership of its agenda. For instance, there was no leverage available during the second period of the South Pacific Tuna Treaty, from 1993 to 2003, to enable the Pacific to bargain for a substantive increase in the financial returns paid by the US. Despite the fact that the value of the fishery had already begun to rise, the Pacific was locked into a 10-year deal of having to distribute US$18 million amongst 16 countries (Aqorau 2014).

The establishment of the FFA and its links with the UNCLOS reveals two key motivations of Pacific diplomacy at the time. One was the Pacific's assertion of ownership over the fish stocks, which was expressed in a united position in the UNCLOS — conforming to the position of coastal states against states such as the United States, which disputed the interpretation of Articles 61 and 64 of the UNCLOS. A second motivation was the economic and financial opportunities made available through the fishery. The FFA's representative force was premised on the fact that it comprised all the Pacific Island states. As such, it was able to represent the Pacific's collective position in regard to the UNCLOS. Through the tuna treaty, the FFA administered financial returns to the Pacific states with various other technical benefits.

The FFA's primary function was to help manage fisheries resources within the Pacific EEZs while seeking to maximise returns from access agreements (Tamate 2003; Tarte 2007). The FFA served to safeguard the Pacific's interests, considering the inherent institutional, diplomatic and technical constraints of the Pacific. The FFA helped focus the Pacific's efforts on the collective agenda, which effectively mediated the Distant Water Fishing Nations (DWFN) 'divide and conquer' strategy of playing Pacific states off with one another (Doulman 1988).

The utility of FFA's assistance to the Pacific was evident when DWFNs cited reservations in negotiating with Pacific states assisted by the FFA. DWFNs stated that negotiations were bilateral and only required the two states concerned without FFA assistance (Doulman 1988). This demonstrated that the DWFNs were recognising the strength of FFA as a galvanising force.

In characterising the Pacific's diplomacy at the time, we can see that the FFA provided important institutional leverage for the island states which enhanced the Pacific's negotiating position and capability. The emergence of UNCLOS led to the Pacific assertion of jurisdiction over its fishery and resource. It created a sense of resource ownership by the Pacific. The establishment of an institutional basis for Pacific representation harnessed the collective leveraging capabilities in negotiations with DWFN (Rayfuse 2004). Such an approach was necessary due to the overpowering influence of the DWFNs in seeking to maximise their profits from exploitation of the fishery.

Negotiating a new Tuna Treaty

The last ten-year agreement of the tuna treaty, spanning 2003–2013, was criticised by Pacific countries for its rigidity. This criticism mostly came from the PNA states[5] which had a larger stake in the fishery, since most of the tuna that was caught in their collective EEZs. On the other hand, the non-PNA states[6] were more comfortable with the status quo because, for very little to no effort, they would still be getting some return from the treaty (Aquora 2014). It became clear that the value of the US tuna treaty, particularly to those countries where US tuna vessels mainly operated, was grossly inadequate. This was evident when the fishery's estimated value rose to US$7 billion (Johnson 2013) and the US vessels, through access provided by the treaty, would catch an estimated US$500 million worth of tuna (Aqorau 2014). The effort on the part of some Pacific countries to pursue bilateral deals outside of the treaty was understandable.

The negotiations for the renewal of the South Pacific Tuna Treaty began in 2009 (Ruaia 2014) and at the time of writing are ongoing. The frustrations of the Pacific were expressed mostly by the states with the most purse seining activity, namely the PNA states. This stemmed from the static nature of the tuna treaty and the increasing financial incentives outside of the treaty. Since the US vessels, through the treaty, are paying a markedly lower price for access compared to other foreign DWFNs (Norris 2013; Aqorau 2014), the Pacific's ability to fully maximise financial returns from the resource is undermined. The treaty also created exemptions for US vessels which undercut conservation efforts focused on the fishery. This has been through the terms and conditions within the tuna treaty which provide immunity from requirements in licensing arrangements (Dunn et al. 2006).

The Pacific's agenda has gravitated around resolving this challenge and a range of related issues. These include the financial returns from the treaty, the full application of national laws, and the acceptance of conservation measures by

5   The Parties to the Nauru Agreement are the tuna-rich states of Federated States of Micronesia, Kiribati, Marshall Islands, Nauru, Palau, Papua New Guinea, Solomon Islands, and Tuvalu.
6   The non-PNA states are the other states in the Pacific Islands Forum Fisheries Agency (FFA), including Australia, Cook Islands, Fiji, New Zealand, Niue, Samoa, Tonga, and Vanuatu.

the US. While details of the full application of national laws and conservation measures are still to be determined, the significant expansion of the financial returns in recent years reflects a notable development for the new Pacific diplomacy.

Considering the massive value of the fishery and the lucrative incentives in bilateral deals outside the treaty, the Pacific began to push for a much higher financial return. It was evident that US$21 million was no longer an acceptable rate of return for the Pacific states. This became clearer as statistics revealed that on a daily rate the US fees provide for US$330 compared to the Japanese access fee to the Pacific of US$3,560 per day in 2011 (Pala 2011). In the negotiations which began in 2009, the initial talks were mostly focused on the financial returns (Roosen 2013). In 2011, the US offered to increase the rate of return to from US$21 million to US$42 million (Aquora 2014). However, this was not well received by the Pacific states, since it was still considered to be insufficient. Additionally, the US chief negotiator had threatened that the US would end all development aid to the region if the Pacific did not agree with the US position (Pala 2011). As a result, in April 2011, Papua New Guinea's acting Prime Minister Sam Abal announced:

> We formally give notice to withdraw from the Multilateral Treaty on Fisheries with the US … This hard line stance by PNG on behalf of smaller Pacific Island countries is set to send direct signals to Washington that the Multilateral Fish Treaty is unsustainable. This is your time, US, to recognize island countries and increase license fees for fishing. The PNG Government's decision is the right thing for the nations in the region. It is about time our friends state clearly and fairly their interest with us. They must give credit where it is due (Hriehwazi 2011).

This statement challenged the US directly because a withdrawal by Papua New Guinea (PNG) would end the existence of the treaty itself. The treaty stipulates that in a situation where the United States, Kiribati, Federated States of Micronesia, or PNG formally withdraw from the treaty, the treaty becomes non-existent (Ruaia 2014). In February 2012, the US offered US$45 million to the Pacific Island parties, aimed at persuading PNG to rescind its application for withdrawal and termination of the treaty (Islands Business 2012). The Pacific had been demanding US$60 million for 7,000 days, while the US was offering US$58 million for 9,000 days of access (Larsen 2012). The negotiations then developed to a point where the US was willing to accept 8,300 days for US$63 million (Matau 2012). After a transitional agreement of 18 months to allow time for the extension of negotiations, the US offered the Pacific US$94.5 million (Ruaia 2014). By late 2014, the US had agreed to pay US$90 million, with 8,300 days, for a period of 12 months, for the year 2015 (FFA 2014). While this amount represents a substantial increase over previous offers, negotiations are still ongoing to fully resolve the various demands of the Pacific countries.

In assessing the recent negotiations, it is clear that the Pacific's bargaining power has substantially increased. This bargaining power has been fortified through internal and external sources of leverage. An external leverage for the Pacific in this regard is the looming presence of China in the region, which provides an opportunity for engagement against the US. Simultaneously, the leverage originating within the Pacific, is the PNA Vessel Day Scheme (VDS), which has elevated and bolstered the Pacific's negotiating position.

The US presence within the South Pacific had been on the decline since the Cold War, until 2007, which was labelled as the 'Year of the Pacific' (Rice 2007). This marked an attempt to invigorate American presence in the South Pacific. The gradual decline was witnessed through the withdrawal of the US Agency for International Development office from Suva and the diplomatic mission in Solomon Islands during the 1990s, coupled with a reduction in high-level engagement with the Pacific Island leaders (McAslan 2013). The US tuna treaty remained the somewhat lone symbol of US commitment to the South Pacific. The treaty was able to provide the US with a multifaceted level of engagement with 16 countries, 14 of which were Pacific Island countries. The multifaceted nature of the treaty not only served the US fisheries interests but also diplomatic, political and geostrategic interests. However, while US presence had begun to decline, Chinese engagement in the region had begun to increase. This was evidenced in the export and import figures in Pacific Island trade, where the US accounted for only 2.2 per cent, while China grew to 4.1 per cent (McAslan 2013). Additionally, China has begun to emerge as a significant aid donor in the Pacific, diversifying its assistance and support (Herr and Bergin 2011). This growing engagement has worried Washington, with former United States Secretary of State Hillary Clinton stating to the US Senate Foreign Relations Committee in 2011:

> We are in a competition with China … They have brought all of the leaders of these small Pacific nations to Beijing, wined them and dined them. I mean, if anybody thinks that our retreating on these issues is somehow going to be irrelevant to the maintenance of our leadership in a world where we are competing with China that is a mistaken notion (Quinn 2011).

Similar to the role of the Soviet Union in the 1980s, China's looming presence has appeared to become a source of external political leverage for the Pacific states. In amongst the international agreements, laws and regimes, major power rivalry provides a useful opportunity for the Pacific. This was evident in late 2014 when the US offered US\$90 million for 8,300 fishing days for 2015, which was agreed amongst the Pacific states. But Kiribati withdrew a portion of its days offered in the 8,300 days pool, to offer to Asian states, which were alleged to have been Taiwan and China (Field 2014). Kiribati has a lot more to gain from engaging outside the treaty, considering it has an extensive EEZ and tuna catch capacity. Once again, the weakened financial incentive in the treaty for states that can claim a larger return, such as Kiribati, was revealed in such an incident. What can be categorised as an economic and financially motivated decision, has provided a perceived political outcome, towards the evident competition for influence in the region, between the US and China.

The crucial role played by the PNA underpins the internal leverage of the Pacific. The PNA constitutes the tuna-rich states of Federated States of Micronesia, Kiribati, Marshall Islands, Nauru, Palau, PNG, Solomon Islands, and Tuvalu (Tamate 2014; PNA 2013). This region is where US purse seine activity is concentrated. The PNA's sub-regional role has provided an important basis for the bargaining power of the Pacific states in the treaty. This is in large measure attributed to the VDS adopted by the PNA. The VDS is a rights-based management mechanism, which was designed by PNA to move to licensing purse seiners on the basis of number of fishing days as opposed to vessel numbers, as was the strategy under the Palau Arrangement (Havice 2010). This means that vessels have to purchase days to fish within waters of the PNA states. It was developed to limit vessel numbers creating competition amongst DWFN, and enabling higher rates of return for the PNA states. The VDS was developed over four years, from 2000–2004, and it went into its implementation stages in 2005 (Aqorau 2009). So far it has more than proven its benefit to the PNA states. In 2010, through the hard limits enforced by the VDS, the revenue gained by PNA rose to US$60 million, then US$104 million in 2011, US$229 million in 2012 and was projected to be US$249 million in 2013 (Aqorau 2014).

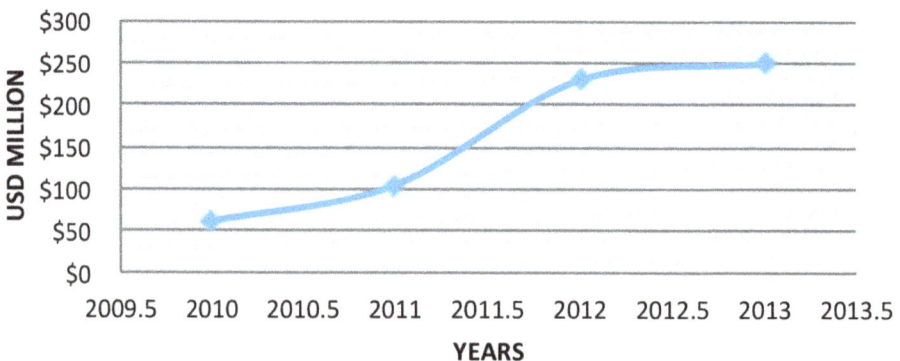

Figure 19.2: PNA revenue from access
Source: Adapted from Aqorau (2014a).

Apart from the substantive financial returns, the VDS finally gave the Pacific states control over their resource, which translated into bargaining and negotiating power. The authority to set the benchmark price on fishing days swung the power balance in favour of the Pacific states.

The VDS is an internally instigated leveraging tool for the resource owners, which has fundamentally transformed the Pacific's negotiating position. It is unprecedented by being a mechanism owned and driven from within the Pacific, and is a crucial marker of the new Pacific diplomacy. The design, manufacture and ownership of VDS as an instrument for, of and by the Pacific, is a testament of the new-found power in negotiation that is internally motivated and controlled.

The combination of the internal and external leveraging exercised by the Pacific has elevated its influence in the negotiations with the US, as witnessed by the rising financial returns accrued during the treaty negotiations since 2009. At the time of writing, the other outstanding issues, such as the full application of national laws and conservation measures, were yet to be finalised. However, considering the external and internal leverage available to the Pacific states, it can be expected the remaining outstanding issues will be resolved in the Pacific's favour.

Clearly, the Pacific has been 'flexing its muscles' (*Islands Business* 2012) and continues to do so with what now appears to be a combination of internal and external sources of leverage. The new Pacific diplomacy, as evident in the South Pacific Tuna Treaty's negotiation with its emphasis on a regionally-owned and controlled diplomacy, has the potential to increase the power of the Pacific in global negotiations. Resource specific sub-regional groups, such as PNA, using a mechanism such as the VDS, elevate the control, ownership and bargaining capacity of the Pacific states. This is aided by external sources of leveraging, such as the looming presence of China, which compels the US to seek an agreement with the Pacific states. A combination of internal control and overarching geopolitical competition has proved advantageous for the Pacific's new diplomacy as seen in the tuna sector.

References

Aqorau, T., 2009, 'Recent Developments in Pacific Tuna Fisheries: The Palau Arrangement and the Vessel Day Scheme', *The International Journal of Marine and Coastal Law* 24(3), pp. 557–81.

Aqorau, T., 2014a, 'Reshaping International Fisheries Development: Assimilating the treaty on fisheries between the governments of certain pacific island states and the United States under the PNA Vessel Day Scheme (VDS)', *International Journal of Marine and Coastal Law* 29(1), pp. 52–76.

Aquora, T., 2014b, personal communication, November.

Chang, K.L., 2007, *A Sustainable Fishery Management Study: The yellowfin tuna fishery in the Western Central Pacific Ocean,* ProQuest Information and Learning Company, Salt Lake City.

Dora, A., 1985, *The South Pacific Islands: New focus needed for U.S. policy,* The Heritage Foundation, Washington.

Doulman, D.J., 1986, *Some Aspects and Issues Concerning The Kiribati/Soviet Union Fishing Agreement,* East-West Center, Honolulu.

Doulman, D.J., 1988, 'In Pursuit of Fisheries Cooperation: The South Pacific Forum Fisheries Agency', *University of Hawaii Law Review* 10(1), pp. 138–50.

Dunn, S., L. Rodwell and G. Joseph, 2006, 'The Palau Arrangement for the Management of the Western Pacific Purse Seine Fishery', presentation at Sharing the Fish Conference, Forum Fisheries Agency, Fremantle.

FFA, 2014, 'Pacific Strikes US90m Tuna Deal for US Treaty in 2015, FFA Applauds Pacific Negotiations', Pacific Islands Forum Fisheries Agency. Available at: www.ffa.int/node/881.

Field, M., 2014, 'Kiribati Deal Shocks Fishing World', *stuff.co.nz.* Available at: www.stuff.co.nz/business/industries/10603447/Kiribati-deal-shocks-fishing-world.

Glebbeek, P., 1990, 'South Pacific Nuclear Free Zone Treaty: A lost battle against the superpowers?' Available at: repub.eur.nl/pub/18836/wp73.pdf.

Gubon, F., 1987, *The 1987 Pacific Island States/United States Fisheries Treaty and its Implications for Fisheries Development, Management and Conservation in the South Pacific Islands Region,* University Of Washington, Seattle.

Havice, E., 2010, 'The Structure of Tuna Access Agreements in the Western and Central Pacific', *Marine Policy* 34(5), pp. 979–87.

Herr, R. and A. Bergin, 2011, *Our Near Abroad: Australia and Pacific islands regionalism,* Australian Strategic Policy Institute. Available at: archives.pireport.org/archive/2011/December/Our_near_abroad.pdf.

Hriehwazi, Y., 2011, 'PNG Tells Mighty US To Go Jump', *Atuna.* Available at: www.atuna.com/NewsArchive/ViewArticle.asp?ID=9501.

Islands Business, 2012, 'Pacific Islands Flexing Muscles?'. Available at: www.islandsbusiness.com/2012/2/fisheries/pacific-islands-flexing-muscles/.

Johnson, G., 2013, 'Tuna Showdown: Pacific tuna stock faces growing crisis of inaction', *Islands Business*. Available at: www.islandsbusiness.com/2013/11/cover-story/tuna-showdown/.

Kengalu, A.M., 1988, *Embargo: The Jeanette Diana affair*, Robert Brown and Associates, Bathurst.

Larsen, E., 2012, 'Fish and Foreign Policy: Renegotiating the South Pacific Tuna Treaty', *cogitASIA*, 26 March. Available at: cogitasia.com/fish-and-foreign-policy-renegotiating-the-south-pacific-tuna-treaty/.

Lugar, R., 2004, 'United Nations Convention on the Law of the Sea: Senate Executive Report', US Government Printing Office, Washington.

Malone, J.L., 1983, 'The United States and the Law of the Sea after UNCLOS III', *Law and Contemporary Problems* 46 (2), pp. 29–36.

Matau, R., 2012, 'Unite for Tuna', *Islands Business*. Available at: www.islandsbusiness.com/2012/10/interview/unite-for-tuna/.

Maw, C.E., 1983, 'The United States and the Law of the Sea after UNCLOS III: Comment', *Law and Contemporary Problems* 46(2), pp. 55–60.

McAslan, H.R., 2013, *China's Increasing Influence in Oceania: Implications for the United States*, United States Government, Philadelphia.

Norris, W., 2013, 'Issues of the South Pacific Tuna Treaty', personal communication.

Pala, C., 2011, 'Islands Revoke US Fish Treaty', *Islands Business*, Suva.

Parties to the Nauru Agreement (PNA), 2013, 'Parties to the Nauru Agreement: About us'. Available at: www.pnatuna.com/About-Us.

Quinn, A., 2011, 'Clinton Says China Seeks to Outflank Exxon in Papua New Guinea', Reuters, 2 March. Available at: www.reuters.com/article/2011/03/02/us-china-usa-clinton-idUSTRE7215UV20110302.

Rayfuse, R.G., 2004, *Non-Flag State Enforcement in High Seas Fisheries*, Martinus Nijhoff Publishers, Netherlands.

Rice, C., 2007, 'Eighth Pacific Island Conference of Leaders', US Department of State Archive. Available at: 2001-2009.state.gov/secretary/rm/2007/may/84414.htm.

Roosen, M.T., 2013, 'Outstanding Treaty Issues', personal communication.

Ruaia, K., 2014, 'The South Pacific Tuna Treaty', personal communication, 1 May.

Tamate, J., 2004, 'Access Agreements: South Pacific Forum Fisheries Agency', FAO Corporate Document Repository, Fisheries and Aquaculture Department. Available at: www.fao.org/docrep/007/y5718e/y5718e07.htm.

Tamate, J., 2014, 'Regionalism: The experience of the Parties to the Nauru Agreement', SSGM, The Australian National University. Available at: ips. cap.anu.edu.au/sites/default/files/SSGM%20IB%202014_31.pdf.

Tarte, S., 1998, 'Regional Strategies: The Pacific Islands and Japan', *The Journal Of Pacific Studies* 22, pp. 159–72.

Tarte, S., 2007, 'Managing Tuna Fisheries in the Pacific: A regional success story', in J. Bryant-Tokalau and I. Frazer (eds), *Redefining the Pacific?: Regionalism past, present and future*, Ashgate Publishing, London, pp. 89–100.

Negotiating Trade and Decolonisation

20

Negotiating Power in Contemporary Pacific Trade Diplomacy

Wesley Morgan

In the two decades following the formation of the World Trade Organization (WTO), Pacific Island countries have pursued an active trade diplomacy agenda. New regional trade agreements have been negotiated and implemented among the island countries themselves. Pacific officials have also pursued their interests at the WTO, and have proved tough negotiators in trade talks with external powers. By driving hard bargains with the European Union (EU), and Australia and New Zealand, Pacific officials have shifted the terms of discussion about trade and development in the Pacific. They have also broadened the agenda of negotiations in the island countries' favour, to include issues such as labour mobility and development assistance.

This chapter highlights the successes of contemporary Pacific trade diplomacy, and explores the agency of island policy-makers. It also emphasises that trade diplomacy and regional geopolitics are intertwined. For Australia and New Zealand in particular, negotiations with Pacific Island countries are linked with an abiding concern to remain 'special insiders' in processes of regional cooperation. To date, new trade agreements have been signed by island members of the Pacific Islands Forum, and among members of the Melanesian Spearhead Group. However Australia, New Zealand (and the EU for that matter) remain on the outer. Pacific officials argue a unique agreement would be required with their wealthy neighbours, one that addresses the island states' unique trade-related constraints. As long as these arguments continue to fall on deaf ears in Canberra and Wellington, trade policy will likely remain an issue-area in which the island countries sail their own way.

Responding to a Changing World

The Uruguay Round of trade negotiations which led to the formation of the WTO had significant and largely negative consequences for Pacific Island economies. Trading partners made commitments that undermined key island exports. For more than a century, Pacific countries had relied on preferential access to metropolitan markets for export commodities — including sugar, coffee, cocoa, oil palm, copra, and canned tuna — and a small range of manufactured exports (see Morgan 2014). As destination countries agreed to lower tariffs to cheaper producers, Pacific exports were increasingly deemed uncompetitive. For Pacific Island governments, the inherent disadvantages of island-based production — high costs, poor transport services, distance from external markets, and exposure to frequent natural disasters — were also brought into sharper relief.

Pacific governments decided the best way to respond to challenges brought about by changes in the global trade regime would be to pursue regional trade integration. Melanesian countries led the way with the formation of the Melanesian Spearhead Group Trade Agreement (MSGTA) in 1993. In 1997, Pacific trade officials proposed a Pacific Regional Trade Agreement (PARTA) among the island country members of the South Pacific Forum. They argued closer economic integration would help the island countries remain competitive in a liberalised global marketplace. As then General Secretary of the South Pacific Forum Noel Levi explained, 'we feel that the free trade area option is the best option for our members to deal with the many issues being raised by globalisation' (Singh 1999). The proposed island-only agreement was particularly favoured by Roman Grynberg, who was appointed in 1997 as the inaugural multilateral trade policy adviser to the South Pacific Forum.

Talk of a Pacific trade agreement that excluded Australia and New Zealand rang alarm bells in Canberra and Wellington. Officials in both countries had long viewed a stable regional order in the South Pacific as a pre-eminent geostrategic priority. Australia provided funding for regional cooperation, at least in part, as a means of maintaining 'a favourable strategic posture in the region' (Fry 1981, p. 480). Crucially, both countries aimed to be 'considered by the Pacific states to be part of the region, and not part of the "outside"' (Fry 1981, p. 480). If the island countries were to negotiate a trade agreement among themselves, particularly through the auspices of the South Pacific Forum, this could be seen as undermining a carefully cultivated perception that they were legitimate insiders. Thus, Australian and New Zealand officials pressed hard to be included in any new Pacific regional trade agreement. When South Pacific Forum trade officials met in March 2000 to consider the legal text of PARTA, the Australian and New Zealand delegations brought their own amended text which included them as parties principle to the agreement.

There is considerable evidence that geostrategic concern (as opposed to strictly commercial interests) underpinned Australian and New Zealand insistence on their inclusion in PARTA. During negotiations around PARTA, Australian Foreign Minister Alexander Downer 'instructed his officials to oppose any agreement that excluded Australia and said nothing could be called "Pacific Regional" unless Australia was involved' (Kelsey 2004, p. 20). Legal experts tasked with drafting the text of a new agreement confirmed 'the desire of Australia and New Zealand to participate as 'parties principle' is driven by political rather than economic considerations' (Johnson 2009, p. 195).

Pacific policy-makers remained concerned about the adjustment costs involved if they included Australia and New Zealand in any new agreement. However they were also sensitive to the political interests of their developed-country neighbours. A compromise was proposed. An 'umbrella agreement' would be negotiated which included Australia and New Zealand as equal parties: the Pacific Agreement on Closer Economic Relations (PACER).[1] A 'subsidiary agreement' would be the trade agreement among island states: the Pacific Island Countries Trade Agreement (PICTA). Taken together, the two agreements would satisfy Australian and New Zealand political interest to be included in any new agreement of the South Pacific Forum,[2] and Pacific concerns to avoid (or at least delay) costly trade liberalisation. As an official from the Australian Department of Foreign Affairs and Trade explained:

> Since Australia had failed to convince Forum island countries of the merits of committing to comprehensive trade integration, there was a need to produce a structure that would allow these countries to go about their business without splitting the Forum permanently, and without alienating Australia and New Zealand completely (Peebles 2005, p. 74).

It should be noted that Australian and New Zealand concern to be included in any Pacific regional agreement was exacerbated when European officials proposed trade preferences for Pacific countries be replaced with a WTO-compatible regional free trade agreement. In June 2000, Pacific governments

---

1   Technically this would not be a trade agreement, but a binding treaty that required consideration of a trade agreement at a future date and guaranteed that island states wouldn't offer better terms to trading competitors.
2   The South Pacific Forum was renamed the Pacific Islands Forum in 2000.

signed a new aid-and-trade treaty between the EU and African, Caribbean and Pacific (ACP) states. The Cotonou Agreement stipulated WTO-compatible Economic Partnership Agreements (EPAs) would be negotiated between the EU and regional country groupings, including Pacific Island countries.

By the turn of the century, Pacific Island trade ministers and officials had cemented their initial response to changes in the global trade regime — by pursuing new trade agreements among themselves. They had also gained experience in trade diplomacy by discussing potential agreements with Australia, New Zealand, and the EU. In addition, island officials had also pursued their interests in multilateral negotiations.

Pacific Trade Diplomacy at the WTO

During the late-1990s, Pacific Island governments spearheaded a campaign for the formation of a new category of states at the WTO. Pacific officials proposed 'small and vulnerable economies' be formally designated among the member-states of the WTO. This would allow developed countries to continue to extend special and favourable treatment to Pacific Island countries — including preferential access to their markets. Technically, the WTO only allowed preferential treatment to be extended to countries recognised by the UN as Least Developed Countries (LDCs). However, during the 1990s, a number of multilateral bodies, including the UN, investigated the unique economic vulnerabilities of Small Island Developing States (SIDS). There was an increasing consensus that these states possessed characteristics that meant they were uniquely vulnerable to economic and environmental shocks. Both the UN and the Commonwealth Secretariat proposed that a 'Vulnerability Index' be developed to reflect the unique needs of SIDS (see Atkins et al. 2001).

Pacific trade officials suggested the unique vulnerabilities of Pacific Island countries should serve as criteria for derogation from more onerous WTO rules, allowing, for example, preferential access to wealthy markets, or special trade-related development assistance. At the 1998 South Pacific Forum Trade Ministers meeting, ministers agreed to pursue the agenda of small island states at the WTO, and to seek WTO observer status for the South Pacific Forum. They resolved to:

> … adopt a common Forum position with the objective of the UN adopting a vulnerability index, and with the aim of having such an index included among the criteria for determining Least Developed Country status, and for deciding eligibility for concessional aid and trade treatment (SPF 1998).

To pursue their interests at the WTO, Pacific trade officials and diplomats formed a strategic alliance with small island states from the Caribbean and the Indian Ocean. In the lead up to the 1999 WTO Ministerial in Seattle, the government of Fiji, working with officials at the forum secretariat, circulated a petition calling for inclusion in the ministerial communiqué language regarding a 'work programme on small states at the WTO' (Grynberg 2001a, p. 7). However, the Seattle meeting was disrupted by 50,000 street protesters and it wasn't until the Doha Ministerial in 2001 that Pacific trade diplomacy achieved its first — albeit limited — success when members agreed to 'frame responses to the trade-related issues identified for the fuller integration of small, vulnerable economies into the multilateral trading system' (WTO 2001, para 35).

Pacific governments won support for the idea that small island countries faced unique trade-related challenges. However, they did not win support at the WTO for any new category of states. Without a formal category it would be difficult for Pacific countries to request differential treatment in multilateral negotiations. Nonetheless, at a subsequent WTO Ministerial in 2005, members were urged to 'adopt specific measures' to help small and vulnerable economies participate in global trade (WTO 2005, para 41).[3] Subsequent proposals in WTO negotiations included: (some) flexibility in tariff negotiations, special assistance for trade facilitation, limited permission to use subsidies (including in fisheries), and a regional pooling of technical assistance required to implement WTO agreements (see Smith 2008; Kaukab 2009).

Having established new trade agreements among themselves, and pursued their interests in global talks, Pacific policy-makers increasingly turned their attention to negotiations with key trading partners from outside the region.

Negotiating with the European Union

Early in the new millennium, Pacific Island countries found themselves negotiating regional trade agreements with the EU, Australia and New Zealand. These talks proved protracted and controversial. Indeed, by 2015, negotiations for an EPA with the EU were effectively a dead letter, and PACER Plus talks with Australia and New Zealand were at a stalemate. Given this state of affairs, one could be forgiven for seeing both negotiations as a failure of Pacific diplomacy. However, a close reading of the motivations of Pacific trade officials suggests they pursued a successful strategy. They delayed proceedings and drove hard bargains, and in doing so broadened the agenda of negotiations in their

---

3   These measures would be proposed for member states on the basis of specific characteristics, and applied to all countries which shared those characteristics, thus circumventing the need for a special category of states.

favour, to include issues such as labour mobility and development assistance. This contrasts markedly with the experience of other island states. In the Caribbean, for example, trade officials quickly acceded to the demands of European officials during regional EPA negotiations and signed an agreement that was subject to heavy criticism in Caribbean capitals (see Bishop et al. 2013).

Faced with a decline in the value of trade preferences, which had for so long underwritten commodity exports, Pacific governments used regional trade negotiations to seek new concessions from wealthy states. As an overarching strategy, island officials demanded their unique trading circumstances be formally recognised in the design of any agreement. They emphasised that they were uniquely disadvantaged in a liberalised global marketplace, and that new treaties should be designed with their trade-related constraints in mind. Grynberg, who returned to the forum secretariat to help coordinate the Pacific's EPA negotiations with the EU, argued what was needed was 'appropriate interventions that will replicate the results of trade preference while avoiding some of the more market-distorting consequences' (Grynberg 2001b).

From 2002 to 2006, Pacific officials fleshed out unique proposals for a deal with the EU. These included sector-specific strategies to encourage investment in Pacific tourism and agriculture; measures to reduce the cost of business finance in the Pacific; temporary access to the EU for Pacific Island workers; and an agreement linking fishing rights for European vessels with measures to encourage downstream processing in island states. These proposals were included in a draft treaty submitted to Brussels in July 2006. The European Commission, however, was not interested in the Pacific's proposals. Officials in Brussels were keen to push their own regulatory barrow, and to avoid precedents that might have implications for their negotiations with other trading partners. With few economic interests in the region, a unique trade agreement was simply not on their agenda. When European officials presented their own draft EPA in mid-2007, it contained none of the proposals developed by island negotiators. The forum secretariat lamented that the EU text 'contained explicit provisions setting out the commission's demands while reflecting almost none of the key written proposals of the [Pacific] group nor the positions put forward and key interests expressed ... during discussions that had been taking place between the two sides over the last two years' (PIFS 2007).

With European officials refusing to countenance their proposals, Pacific officials went cold on a regional agreement with the EU. Discussions turned instead to preventing serious disruption to export sectors reliant on European trade preferences. A WTO waiver for those preferences was due to expire on 31 December 2007 and any tariff increase threatened tuna exports from Papua New Guinea and sugar exports from Fiji. During intense negotiations in Brussels in late 2007, the EU proposed interim EPAs — covering goods only —

that would allow Pacific countries to continue to access EU preferences. Island officials were concerned that these interim arrangements were ill-conceived, and argued a number of provisions would need subsequent revision or removal (Primack 2007). However, in perhaps the only significant gain for the Pacific to come from the EPA negotiations, the EU did agree to island proposals to revise rules of origin requirements for processed tuna. In effect, these changes meant fishing vessels from anywhere in the world could land, and process, their catch in a Pacific Island country and gain preferential access to EU markets. In the short term it was expected this change would allow for the establishment of tuna canneries in Madang and Lae in northern Papua New Guinea.

The breakdown in regional negotiations for an EPA frayed diplomatic relations between Pacific Island countries and the EU. When the Cook Islands Trade Minister Wilkie Rasmussen explained to a sitting of the ACP–EU Joint Parliamentary Assembly that the EU Trade Commissioner Peter Mandelson had been insensitive to the needs of Pacific Island countries, Mandelson wrote to Rasmussen suggesting he had been misquoted, and that might he consider a public correction (Mandelson 2008). This raised the ire of Rasmussen who, in a strongly worded reply, told Mandelson:

> the common impression you left on all the Pacific Island Trade Ministers was that you are insensitive to our protocols and issues … I can assure you that the general feeling is that Papua New Guinea and Fiji initialled the Interim Agreement because of fear that they would lose their preferential trade arrangements with the European Union (PANG 2008).

Dealing with Big Brothers

Australian and New Zealand representatives insisted they would be more sympathetic to the ideas of Pacific officials than their European counterparts. In the lead up to a formal launch of PACER Plus negotiations, Australian Trade Minister Simon Crean explained Australia had 'learnt the lessons of the EPA negotiations with the European Union … We have learnt from that experience and are not going to repeat it … unlike the EPA, PACER-Plus is not just a trade agreement' (Crean 2009). For their part, the Pacific trade ministers resolved PACER Plus negotiations could only proceed if Australia and New Zealand formally agreed that unique and additional measures would be included in a final agreement. They were particularly keen to include measures permitting Pacific Islanders to work in Australia and New Zealand on a temporary basis. Indeed, island ministers decided that market access offers on goods and services would be conditional on 'a commitment from Australia and New Zealand to discuss labour market access, and the broad parameters of that access is agreed' (OCTA 2011, p. 6).

As it turned out, labour mobility proved to be the key stumbling block for the PACER Plus talks. Pacific officials proposed legally binding measures that would facilitate the movement of workers to ameliorate labour shortages in horticulture and tourism sectors in Australia and New Zealand. Given Pacific Island countries already enjoyed tariff-free access to both countries, many island officials felt a treaty without labour mobility would not be worth signing. Initially, Australian negotiators seemed to agree labour mobility should be included 'in the context of a comprehensive fully WTO-consistent Agreement' (DFAT 2006, p. 2). However, after further consideration, Australian and New Zealand officials became concerned that including labour mobility in PACER Plus would create a precedent that would be difficult to contain in other negotiations. Furthermore, both countries proceeded to implement labour mobility schemes for Pacific Island workers outside of a regional trade agreement. The New Zealand Recognised Seasonal Employer scheme, launched in 2007, and the Australian Seasonal Worker Program, launched in 2009, both allowed employers to recruit Pacific Islanders on a temporary basis.

At the time of writing, intransigent negotiating positions on both sides with regard to labour mobility marked a stagnation of the PACER Plus talks.[4] Furthermore political commitment to the negotiations was on the wane. Papua New Guinea Trade Minister Richard Maru indicated his country was considering pulling out of the talks altogether, labelling them a 'complete waste of time' (Pareti 2013). Australian and New Zealand diplomats had spent nearly 20 years trying to convince Pacific countries of the merits of including them in a regional free trade agreement. However, the message from island governments remained clear: they would do so only if they deemed such a move to be in their interests.

Trade Negotiations and the New Pacific Diplomacy

Pacific Island countries have more agency in international trade negotiations than is commonly understood. Many observers have characterised Pacific countries as powerless actors in the global trade regime. They suggest island governments have had little choice but to adapt to changes in the global economy, to embrace trade liberalisation, and to sign free trade agreements with metropolitan powers. However, Pacific officials have resisted pressure

---

4   As the Pacific's Chief Trade Adviser Edwini Kessie explained: 'Australia and New Zealand want to treat labour mobility outside of PACER Plus and the Pacific Island countries want legally binding commitments, so that is the main issue dividing the parties' (Radio New Zealand 2013). Or as another regional commentator put it: 'Begun in 2009, PACER-Plus is argued dry … The one thing the Islands want from Australia and New Zealand — labour mobility — is the one thing Australia and New Zealand won't give … Stalemate' (Dobell 2014).

to sign orthodox trade agreements. Instead, they have demanded recognition of their unique trading circumstances and have argued for concessions from wealthy states. This strategy has borne some fruit. European policy-makers agreed to changes allowing more fish from the Pacific to enter European markets tariff-free, a move that has expanded tuna-processing facilities in the region. More significantly, governments in Australia and New Zealand have taken heed of arguments that island workers should be allowed temporary access to their labour markets. This has seen tens of thousands of Pacific Islanders earn incomes abroad, which have been spent or saved at home.

Finally, it should be remembered that trade diplomacy in the Pacific is inextricably linked with regional geopolitics. As elsewhere in the world, consideration of the economic merits of trade arrangements occurs against a political backdrop. In recent years, Pacific Island countries have indicated a greater willingness to pursue an independent foreign policy — a trend described in this book as the new Pacific diplomacy. Pacific diplomats have pursued their particular interests at the United Nations, and with regard to issue-areas such as climate change, fisheries management and decolonisation. Discussions on trade have been no different. Pacific officials have demanded their unique circumstances be taken seriously. Until they are, Pacific governments appear to be in no hurry to extend regional trade arrangements to include their wealthier neighbours.

References

Atkins, J.P., S.A. Mazzi and C.D. Easter, 2000, *Commonwealth Vulnerability Index for Developing Countries: The position of small states*, Economics Paper No. 40, Commonwealth Secretariat, London.

Bishop, M., T. Heron and A. Payne, 2013, 'Caribbean Development Alternatives and the CARIFORUM–European Union Economic Partnership Agreement', *Journal of International Relations and Development* 16, pp. 82–110.

Crean, S., 2009, 'Enhancing Prosperity in the Pacific', speech to the Third Informal Meeting of Officials on PACER-Plus, Adelaide, 16 February.

Department of Foreign Affairs and Trade (DFAT), 2006, 'Pacific Region Seasonal Contract Labour', submission by the Department of Foreign Affairs and Trade to the Senate Committee on Employment, Workplace Relations and Education, April. Available at: www.aph.gov.au/~/media/wopapub/senate/committee/eet_ctte/completed_inquiries/2004_07/contract_labour/submissions/sub042_pdf.ashx.

Dobel, G., 2014, 'Rethinking Australia's Economic Role in the Pacific', *The Strategist*, Australian Strategic Policy Institute, 1 December. Available at: www.aspistrategist.org.au/rethinking-australias-economic-role-in-the-pacific/.

Fry, G., 1981, 'Regionalism and International Politics of the South Pacific', *Pacific Affairs* 54(3), pp. 455–84.

Grynberg, R., 2001a, 'The Pacific Island States and the WTO: Towards a post-Seattle agenda for small vulnerable states', in D. Peretz, R. Faruqi and E.J. Kisangs (eds), *Small States in the Global Economy*, Commonwealth Secretariat, London, pp. 329–42.

Grynberg, R., 2001b, 'A Theory of Trade and Development of Small Vulnerable States', *Journal of Pacific Studies* 25(1), pp. 155–72.

Johnston, A., 2009, 'Explaining PICTA, PACER and Cotonou: Trade policy in the Pacific (1996–2006)', unpublished PhD thesis, School of Philosophy, Anthropology and Social Inquiry, University of Melbourne.

Kaukab, R., 2009, *Development Effects of the Doha Round on Small and Vulnerable Economies*, CUTS Geneva Resource Centre, Geneva.

Kelsey, J., 2004, *A People's Guide to PACER: The implications for the Pacific Islands of the Pacific Agreement on Closer Economic Relations (PACER)*, Pacific Network on Globalisation, Suva.

Mandelson, P., 2008, 'Letter from EU Trade Commissioner Peter Mandelson to the PACP Trade Ministers' Lead Spokesperson for the EPA Negotiations with the EU, Samoa's Associate Minister for Commerce Industry and Labour, Hans Joachim Keil', 16 July.

Morgan W., 2014, 'Trade Negotiations and Regional Economic Integration in the Pacific Islands Forum', *Asia and the Pacific Policy Studies* 1(2), pp. 325–36.

Office of the Chief Trade Adviser (OCTA), 2011, 'Forum Island Country Trade Ministers' Meeting — Outcomes Document (FIC Eyes Only)', 17 May, Vava'u, Tonga, OCTA, Port Vila.

Pacific Islands Forum Secretariat (PIFS), 2007, 'Pacific ACP Countries Express Deep Concern at EU Trade Deal Proposal', press statement (106/07), 28 August.

Pacific Network on Globalisation (PANG), 2008, 'Pacific Trade Ministers Slam EU Bullying in Trade', press release, Suva.

Pareti, S., 2013, 'Pacific Trade Talks "Waste of Time": PNG', ABC News, 21 May. Available at: www.abc.net.au/news/2013-05-20/an-png-considering-withdrawing-from-pacer-talks/4701402.

Peebles, D., 2005, *Pacific Regional Order*, Asia Pacific Press, Canberra.

Primack, D., 2007, 'EPA Fails to Draw the Pacific Closer to the International Trading System', *Trade Negotiations Insights* 6(8).

Radio New Zealand, 2013, 'Pacific's Chief Trade Advisor Believes Parties can Compromise', 2 December. Available at: www.radionz.co.nz/international/programmes/datelinepacific/audio/2578392/pacific's-chief-trade-advisor-believes-parties-can-compromise.

Singh, D., 1999, 'South Pacific: As Lome Pact Fades, Push for Free Trade Area Grows', Inter Press Service News Agency, August 24. Available at: www.ipsnews.net/1999/08/south-pacific-as-lome-pact-fades-push-for-free-trade-area-grows/.

Smith, R., 2008, *WTO Doha Round: Small Economies and Their Interests*. Trade Hot Topics no. 55, Commonwealth Secretariat, London.

South Pacific Forum (SPF), 1998, 'Twenty-Ninth South Pacific Forum: Forum Communique', 24–25 August, Pohnpei, Federated States of Micronesia.

World Trade Organization (WTO), 2001. 'Doha WTO Ministerial 2001: Ministerial Declaration', (WT/MIN(01)/DEC/1).

.

21

Pacific Diplomacy and Decolonisation in the 21st Century

Nic Maclellan

Introduction

The issue of political independence and sovereignty was a central element in the establishment of the South Pacific Forum in 1971, as four independent island nations moved out of the confines of the South Pacific Commission. Self-determination was extensively debated at the forum throughout the 1980s.

Today, well into the 21st century and the United Nations' Third International Decade for the Eradication of Colonialism, decolonisation has largely faded from the international agenda. Despite this, 16 territories remain on the United Nations' (UN) list of non-self-governing territories, including six in the Pacific: New Caledonia and French Polynesia (under French administration); Tokelau (New Zealand); Pitcairn (United Kingdom); and Guam and American Samoa (United States). Developments in these territories are monitored by the seminars, missions and annual resolutions of the UN Special Committee on Decolonisation.[1]

---

1   The generic term 'territories' is used for convenience, but these dependencies have a variety of political and constitutional structures. France describes its Pacific dependencies as 'collectivities', while Indonesian and Papua New Guinea governments bridle at the suggestion the provinces of Papua, West Papua or Bougainville require 'decolonisation'.

Across the region there are also 'second order' self-determination struggles in postcolonial states that do not fall under the mandate of the UN special committee, such as Bougainville (Papua New Guinea), Rapanui (Chile), and West Papua (Indonesia).

While the UN is an important institution for setting human rights norms, it has limited enforcement capacity. The United Nations can act with the support of the administering power, as shown with New Zealand's extensive work with the UN decolonisation unit over Tokelau (Huntsman and Kelihian 2007). But Paris and Washington have long ignored UN criticism of their colonial policies, prioritising strategic interests such as US military deployments in Guam or France's control of the resources in its seven-million-square-kilometre Exclusive Economic Zone in the Pacific (Mrgudovic 2008). Moreover, the UN decolonisation unit is starved for funds and staff, and reluctant to implement an assertive agenda.[2]

Since the end of French nuclear testing in 1996 and the signing of New Caledonia's Noumea Accord in 1998, the Pacific Islands Forum has developed new policies on engagement with the territories. New Caledonia (1999) and French Polynesia (2004) gained forum observer status, then both upgraded to 'associate membership' at the 2006 forum meeting in Apia. Tokelau also upgraded its 2005 observer status to associate membership in 2014. Other nations remain as forum observers, including Timor-Leste (2002), Wallis and Futuna (2006) and the US dependencies of Guam, American Samoa, and the Commonwealth of the North Marianas (2011).

The policies of Australia and New Zealand (and, on occasions, other forum members) have constrained a more active role for the forum on decolonisation. Australia has increasingly backed France's regional role and proposed that territories such as New Caledonia should become full members of the forum, even before their final political status is determined.[3] This significant policy shift was endorsed in the 2013 Morauta Review of the Pacific Plan for Strengthening Regional Cooperation and Integration, which argues that original forum priorities such as decolonisation and a nuclear-free Pacific 'have either been resolved or moved to other platforms for debate and determination'.[4]

---

2   For a more ambitious agenda, see Corbin (2010).

3   Interview with Parliamentary Secretary for Pacific Island Affairs Richard Marles, May 2012. See also Maclellan (2013d).

4   'The contemporary debate about regionalism has rather less intrinsic association with self-determination. Most of the issues being debated in contemporary Pacific regionalism (trade and transport, for example) are entirely within the mandate of even the non-self-determining territories to resolve, and regionalism would be better served by fully including, not excluding, such territories in the debate and in its implementation' (Pacific Plan Review 2013, p. 78).

For this reason, island leaders have increasingly used other mechanisms to take diplomatic initiatives on decolonisation, such as the Melanesian Spearhead Group (MSG) and Pacific Small Island Developing States (PSIDS) ambassadors. This chapter documents two recent examples of this new Pacific diplomacy on decolonisation: the work of PSIDS for the reinscription of French Polynesia at the UN General Assembly; and the MSG's current debate on self-determination in West Papua.

These initiatives do not guarantee that independence will be achieved — indeed, there are many economic, demographic and strategic barriers to decolonisation for the remaining Pacific territories. The diversity and small size of some territories is a constraint on advancing the decolonisation agenda, and significant parts of some local populations welcome immigration rights, federal grants and other benefits of territorial status (Firth 2013). In other cases — Guam, West Papua, and New Caledonia — indigenous peoples have been made a minority in their own country, constraining advances through elections or referenda.

Rather than assuming a unified Pacific response to decolonisation, it is important to analyse varying reactions by regional organisations and governments. Solidarity can be trumped by countervailing influences, such as Papua New Guinea's and Fiji's relationship with Indonesia or trade ties to the European Union. As new players such as Indonesia and Timor-Leste enter Pacific regional networks, island leaders are forced to juggle more complex obligations. Fiji and Papua New Guinea (PNG) are active members of the UN Special Committee on Decolonisation, but growing ties with Asia affect their actions on decolonisation. Melanesian governments have actively supported independence movements in New Caledonia and French Polynesia, but have maintained a diplomatic silence about decolonisation in the US territories.

Canberra's strategic support for Paris and Washington is a significant roadblock to advancing the decolonisation agenda, but the following two studies of contemporary Pacific diplomacy on decolonisation also highlight the tension between principle and national interest for island governments. The first relates to the campaign to have French Polynesia reinscribed on the UN list of non-self-governing territories, in the face of French opposition. The second study looks at ongoing diplomacy through MSG and PSIDS to deal with West Papuan self-determination.

French Polynesia's Reinscription with the United Nations

For many years, the French State has resisted international scrutiny of its colonial policies and ignored international obligations created by UN decolonisation resolutions. As noted in a November 1986 internal memo from the French Ministry of Foreign Affairs:

> We have never accepted resolutions 1514 (XV) and 1541 (XV), for which we abstained … We have never accepted the legitimacy of the Special Committee on Decolonisation, as directed by resolution 1564 (XVI), to propose the inscription of territories on the list of non-self-governing territories (Regnault 2013, pp. 69–70).

In the face of this French opposition, the Pacific Islands Forum played a crucial role in supporting the reinscription of New Caledonia on the UN list in the mid-1980s.[5] The passage of UN General Assembly resolution 41/41 in December 1986 came at the height of armed conflict between the French armed forces and supporters of independence during 1984–1988.

France launched extensive diplomatic manoeuvres to ignore, delay and then derail the 1986 forum initiative, using its political and economic weight to encourage countries to abstain or oppose the resolution. Cuba, although a member of the UN Special Committee on Decolonisation and the Non-Aligned Movement, was promised a soft ride at the next UN Human Rights Commission. Tunisia and French-speaking African nations were wooed, based on solidarity to 'francophonie'. Newly independent Vanuatu was threatened with aid cuts, while Argentina was lobbied with offers of support in their dispute with United Kingdom over the Falklands/Malvinas islands (Regnault 2013, p. 99).

After years of lobbying, Australia and New Zealand only joined their island neighbours to support New Caledonia's reinscription after the election of a conservative government in Paris in 1986. Canberra and Wellington shifted policy in part due to concerns about perceived Soviet and Libyan advances in the South Pacific. Australia's then Deputy Prime Minister Lionel Bowen had stated: 'If France drags its feet too much over decolonisation, the independence movement will become increasingly radicalised and perhaps open to Soviet influence and manipulation' (*The Australian* 1982).

---

5   The list was created in 1946, but from 1947 France refused to transmit information on its overseas territories to the General Assembly, as required under Article 73e of the UN Charter. A revised UN list of territories in 1963 ignored France's Pacific dependencies, apart from the joint Anglo-French condominium of the New Hebrides.

Since reinscription nearly 30 years ago, New Caledonia has been scrutinised by the UN Special Committee. A UN monitoring mission travelled to New Caledonia in 1999 and the governments of France and New Caledonia hosted a regional seminar of the UN Special Committee in Noumea in 2010.[6] Another UN mission travelled to Noumea in March 2014, to monitor the electoral roll for New Caledonia's May 2014 provincial and congressional elections.

Despite this engagement on New Caledonia, France has continued to resist decolonisation for French Polynesia. In 2010, then French President Nicolas Sarkozy stated that France's overseas territories 'are French and will remain French'. He stressed that for French Polynesia, there is 'one red line that I will never accept should be crossed: that of independence' (Sarkozy 2010). Despite this, active Pacific diplomacy led to an historic decision on 17 May 2013, when the UN General Assembly adopted a resolution to reinscribe French Polynesia on the UN list of non-self-governing territories.[7]

The resolution, sponsored by Solomon Islands, Nauru and Tuvalu with support from Vanuatu, Samoa and Timor-Leste, was adopted by the UN General Assembly without a vote. It called on the French government 'as the Administering Power concerned, to intensify its dialogue with French Polynesia in order to facilitate rapid progress towards a fair and effective self-determination process, under which the terms and timelines for an act of self-determination will be agreed'.[8]

Even as a symbolic measure, the UN resolution sparked fury in Paris. After writing to all member states in an unsuccessful bid to delay the resolution, France's UN Ambassador Gérard Araud boycotted the general assembly session. The French Ministry of Foreign Affairs raged: 'This resolution is a flagrant interference with a complete absence of respect for the democratic choice of French Polynesians and a hijacking of the decolonisation principles established by the United Nations' (Ministry of Foreign Affairs 2013).

The French government has maintained its stubborn refusal to acknowledge any role for the UN over self-determination in French Polynesia, failing to meet its obligations as an administering power. Each year, under Article 73e of the UN Charter, colonial powers are required to submit information to the United Nations relating to the economic, social and educational conditions in their

---

6   French Polynesian independence leader Oscar Temaru was refused entry to this UN seminar in New Caledonia's capital, a symbol of ongoing French opposition to Maohi self-determination.
7   This section draws on interviews with former Presidents of French Polynesia Gaston Flosse (Majuro 2013) and Oscar Manutahi Temaru (Noumea 2013) and Senator Richard Tuheiava (Suva 2013).
8   'Self-determination of French Polynesia', UN General Assembly Resolution, A/67/L.56, 17 May 2013. See Maclellan (2013a).

territories. France formally submitted information about New Caledonia in 2014 and 2015, but refused to submit information on French Polynesia in either year (UN General Assembly 2015).

The 2013 decision on French Polynesia came after decades of lobbying by the independence party Tavini Huiraatira. As leader of the Polynesian Liberation Front, Oscar Temaru first lobbied at the UN in 1978. He patiently sought support throughout the 1980s and 1990s, gaining solidarity from the Pacific Conference of Churches and the Nuclear Free and Independent Pacific (NFIP) movement, but little action from neighbouring Polynesian governments.[9]

Temaru won office as president of French Polynesia in 2004 and despite 11 changes of the presidency over a decade, continued to campaign for reinscription. In 2011, for the first time, the French Polynesian Assembly narrowly voted to support Temaru's call.

The governing Union for Democracy and Social Progress coalition (*Union pour la Démocratie et le Progrès Social* (UPLD)) looked to the French Socialist Party for recognition of the Maohi people's right to self-determination. The UPLD decided to soft-pedal their reinscription campaign during 2012 in order to avoid embarrassing Socialist Party candidate Francois Hollande in his successful bid for the French presidency. Once elected, however, Hollande began to back away from the interparty accord between the Socialist Party and Tavini Huiraatira.

A number of Pacific governments took up the issue of French Polynesia's self-determination at the 2011 'Engaging with the Pacific' summit, a meeting initiated by the Bainimarama regime that led to the creation of the Pacific Islands Development Forum. The 2011 summit in Nadi 'welcomed increasing social and cultural linkages between French Polynesia/Tahiti Nui and PSIDS', and 'supported the re-inscription of French Polynesia/Tahiti Nui on the UN decolonisation committee's list as the first step in the process of self-determination.'[10]

With Australia and France signing a Joint Statement of Strategic Partnership in January 2012, Canberra was less than enthusiastic about Temaru's reinscription initiative. In 2012, Australia's then Parliamentary Secretary for Pacific Island

---

9   NFIP supported publication of a booklet in English for Maohi leaders to use in lobbying Pacific governments: 'Independence and sovereignty for Te Ao Maohi / French Polynesia' (Tavini Huiraatira no Te Ao Maohi, Papeete, 1997). After the end of French nuclear testing in 1996, NFIP held its next regional conference in Tahiti in 1999. See Maclellan (1999).

10   Section 2, Final communiqué, Engaging with the Pacific leaders meeting, Tanoa hotel, Nadi, 1–2 September 2011.

Affairs, Richard Marles, described France as a long-term stable democratic partner in the Pacific and reaffirmed Australian opposition to reinscription: 'We absolutely take our lead from France on this.'[11]

Meeting in Rarotonga in August 2012, forum leaders reiterated their support for the principle of self-determination but didn't endorse the call for reinscription.[12] A month after the forum, without the restraining influence of Canberra and Wellington, the leaders of Samoa, Solomon Islands, Fiji and Vanuatu lined up at the UN General Assembly, calling for action on decolonisation.

Vanuatu's then Prime Minister Sato Kilman called on 'the independent and free nations of the world to complete the story of decolonisation and close this chapter'. He urged the UN 'not to reject the demands for French Polynesia's right to self-determination and progress' (Livtuvanu 2012).

Samoan Prime Minister Tuilaepa Sailele Malielegaoi told the general assembly: 'In the case of French Polynesia, we encourage the metropolitan power and the territory's leadership together with the support of the United Nations to find an amicable way to exercise the right of the people of the territory to determine their future' (Malielegaoi 2012).

Outside the forum, Fiji's new membership of the Non-Aligned Movement (NAM) opened the way for Foreign Minister Ratu Inoke Kubuabola to attend the 16th NAM Summit in Tehran in August 2012, which issued a new policy on French Polynesia's decolonisation: 'The Heads of State or Government affirmed the inalienable right of the people of French Polynesia–Maohi Nui to self-determination in accordance with Chapter XI of the Charter of the United Nations and the UN General Assembly resolution 1514 (XV).'[13]

Opinion was also shifting at home. The Eglise Protestante Maohi, the largest Christian denomination in French Polynesia, voted for the first time in August 2012 to support Temaru's call for reinscription.[14] The following month, the Central Committee of the World Council of Churches added its voice, calling on 'France, the United Nations, and the international community to support the reinscription of French Polynesia on the UN list of countries to be decolonised, in accordance with the example of New Caledonia' (WCC Central Committee 2012; see also Bhagwan 2012).

---

11   Interview with Richard Marles, May 2012. See Maclellan (2012).
12   The forum communiqué simply welcomed 'the election of a new French government that opened fresh opportunities for a positive dialogue between French Polynesia and France on how best to realise French Polynesia's right to self-determination.' Item 70, Communiqué, 43rd Pacific Islands Forum, Rarotonga, Cook Islands, 2012.
13   Final communiqué, 16th Summit of the Non-Aligned Movement, 26–31 August 2012, Tehran, Iran.
14   'The re-inscription of Maohi Nui on this list constitutes one way to protect the people from decisions and initiatives of the French State that are contrary to their interests' (EPM 2012).

With increasing regional support, the formal bid for reinscription was relaunched in early 2013, with extensive lobbying in New York by Oscar Temaru and France's then Senator for French Polynesia, Richard Ariihau Tuheiava. In January, Temaru addressed a meeting of the NAM Coordinating Bureau in New York:

> This is yet another case of David against Goliath, and the reason why we want our country back on the UN's list of non-self-governing territories. Without the UN as a referee between France and us, this is once again an unfair and uphill battle (Temaru 2013a).

In February, the PSIDS ambassadors for Solomon Islands, Tuvalu and Nauru formally lodged a draft resolution at the UN General Assembly. France's UN Ambassador Gérard Araud lobbied hard to have the resolution delayed in the hope that it would lapse after May 2013 elections in Papeete. In the interests of compromise, the sponsoring states issued a revised version of the resolution on 1 March, but France sought for weeks to keep the resolution out of the general assembly.

In a memo to Paris, Ambassador Araud stated:

> The question raised by Oscar Temaru must remain a franco-French affair, and the United Nations should not interfere with French political life, because France recognises the right of people to self-determination. France challenges the legitimacy of the Decolonisation Committee, as it has done since its creation in 1961 (Regnault 2013, p. 77).

Some UN member states were astounded by the way France pressed its case. Denouncing the 'violence and condescension' of Araud's interventions, Temaru wrote to President Hollande on 27 March, calling on him to bring the ambassador to heel:

> I would draw to your attention the growing frustration and incomprehension over France's position, which we have been informed of by several UN member states … The French pressure towards the President of the General Assembly is similarly perceived as the denial of the democracy that is at the heart of the General Assembly … If some of your confreres in the P5 [permanent members of the Security Council] seem to be accepting the French action on our dossier, others have shared their astonishment with us (Temaru 2013b).

French Polynesia's local elections on 5 May 2013 saw the defeat of President Temaru's UPLD coalition and the return of long-serving leader Gaston Flosse (since removed from office for misuse of public funds). After his election, Flosse immediately wrote to the president of the UN General Assembly in an unsuccessful attempt to delay action on the resolution. France's ambassador boycotted the session on 17 May — but the resolution was passed without a recorded vote.

Britain, the United States, Germany and the Netherlands all disassociated themselves from the decision. Fearful of a growing regional debate about West Papua, Indonesia's representative also stressed that the 'adoption was solely based on a specific historical context and should not be misinterpreted as precedence by other territories whose cases were pending with the Decolonisation Committee'.

Regional Diplomacy and West Papua

The diplomacy of decolonisation has bedevilled Pacific governments and regional organisations in recent years. While they have actively supported decolonisation for 'blue water' European colonies like French Polynesia, many governments have been reluctant to address struggles for self-determination in postcolonial nations such as Indonesia and PNG.

Since its founding in 1988, the MSG has actively supported the Kanak independence movement in New Caledonia. Indeed, the *Front de Libération Nationale Kanak et Socialiste* (Kanak and Socialist National Liberation Front (FLNKS)), rather than the Government of New Caledonia, is the full member of the sub-regional body. At the 2013 MSG summit, FLNKS spokesperson Victor Tutugoro was appointed as MSG chair, taking the role at a crucial time as the French dependency moves to a referendum on self-determination, scheduled for 2018. The MSG has also established an FLNKS unit in its Port Vila secretariat, appointing a Kanak activist as political counsellor.

In contrast to this long-standing solidarity with the FLNKS, the MSG had been largely silent on the more sensitive issue of West Papua — until now.

After more than 100,000 deaths in West Papua, there is significant popular support for West Papuan independence in the independent Melanesian nations. Even after the fall of Suharto's new order regime, there are ongoing human rights abuses by the Indonesian police and military.[15] This has led to new advocacy across Melanesia, with Facebook and other social media spreading information from inside West Papua across the region. This solidarity movement has forced a complex and unresolved debate over relations with Indonesia onto the agenda of recent MSG summits.

The MSG's unity has been stressed by this debate, at a time of other trade and diplomatic disputes (Webb-Gannon and Elmslie 2014). There have been some tensions between the larger states of PNG and Fiji — which are moving closer

---

15   Dominic Berger says, 'Reducing political tensions and ending human rights abuses in Papua remained elusive throughout [SBY's] tenure' (Berger 2015, p. 230).

to Jakarta — and Vanuatu and the FLNKS, which openly express solidarity with the West Papuan nationalist movement (with the Solomon Islands wavering between) (Maclellan 2015b, pp. 10–11).

Despite these rifts, the MSG's new engagement contrasts with the silence of the Pacific Islands Forum over the last decade. For nearly 30 years after its founding, the forum avoided the issue of West Papua. Action was always constrained by governments in Australia and PNG, which reaffirm the 'territorial integrity' of Indonesia and (incorrectly) state that Indonesia has always held sovereignty over West Papua.[16] Trade links are growing between Canberra, Port Moresby, Suva and Jakarta, adding to other strategic concerns, such as PNG's control of its land border and Canberra's fixation with boat people.

Despite this, forum leaders could not ignore the fall of the Suharto dictatorship in 1998, Timor-Leste's independence and the organising by West Papuan nationalists that created a brief 'Papua Spring' in Jayapura at the beginning of the 21st century.[17] At the September 2000 UN Millennium Summit in New York, Nauru, Vanuatu and Tuvalu were the first countries to declare support for West Papuan self-determination at the United Nations.

Four West Papuan activists were given official delegate status at the October 2000 forum in Kiribati as members of the Nauru delegation. At the Tarawa forum, Vanuatu, Nauru and other countries supported the push for human rights in the troubled country, even as they deferred to Australian and PNG sensitivities by acknowledging Indonesia's sovereignty. Forum Chair President Teburoro Tito of Kiribati said: 'Personally, I have great sympathy for the cause of the West Papuan people, just on the basis of culture alone.'[18]

The forum issued an unprecedented statement calling for peaceful dialogue on the future of the country and an end to human rights abuses. At the time, Papua Presidium member FranzAlbert Joku welcomed the statement: 'After four decades, we are back in our natural habitat, the South Pacific.'[19]

Joku was looking back to earlier pan-Melanesia engagement that existed before Indonesia's 1969 Act of Free Choice. Papuan delegates Marcus Kaisiepo and Nicolas Jouwe represented Dutch New Guinea at the first South Pacific Conference in 1950.[20] Dutch evangelical Christian church Reverends Kabel and

---

16   Australian support for Dutch sovereignty in the 1950s is discussed in Lijphart (1966).
17   For details of the Papua Spring, see Chauvel (2005).
18   Interview with President Teburoro Tito, Tarawa, September 2000. See Maclellan (2000).
19   Interview with FranzAlbert Joku, Tarawa, September 2000.
20   For photos of the West Papuans at the 1950 SPC meeting, see (DFAT 2000).

Maloali were active at the 1961 Malua Conference of Churches and Missions in Samoa (which led to the founding of the Pacific Conference of Churches). West Papuans studied at the Fiji School of Medicine in the 1960s.[21]

In April 2001, the forum decided to accept Indonesia as a post-forum dialogue partner. West Papua was discussed at forum meetings between 2001 and 2003, but Indonesian repression of the Papua Spring led to an end to discussion at the forum (apart from a brief mention in the 2006 communiqué). For a decade, forum communiqués have been silent on West Papua, despite possible openings for engagement as post-Suharto presidents established a Special Autonomy Law and divided the western half of New Guinea into the two provinces of Papua and West Papua.

In recent years, the issue has shifted to the MSG, leading to unprecedented debates amongst the five MSG members. This engagement was accelerated by the decision of then MSG Chair Voreqe Bainimarama to invite Indonesia and Timor-Leste to become MSG observers at the March 2011 summit in Fiji.[22]

Following Fiji's 2009 suspension from forum activities, the Bainimarama regime had been extending economic and political links with Asian nations, opening an embassy in Jakarta in August 2011. Ties between Suva and Jakarta are growing, highlighted by the then Indonesian President Susilo Bambang Yudhuyono opening the 2014 Pacific Islands Development Forum and Indonesia's role in co-chairing the Multinational Observer Group for Fiji's 2014 elections. Fiji's global ambitions — including membership of the NAM and its 2013 role as chair of G77 plus China — have introduced new complexities into the regional decolonisation agenda, given Indonesia is a key player in both networks.

PNG governments have long juggled competing tensions: public sentiment in support of West Papuan rights, growing economic links with Indonesia and ASEAN, and border security along the region's only land border. PNG's policy on West Papua is complicated by concerns over its own resource-rich province of Bougainville. With the 2015 re-election of John Momis as President of the Autonomous Bougainville Government, complex debates over the reopening of the Panguna mine and a five year window before a vote on political status, Bougainville will soon pose challenges for PNG's regional leadership — and the MSG.

---

21   Some West Papuans remained in Fiji after Indonesia's takeover. Interview with Dr Welby Korwa, Suva, 1998.

22   In February 2011, MSG foreign ministers 'endorsed applications for observership by Indonesia and Timor-Leste and agreed to seek an "out of session" decision from the leaders to allow Indonesia and Timor-Leste to attend as observers at the March 2011 [MSG] leaders' summit'. (Fiji Ministry of Information press release, February 2011).

Jakarta's bid for greater involvement in the MSG reflects Indonesia's mounting diplomatic efforts in the region. For many years, the Indonesian embassy in Port Moresby was the main hub for activity in forum island countries, with Indonesian officials lobbying the islands from embassies in Canberra, Wellington, Beijing and Tokyo (from 1974 until 2002, Indonesian diplomats travelled to Fiji from Wellington, until an embassy was opened in Suva).

Today, Jakarta is deploying more effort on the ground, to build economic ties but especially to counter West Papuan diplomacy. Former independence activists FranzAlbert Joku and Nick Messet now act as Indonesian diplomats and join delegations to regional and international summits, to showcase Jakarta's initiatives and argue against independence.

On the international stage, Indonesia, PNG and Fiji are all members of the UN Special Committee on Decolonisation. The two Pacific countries use the special committee as a platform to support the FLNKS, but join Indonesia in opposition to calls for West Papua to be relisted with the UN.[23]

In contrast, the Kanak independence coalition has long supported a fellow liberation movement in West Papua, wary of Indonesia's growing role in the MSG. Outgoing MSG chair Victor Tutugoro of the FLNKS told the author in 2015: 'For the FLNKS, the MSG is an organisation of Melanesian countries. As I see it, Indonesia is not part of the Melanesian bloc.'[24]

Vanuatu too has long backed the West Papuan nationalist movement with practical and diplomatic aid, hosting an office for the West Papua nationalist movement. In 2011, the Sato Kilman Government briefly moved closer to Indonesia, with the signing of a Vanuatu–Indonesia Development Cooperation Agreement. These moves dismayed West Papuan activists, especially as the cooperation agreement stressed Indonesian territorial integrity and sovereignty over West Papua, and prohibited Vanuatu from interfering in Indonesia's 'internal affairs'. This decision contributed to a backlash in Port Vila and the election of a new government under Moana Carcasses Kalosil, who proceeded to launch a series of attacks on Indonesia in UN forums.[25]

In March 2013, the Port Vila-based West Papua National Council for Liberation (WPNCL) lodged a formal membership application to join the MSG, and the existing members began to position themselves.

---

23   Indonesia provided funds to Fiji for the costs of the UN Special Committee's 2014 Pacific Regional Seminar, held in Nadi. On UN policy on self-determination and the 1969 Act of Free Choice, see Saltford (2002).

24   Interview with Victor Tutugoro, Honiara, June 2015. See Maclellan (2015a).

25   In an interview (Port Vila, July 2013), incoming Justice Minister Ralph Regenvanu stressed that the West Papua issue was a central reason for public disenchantment with the Kilman Government (although many other issues contributed to its electoral defeat).

In early June 2013, Fiji's Prime Minister Bainimarama held a meeting in Nadi with Djoko Suyanto, Indonesia's Coordinating Minister for Legal, Political and Security Affairs, and a former commander of Indonesia's armed forces. Soon after, to the disquiet of some delegates, Fiji arrived at the June 2013 MSG Summit in Noumea with a roadmap to drive the West Papua debate.

However, the host organisation FLNKS also formally invited the WPNCL to attend the summit. FLNKS representative Caroline Machoro-Reignier told the author:

> If this issue came up today within the MSG, it's because the FLNKS requested it. We asked the representatives of West Papua to come to New Caledonia to explain the situation to us. We cannot just leave the issue aside, with all the exactions, the violations of human rights that West Papua is suffering … However this is a very sensitive topic that affects relations between Indonesia and the other member states in the Spearhead Group.[26]

Indonesia sent a large delegation to press its case, including FranzAlbert Joku and Nick Messet, while a five-person delegation led by WPNCL Vice President John Otto Ondawame and Secretary-General Rex Rumakiek arrived to lobby for support of their bid for MSG membership. In a striking diplomatic gesture, PNG Prime Minister Peter O'Neill and Foreign Minister Rimbink Pato were absent from the summit, leading a large business delegation to Indonesia. Their presence in Jakarta as the MSG debated West Papua shows the priority given to relations with PNG's powerful neighbour (Maclellan 2013c).

After extensive lobbying in the corridors, MSG leaders agreed to defer a decision on the West Papua application. A decision would only be made after a delegation of Melanesian foreign ministers visited Jakarta and Jayapura and reported back to the leaders within six months (Maclellan 2013b). WPNCL's Ondawame expressed disappointment about the delay, arguing that the Indonesian government and military would stage-manage the MSG mission. However, he said he valued the opportunity to address the summit plenary and highlighted positive commitments by the MSG leaders.[27]

Despite these delaying tactics, the MSG summit communiqué included unprecedented language on West Papua, supporting 'the inalienable rights of the people of West Papua towards self-determination' and criticising 'human rights violations and other forms of atrocities relating to the West Papuan people'.[28]

---

26 Interview with Caroline Machoro-Reignier, FLNKS representative to the 2013 MSG foreign ministers meeting, Lifou, June 2013.
27 Interview with John Ondawame, Noumea, 20 June 2013. Sadly, Ondawame died in September 2014, a significant loss to the nationalist movement.
28 Final communiqué, 19th MSG leaders' summit, Escapade resort, Noumea, 20 June 2013.

Indonesia then wooed Solomon Islands, with then Prime Minister Gordon Darcy Lilo travelling to Jakarta in August 2013 on a trade mission, which the Vanuatu government perceived as an effort to undercut the foreign ministers' delegation. Vanuatu later boycotted the mission to West Papua, which travelled to Jakarta and Jayapura from 11–15 January 2014, led by Fiji Foreign Minister Ratu Inoke Kubuabola. The Vanuatu government was angered by the way Indonesia transformed the trip into a trade mission and refused access to pro-independence church and civil society representatives during a brief visit to Jayapura.[29]

Indonesia's diplomatic efforts were rewarded at a special MSG leaders' summit in Port Moresby in June 2014, which deferred the WPNCL application for membership and agreed 'to invite all groups to form an inclusive and united umbrella group in consultation with Indonesia to work on submitting a fresh application'.[30] The summit agreed on a range of activities to ensure 'that the MSG and Indonesia take a more proactive approach in addressing the issue of West Papua and Papua', broadly endorsing Indonesia's Special Autonomy Law and welcoming the involvement of West Papuans in a range of MSG sporting, cultural and development activities.

Despite this, Vanuatu continued to show its support for West Papuan self-determination. Vanuatu churches and customary chiefs, supported by the government, hosted a December 2014 meeting to bring together Jayapura-based activists and exiled campaigners and form a united front between competing groups. The newly created United Liberation Movement for West Papua (ULMWP) unites three strands of the West Papuan nationalist movement: the WPNCL, Federal Republic of West Papua, and the National Parliament of West Papua, which incorporates the National Committee for West Papua. In February 2015, the ULMWP resubmitted its application for full MSG membership.

In a major speech the same month, PNG Prime Minister Peter O'Neill said his country needed to do more to address human rights in West Papua. Proposing that his country take a lead in discussions with Indonesia 'in a mature and engaging manner', he added:

> Sometimes we forgot our family, our brothers and sisters, especially those in West Papua. I think as a country the time has come for us to speak about oppression of our people. Pictures of brutality of our people appear daily on social media and yet we take no notice. We have the moral obligation to speak for those who are not allowed to talk. We must be the eyes for those who are blindfolded (O'Neill 2015).

---

29   Discussions with Vanuatu Foreign Minister Edward Natapei (New Caledonia, June 2013) and Prime Minister Joe Natuman (Port Vila, July 2014). The communiqué of the June 2014 Special MSG Summit noted: 'Vanuatu was of the view that the Mission's program would not allow the MSG to obtain credible information to fulfil the MSG Leaders mandate.'
30   Final communiqué, special MSG leaders' summit, PNG National Parliament, Port Moresby, June 2014.

Indonesia continued to work to blunt the diplomatic advances of the West Papuan nationalist movement. In March 2015, during the lead up to the MSG summit, Indonesia's Foreign Minister Retno Marsudi travelled to PNG, Solomon Islands and Fiji. In May, a month before the summit, President Joko Widodo visited West Papua and PNG, announcing clemency for five political prisoners and making other concessions.[31]

At a press conference in Merauke, Jokowi addressed longstanding restrictions on international media travelling to West Papua: 'Starting from today, foreign journalists are allowed and free to come to Papua, just as they can [visit] other regions.' This pledge was immediately undercut by his Minister for Political, Legal and Security Affairs, Tedjo Edhy Purdijatno, who confirmed that foreign journalists would still be screened and must obtain permission from the security forces to travel to the highlands:

> We'll allow it, on condition that they report on what they see, not go around looking for facts that aren't true from armed groups … There's a lot of news out there that makes it look like [human rights] violations are taking place here all the time, but I don't think that's the case (Jakarta Globe 2015).

The diplomatic issue came to a head at the June 2015 MSG Summit in Solomon Islands, where leaders made an historic decision to expand the MSG's reach. With divergent views continuing amongst the five members, an uneasy consensus led to the granting of associate member status to Indonesia and observer status to the ULMWP.

To dodge questions over Indonesian sovereignty, the MSG leaders agreed that 'the ULMWP be admitted as an observer under the regional and international category representing Melanesians living abroad' (despite the ULMWP representing groups both inside and exiled from West Papua). In the presence of a large delegation led by Indonesian Vice Foreign Minister A.M. Fachir, the island leaders approved 'that associate membership be accorded to Indonesia representing the five Melanesian provinces in Indonesia' (Papua, West Papua, Maluku, North Maluku, and East Nusa Tenggara).

Describing the ULMWP as an 'external non-government organisation', Fiji Prime Minister Bainimarama stated:

---

31 Ironically, Jakarta has long argued there are no political prisoners in West Papua. Many prisoners refused presidential clemency (which requires an acknowledgement of guilt), arguing that they were falsely convicted for political reasons and that alleged acts — such as raising or displaying the Morning Star flag — were not crimes.

> Indonesian sovereignty over West Papua cannot be questioned … the MSG has no choice but to deal with Indonesia in a positive and constructive manner. The best hope for improving the lives of the people of West Papua is to work closely with the Indonesian government, one of the most vibrant democracies in the world (Bainimarama 2015).

The 20th MSG summit communiqué noted that the 'Indonesian President is someone whom the MSG can dialogue with'.[32] But despite recent initiatives by President Joko Widodo, Indonesia's development policies in West Papua will continue to drive calls for change, as customary landowners fight to protect their land and restrict ongoing immigration. The future role of the five governors in MSG is unclear, given the historic difference between Papua and West Papua (which remained under Dutch administration until the 1960s) and the other three provinces (which were part of Indonesia from independence in 1949). Governors Lukas Enembe of Papua and Bram Atururi of West Papua were both absent from the 2015 summit; as they seek a different political status within Indonesia, more debate is on the cards within the MSG.[33]

The creation of the ULMWP as a united coalition will also pose diplomatic challenges for Pacific governments, as the MSG observer highlights historic grievances and ongoing human rights violations. ULMWP Secretary-General Octo Mote says observer status is 'a foot in the door' for dialogue between West Papuan nationalists, Melanesian governments and Indonesia: 'We're a nation in waiting, and we're not going away!'[34]

Conclusion

The recent flurry of diplomatic activity on decolonisation by MSG and PSIDS is a striking example of ways that new Pacific diplomatic structures have allowed action on questions that governments have been reluctant to address through the Pacific Islands Forum for many years.

Over the next five years, there will be major political and constitutional changes in two Melanesian nations, as New Caledonia and Bougainville vote on a new political status. Under the 1998 Noumea Accord, New Caledonia is scheduled to hold a referendum on self-determination in late 2018, with two other votes

---

32   Final communiqué, 20th MSG summit, Heritage Park Hotel, Honiara, Solomon Islands, 26 June 2015, p. 6.
33   Indonesian proposals to create even more provinces in the western half of the island of New Guinea are disrupting moves towards a strengthened autonomy law known as Otsus Plus. See IPAC (2014).
34   Interview with Octavius Mote, Honiara, June 2015.

possible up until 2022. In a similar period, Bougainville will come to the end of its 10–15 year transition after the 2005 election of the Autonomous Bougainville Government.

These referenda have important implications for neighbours such as Australia, New Zealand and the island members of the Pacific Islands Forum and MSG. The issue of self-determination will again force itself onto the regional agenda.

References

The Australian, 1982, 'Act now before Russians move in, says Bowen', 20 February.

Bainimarama, F., 2015, 'Speech to MSG Summit Plenary Session', Honiara, 26 June.

Berger D., 2015, 'Human Rights and Yudhyono's Test of History', in E. Aspinall et al. (eds), *The Yudhoyono Presidency: Indonesia's decade of stability and stagnation*, Institute of South East Asian Studies, Singapore.

Bhagwan, P.J., 2012, 'The Struggle for Self-Determination', *Fiji Times*, 12 September.

Chauvel, R., 2005, *Constructing Papuan Nationalism: History, ethnicity, and adaptation*, East-West Centre, Washington.

Corbin, C., 2010, 'An Analysis of Implementation of the United Nations Decolonisation Mandate during the Second International Decade for the Eradication of Colonialism (2001–2010) and Strategies for Completion of the Decolonisation Mandate', *Overseas Territories Report* 9(5).

Department of Foreign Affairs and Trade (DFAT), 2000, *The South Pacific Commission: The first fifty years*, DFAT, Canberra.

Eglise Protestante Maohi (EPM), 2012, media release, August.

Fiji Ministry of Information, 2011, press release, February.

Firth, S., 2013, 'Political Status and Development: The implications for Australian foreign policy towards the Pacific Islands', SSGM discussion paper 2013/6.

Huntsman J. and K. Kelihian, 2007, *The Future of Tokelau: Decolonising agendas 1975–2006*, Auckland University Press, Auckland.

Institute for Policy Analysis on Conflict (IPAC), 2014, 'Papua Update: The latest on Otsus Plus', IPAC Report No. 7, 27 February.

Jakarta Globe, 2015, 'In President's Promises on Papua, Little Sign of Meaningful Change', 10 May.

Lijphart, A., 1966, *The Trauma of Decolonisation: The Dutch and West New Guinea*, Yale University Press, New Haven.

Livtuvanu, M.S.K., 2012 'Statement by Prime Minister of Vanuatu', 67th Session of the UN General Assembly, New York, 28 September, p. 3.

Maclellan, N. (ed.), 1999, *No Te Parau Tia, No Te Parau Mau, No Te Tiamaraa*, PCRC, Suva.

Maclellan, N., 2000, 'Historical Moment for West Papua at Forum', *Pacific News Bulletin*, November.

Maclellan, N., 2012, 'Partenariat stratégique entre l'Australie et la France', *Tahiti-Pacifique magazine*, August.

Maclellan, N., 2013a, 'Hijacking Decolonisation: French Polynesia at the United Nations', *Inside Story*, 31 May.

Maclellan, N., 2013b, 'MSG to Send Mission to Jakarta and West Papua', *Islands Business*, 18 June.

Maclellan, N., 2013c, 'MSG Aims "to restructure the Pacific landscape": Summit supports Kanak and West Papuan self-determination', *Islands Business*, July.

Maclellan, N., 2013d, 'Forum to Discuss New Caledonia's Membership Bid', *Islands Business*, 4 September.

Maclellan, N., 2015a, 'FLNKS Supports West Papuan Membership Bid', *Pacnews*, 24 June.

Maclellan, N., 2015b, 'Competing Pressures Over West Papua', *Islands Business*, July.

Malielegaoi, T.S., 2012, 'Statement by Prime Minister of Samoa', 67th Session of the UN General Assembly, New York, 28 September, p. 1.

Ministry of Foreign Affairs, 2013, 'Résolution adoptée par l'Assemblée générale des Nations unies sur la Polynésie française', press release, 17 May.

Mrgudovic, N., 2008, *La France dans le Pacifique sud: Les enjeux de la puissance*, L'Harmattan, Paris.

O'Neill, P., 2015, 'Speech by Hon. Prime Minister Peter O'Neill CMG MP', 2015 Leaders Summit, Port Moresby, 5 February.

Pacific Plan Review, 2013, 'Report to Pacific Leaders, Volume 1', Pacific Islands Forum Secretariat, Suva.

Regnault, J.-M., 2013, *L'ONU, la France et les décolonisations tardives: l'exemple des terres françaises d'Océanie*, Presses universitaires d'Aix-Marseille, Aix-en-Provence.

Saltford, J., 2002, *United Nations and the Indonesian Takeover of West Papua, 1962–1969: The anatomy of a betrayal*, Routledge Curzon, London.

Sarkozy, N., 2010, 'Voeux à la France d'Outre-mer', speech presented at Saint Denis de la Réunion, 19 January.

Temaru, O.M., 2013a, 'Presentation to Non Aligned Movement Coordinating Bureau meeting', New-York, January.

Temaru, O.M., 2013b, 'Réinscription de la Polynésie française sur la liste des pays non-autonome', letter from President Oscar Manutahi Temaru to President François Hollande, 27 March.

UN General Assembly, 2015, 'Information from Non-Self-Governing Territories transmitted under Article 73e of the Charter of the United Nations', Report of the Secretary General, 7 March, A/70/67.

WCC Central Committee 2012, 'Statement on Re-Inscription of French Polynesia (Maohi Nui) on UN List of Countries to be Decolonized', 4 September.

Webb-Gannon C. and J. Elmslie, 2014, 'MSG Headache, West Papuan Heartache? Indonesia's Melanesian Foray', *The Asia-Pacific Journal* 12(46).

Appendices

Thinking 'Outside the Rocks': Reimagining the Pacific[1]

Hon. Henry Puna

This obvious play on words is a home-grown attempt to capture the way in which our region faces enormous challenges in trying to find its own way in the world — defining itself while grappling with the constraints associated with remoteness, size, and resources.

A changing world demands changing mindsets, and those demands are pressing for a renewed effort on our part to redefine our thinking in ways that reflect who we are, and what we want to be, on our own terms.

Thinking 'outside the rocks' is how we need to reverse a self-imposed limitation of believing we are simply 'dots on a map'. For too long we've allowed a sense of smallness to underscore our outlook and projection to the rest of the world.

On the contrary, our island nations carry enormous significance well beyond tiny volcanic specks and atolls in what is a vast, collective territory of the Pacific Ocean. This is our course for the future — thinking beyond the rocks.

---

1   Address to students of the University of the South Pacific, Suva, Fiji, 19 October 2012.

Reimagining Ourselves

I think the time is right that we take on a more concerted effort, as a region, to define ourselves on our own terms. After all, this global community of ours is continuing to shrink rapidly, thanks to the marching advancement of internet technology and the uptake of mobile devices, which can basically run and organise a business or organisation — on the run!

The conduct of business is evolving in competitive ways that demand new thinking. And the structures of professional fields in media information and dissemination can no longer be called 'traditional' — they're constantly reinventing themselves into challenging spheres of competitive space. Just ask dot com!

For me, as a leader, and us as governments, our collective interests are being pressured and shaped toward a new Pacific order — one that won't necessarily meet the expectations of others — or the perceptions of outsiders. What is important is that we choose what's best for us. We have the ability to define what's good, and we have the right to take commanding ownership of our future.

Large Ocean Island States

I am, of course, partly alluding to the theme of the Pacific Islands Forum this year — a theme we chose as hosts to help encourage a greater sense of our region as home to large ocean island states.

And as I made a point of mentioning during the forum opening in August, our collective territories are nearly two times the size of Russia, and more than three times the size of the People's Republic of China. It's time we refocused our lens on the world and sharpened our strategy toward greater economic growth and sustainability.

Our thinking — our very identity as Pacific Islanders — must project from a more advanced, self-awareness of our presence in the world. And I think we're off to a good start.

The Pacific Islands Forum is registering higher, more significant levels of engagement with the broader international community. Just last month, I was joined by several Pacific leaders in the first ever joint dialogue with the United Nations Secretary General and his leadership team. This was a very important first step in ensuring the Pacific Islands have a firm fix on inroads to the UN system.

The Pacific bloc of Small Islands Developing States (SIDS) plays a key role in the UN. As members of the Alliance of Small Islands States, we are bound to the processes associated with the ongoing climate change negotiations, and adaptation funding mechanisms.

This ongoing struggle is absolutely crucial to our survival. It's vital that we — as a solid, united front — present our case with an effective voice. And my underlying concern is to ensure that all the SIDS are represented equally, and with conviction, in the UN processes, particularly leading up to and participating in the 2014 global SIDS summit in our region.

The forum is also beginning to ignite groundbreaking steps in the sound management of our oceans and natural resources, and push the boundaries of regional integration to cooperate in new and challenging fields.

For example, international interest in the recent establishment of the biggest Marine Park in the world in the Cook Islands has been tremendous. The principles of sound management and conservation of our ocean are being strengthened across the Pacific as more nations look to strike a careful balance between exploiting natural resources and sustaining their value through conservation measures.

In renewable energy, many Pacific nations are capitalising on available expertise and resources to realise their goals. New priorities for energy security in countries like Tonga, Tokelau, Samoa, Vanuatu, and Fiji, have resulted in terrific progress, increasing the share of renewable energy generation, improving levels of energy efficiency, and slicing back the dependency on environmentally-damaging fossil fuels.

The Cook Islands has joined this trend in setting ambitious targets and we are poised to commence solar energy projects in our isolated Northern Group Islands. Niue too, recently signed on for major development in renewable energy projects, assisted by the Japan-supported Pacific Environment Community Fund.

The forum's strategic engagement with its external partners is being rewarded. Close working relationships and beneficial outcomes are largely due to the effectiveness of our cooperative frameworks like the Forum Compact, and Pacific Plan.

Pacific Plan Optimism

And as you may already be aware, the Pacific Plan will be the subject of major review in the coming months. My presence here in Suva is to help promote and speak to the significance of the plan and what it means to the island countries of the Pacific, and their aspirations for the future.

Yesterday, at the Forum Secretariat Headquarters, I utilised the honour of the annual public lecture to highlight my perspectives on an emerging sense of new optimism in the Pacific — and that this positive theme should be harnessed to instil more dynamism into the Pacific Plan.

Are we thus looking at a new period of renaissance in the Pacific? Perhaps. There may be value in arguing that point although it will be problematic to isolate a particular point in time that this new optimism arose.

Leaders before me have spoken of a Pacific reawakening, a rebirth of sorts, particularly as evidenced in the way we celebrate our heritage, culture and traditions in the region — through performing arts and crafts festivals, language preservation, and voyaging.

Voyaging as Reimagining

Voyaging and the celebration of migratory peoples across this vast ocean of ours, is close to the heart of Cook Islanders, and to many of you also. In fact, this centuries-old navigation of the seas has been the subject of its own debate in past years for the way it has been revitalised and thrust to the forefront of our cultural consciousness.

Sailing by traditional means is firmly part of our identity — an identity that is transported across the Pacific, east to west, north to south. I, for one, was very proud to be a part of the welcoming reception of a flotilla of seven *vaka* that arrived in the United States last year — a remarkable voyaging accomplishment, which brought many of our nations together as one.

Traditional voyaging is also firmly entrenched in the way the Pacific region has been reimagining itself over many years of dominant ideals and tropes that originated from a Eurocentric view of the world. Europeans have imagined and constructed the Pacific and its peoples in ways that have endured for centuries.

But we're not denying that this is part of who we are. This is part of our history. In fact, we would be among those to uphold one of the greatest European voyagers of the Pacific: Captain James Cook.

This Yorkshire-born navigator of the seas is still making headlines today — and not just because our country was renamed in his honour. Cook's charts and maps of the Pacific are everlasting, coexisting today in a world where Pacific Islands' voyagers need only the stars to cross the Pacific.

These ironies live on, throughout our region today. The very categorisation of our islands into convenient blocs by French voyager Dumont d'Urville, for instance, has long been accepted, reappropriated with robust political purpose.

Today, those European constructs of Polynesia, Melanesia, and Micronesia instil pride within us all, and evoke a dignity associated with diverse, natural beauty and strength. We simply took ownership, and made it ours.

Tourism

And what's interesting about this twist, is the way that Small Island Developing States, which are experiencing economic growth in industries like tourism, are essentially delivering a product that was imagined by European Romanticists in the 18th century.

The very notion of an idyllic paradise of sensual beauty and charm is exactly how we tend to portray the serenity of our attractive islands and their people to the tourist markets overseas today.

The desire for the Pacific that emerged centuries ago to lure outsiders to these shores, is now allowing us the means with which to secure economic strength. For the Cook Islands, tourism is the backbone of our national economy, and the leader and driver of our potential and growth.

But in the true nature of Pacific paradoxes, tourism is both our strength, and weakness. Our unspoilt islands remain vulnerable, fragile to climate change, the incessant drive of development in modern infrastructure, and the debilitating trend of population drift, which impacts upon our ability to sustain resources.

The narrowness of our existence in the Pacific requires broadening — a widening of both opportunity and the way in which we must take on these tasks.

For these reasons I ask for encouragement to accept this responsibility to think beyond the constraints — rise above, explore 'outside the rocks', and progress with a boldness founded on who we can be, as large ocean island states.

Melanesian Spearhead Group: The last 25 years[1]

Sir Michael Somare

Much has been said about the achievements of the Melanesian Spearhead Group (MSG) over the last few months as we celebrated our 25 years anniversary in our various capitals. I will therefore not dwell much on them today. However, it is fair to say that from what started as a political sub-grouping, MSG's cooperation now covers most areas of human pursuit and endeavour. It is no exaggeration that MSG's cooperative efforts in political and security, trade and economic, social, cultural and sports activities have increased and strengthened in ways that our founders never imagined.

I am told that even Honourable Ezekial Alebua admitted recently that when they first met in Goroka in 1986, he never imagined the MSG would grow from a simple political 'pressure group' to a vibrant and successful organisation as it is today. We are the only sub-regional grouping within the Pacific Islands Forum (PIF) area that has a formal secretariat and headquarters.

MSG into the Future

I was fortunate to be given the opportunity to share my thoughts and listen to the Eminent Persons Group established by our leaders to draw up a vision and future plan for our organisation. I was encouraged by what I heard: MSG must be inclusive. It must be compassionate. It must have integrity.

---

1 Keynote address by Grand Chief Sir Michael Somare on the occasion of the Melanesian Spearhead Group 25th anniversary celebrations in Noumea, New Caledonia.

All our efforts in regional cooperation and integration must mirror these principles. Just as important is the principle that MSG must seek to help itself first. MSG must only seek outside assistance if its own resources are inadequate or its capacity is found wanting. Experiences in our region and elsewhere suggest that this approach provides some insurance against outside influence — influence that could easily lead to distortion of MSG's priorities and development agenda.

MSG must be in the Driver's Seat

As we search to find areas of common interest, to pursue our quest for more enhanced cooperation and deeper integration, we must ensure that our national resources and energies are not wasted. Our MSG Secretariat, that is entrusted to help us in our undertaking to better serve our peoples, must be appropriately resourced to discharge its responsibilities. To help improve communications and implementation of the work program, MSG members should seek to open resident representative offices in Port Vila.

The last 25 years have given us valuable experience on collective action in pursuit of identified development goals — be they political, economic, trade, social, cultural, etc. That many of our neighbours, sub-groups and Melanesian communities elsewhere have expressed an interest in joining MSG is a strong validation of how well we have organised ourselves. The interest shown manifest the value others attach to MSG's role in the pursuit of common development objectives. It is no exaggeration that some critics that initially thought the Melanesian Spearhead Group enterprise was overly ambitious now consider MSG cooperation as a viable enterprise in sub-regionalism in the Pacific.

MSG is fortunate in that it can, and must, extract lessons from the workings of PIF and learn from the experience of other similar organisations elsewhere. We must avoid creating new MSG institutions to provide a public good or service if another regional or national institution is already providing them. It is no epiphany to suggest that we would be better off accessing the services from the existing regional or national institutions. What might be necessary, though, is to channel more resources to these institutions to bolster their capacity to better serve our collective interests and needs.

We must only create new institutions either because none exists to provide that public good or service, or if by doing so, it adds considerable value to existing efforts.

If experience elsewhere, by similar organisations like ours, demonstrate that binding ourselves to decisions would improve implementation of our initiatives then we should find ways to legally bind ourselves to the decisions we make. This would help strengthen MSG's credibility.

Political and Security

Political and security concerns, namely decolonisation of New Caledonia and cessation of nuclear testing in Moruroa were the main reasons MSG was formed. New Caledonia's right to self-determination, and independence, championed by the Kanak and Socialist National Liberation Front (FLNKS), was perceived as not getting the serious attention it deserved. In addition, the then MSG leaders felt that some regional partners were undermining efforts to adopt a stronger position within the PIF.

New Caledonia's reinscription as a non-self-governing territory within the purview of the United Nations Committee of 24 is largely due to the change in approach and the concerted efforts of the MSG. It is also arguable that the Noumea Accord, and the processes leading up to it, would not have come about without the deliberate international campaign mounted by the MSG countries in support of New Caledonia's right to self-determination. These included persistent representations to the metropolitan power and the United Nations.

The Noumea Accord offers a glimmer of hope for the Kanaky people and their aspirations. It would be a sad indictment on MSG's resolve if we do not ensure the FLNKS is positioned to win the provincial elections next year. MSG has that obligation and, as a member, FLNKS is entitled to expect nothing less from the other MSG members.

MSG's responsibility extends beyond the FLNKS leadership of today. MSG owes it to the FLNKS leaders of yesteryears whose pioneering work has helped us come this far. At this juncture, I wish to pay tribute to the likes of Uregei, Machoro, Tjibaou, Yéwéné Yéwéné, and the young Kanaks in Ouvéa who paid the ultimate price for championing justice and the emancipation of the Kanaky people. MSG countries owe it to the Kanaky people to remain true to their commitment to defend and promote independence as the inalienable right of indigenous peoples of Melanesia as espoused in the agreement establishing our organisation.

Political and parliamentary instability in MSG countries continue to undermine our efforts in promoting our region as a region of opportunity, stability and prosperity. More energy must be directed in the next 25 years towards strengthening our governance institutions and good governance processes.

It is worth clarifying, though, that in many instances in MSG, political and parliamentary instability occur as a result of the democratic process at play, in particular the exercise of democratic rights. They are not indicative of the absence of democracy in MSG but simply reflect symptoms of weak governance institutions and processes.

As a group, the West Papua issue will continue to test MSG's commitment to defend and promote independence as the inalienable right of indigenous peoples of Melanesia as well as to promote their human rights. There is strong and growing support among the MSG peoples for West Papua's membership to MSG and West Papua's aspirations to self-determination.

Obviously, Papua New Guinea government's position on this issue will very much weigh on MSG's considerations in terms of how it deals with West Papua. For me personally, I believe that MSG should actively make representations to Indonesia to address the human rights abuses in West Papua. MSG must also involve West Papua in some of MSG's cultural events, sporting activities and technical skills exchanges. West Papua after all has a significant Melanesian community.

But, should the MSG leaders decide on granting West Papua 'membership', in one form or another, it should be done only on the basis that it is a Melanesian community and not because MSG countries recognise West Papua as a sovereign independent state.

MSG already has a non-state entity as a member in FLNKS. A not too dissimilar arrangement can be found in Asia-Pacific Economic Cooperation (APEC) where Taiwan and Hong Kong, regarded by many as part of China, participate as partners in development with independent sovereign. The point here is that we have to be inventive. Again, should a decision be made for West Papua to be a 'member' of MSG, it is not hard to imagine this serving as a venue for both Indonesia and West Papua to engage in dialogue and regularly brief MSG countries of developments in West Papua.

Fiji's current political situation is another case that will continue to test MSG solidarity as a group. It is no secret that regional decisions and approaches to Fiji have caused polarisation of views in the PIF. Even within our MSG grouping, I can sense a tenuous unity of purpose on Fiji. There is a real risk of a chasm developing between MSG members if we are not careful. I have always maintained that Fiji requires our understanding and support.

Time should not be the essence for Fiji to return to elective government. Ensuring Fiji develops a strong culture of enduring democracy, with robust democratic institutions, is most important. Melanesian values of dialogue and patience, although protracted in process, have the greatest potential to bring about the changes we want in Fiji. This is in stark contrast to the effects that condescending tactics and heavy handed punitive actions advocated by some have had on Fiji. I would also suggest that the changing geopolitical situation in the region is a result of this.

MSG must also resist the temptation of using high 'moral ground' reasons to justify calls for it to criticise Fiji's slow return to parliamentary democracy. Although pious principles are noble they are very often void of reality on the ground. MSG needs to be pragmatic in its approach to Fiji.

With regards to the issue of nuclear testing, MSG will need to continue to be interested in the transhipment through our waters of nuclear weapons and nuclear waste material.

We must be vigilant over the mechanisms established to compensate coastal states in the event of disasters. Even with all the advances made in technology, disasters will happen and we need to ensure provision of assistance is predictable, swift and adequate under these mechanisms.

The interest shown and the entry by non-traditional powers in our region will inevitably reconfigure the geopolitical landscape and usher in new security challenges. But the notion of security extends beyond the realms of external physical threats to territorial integrity and sovereignty. Globalisation has given birth to new security issues. The resulting better communications, and easier movement across national borders of capital, goods, services and persons, has brought along with it challenges in cybercrime, money laundering, illicit cross-border trade, human trafficking, health, etc. Lack of food, absence of proper sanitation, inadequate housing and unemployment are security threats in themselves.

Another security issue concerns our porous borders. Lack of national capacity to undertake effective surveillance, means that our rich marine and land resources may be exploited in ways that are unsustainable. Even if they are developed within the legal limits there is no guarantee that fish-catch data, forest-harvest figures and mineral-export statistics reveal the true picture, thus denying us optimum benefits from our resources.

These sets of challenges I have just described require us to address them collectively as MSG and as a region. They know no borders.

Global warming and sea level rise is posing serious, if not imminent, danger to the very survival of our people on our coastlines and the low-lying islands in our region. This threat scenario calls for MSG to commit itself, and lead the way, in undertaking sustainable development practices. Having the largest landmass in the PIF region — 99 per cent (excluding Australia and New Zealand) — MSG countries have a moral duty to resettle climate refugees from the other small island countries of the Pacific.

Economic and Trade

Our cooperation in trade and economic activities has become somewhat the talking point of many of our colleagues in the region. And rightly so! It is the only regional trading agreement that is working in the Pacific. MSG must always remind itself of the initial cynicism which accompanied the reactions of many of our regional partners when we concluded a trading agreement with only three items to trade. The announcement generated considerable scepticism. Some, less generous, even suggested that the idea to trade with only three items was bordering on delusional.

I only belabour this point, not to disparage our critics, but to encourage us to draw inspiration from this experience as we embark on more enhanced cooperation and greater integration. There is nothing wrong with having a dream. Nor is it silly to be ambitious. MSG efforts in collective bargaining, joint provision of certain public goods and services, and general regional cooperation and integration will always attract its antagonists. But should we allow this to determine what we can and cannot do? I think the answer is obvious: we cannot and we must not!

MSG intra-trade continues to grow. Currently all items traded do not attract tariff in Fiji and Vanuatu. Papua New Guinea only has a negative list of three items and Solomon Islands is working on reducing its tariffs by 2017, a differentiated treatment granted to it by the other members because of its least developed country status. MSG countries' trade with the outside world is also growing. This is an indication of the positive growth experienced by the MSG over the last few years. There is strong indication that these growth trends will continue.

But let us not delude ourselves. It would be naïve to think that trade liberalisation, or regional cooperation and integration, are without perils. For the future, the challenges that MSG will need to address include diversifying our economic activities, growing the SMEs' (small, and medium-sized enterprises) share of our economies and further developing our export capability.

We must aggressively create an enabling environment for investment by providing reliable and affordable infrastructure, such as public utilities. This might require time-bound affirmative action by our governments to allocate resources to the development and roll-out of public goods and services to the rural areas where a large part of our populations reside.

New Caledonia, from where a member of our group comes, remains outside the MSG Trade Agreement. This is an anomaly that requires correcting. With a bit of innovation, MSG can extend the benefits of the trade agreement to the New Caledonian business community. An idea worth considering is for parties to the trade agreement to conclude a protocol with FLNKS. This protocol can provide the framework for the business community in New Caledonia to benefit from the provisions of the MSG Trade Agreement.

Social and Humanitarian

MSG countries, despite their best efforts, still have data showing their social indices to be less than enviable. Thus, improving health, education, water, sanitation, transport and communication facilities must continue to receive our serious attention. But more importantly, MSG needs to ensure that these public goods and services are extended to reach and cover our rural populace and disadvantaged communities.

Cultural, Traditional and Sporting

The Framework Treaty on the Protection of Traditional Knowledge and Expressions of Culture signed in 2011 is a good starting point for MSG.

The Melanesian Cup must be revived and made more permanent on the calendar of MSG. I am happy to note that New Caledonia will host the Melanesian Cup next year. The Melanesian Festival of Arts must continue to be a major event for MSG. Papua New Guinea plays host to this event next year. We must ensure that this occasion provides the opportunity for our peoples to have exchanges with a view to promoting better appreciation of the different Melanesian cultures and traditions. The educational value of these exchanges must be exploited to the maximum by ensuring that both the young and old form part of our national delegations so that the old can impart traditional knowledge to the young.

Many of our sacred cultural properties were illegally exported and are currently being held overseas in museums and private collections. It would help with national efforts if MSG were to develop a common strategy to address this issue of restitution. These sacred objects of art, in some cases human remains, need to be brought back home to rest. Adequately resourcing our museums and cultural institutions to research, document, preserve and promote our cultures and traditions would ensure that our future generations continue to have a Melanesian identity. Just as important is the need to develop appropriate curricula to teach in our schools. Traditional institutions, such as the customary chiefs, and customary practices, such as reconciliation ceremonies, can be better leveraged for policy dissemination and conflict resolution.

Conclusion

MSG has come a long way from its humble beginnings in Goroka. But we certainly have not reached the 'promised land' that our people deserve and expect us to deliver. The Kanaky peoples' dream of emancipation has not been realised yet. As we go forward, we must not forget that there are perils associated with regional cooperation, regional integration and trade liberalisation.

We must therefore recommit ourselves to the goals and objectives set by our leaders. There is need to redouble our efforts towards greater cooperation and integration within our national boundaries, between ourselves and with our brothers in our region.

MSG cooperation and integration has been successful because there are willing partners determined to share resources, best practices and, in certain instances, prepared to extend differentiated treatment to one another in recognition of their peculiar development needs.

I would further propose that the bigger and more well-endowed of the MSG countries, like Papua New Guinea, must accept asymmetric responsibilities if MSG cooperation and integration is to be sustained. Those well off in our group must be prepared to make sacrifices, forego certain short term benefits, for the common good and the long-term solidarity of MSG.

MSG must provide the leadership in advancing wider regional interests and concerns. It must provide the building block for wider regional cooperation and economic prosperity. Our interests are mutually reinforcing. The willingness to extend a helping hand must continue to guide MSG's approach to regional cooperation. In fact, I would venture to suggest that this sense of compassion should underpin our every effort in regional cooperation and integration.

As such, MSG must, wherever possible, employ its size and strength in the service of the wider region, especially the small island states. An MSG without the Pacific is the weaker, just as a Pacific without the MSG is the poorer. At all costs we must resist the temptation of being inward looking — there is so much to be gained from being inclusive.

The future of MSG is destined to be nothing but better. We must aim to make MSG the paragon of Pacific sub-regionalism. Together we have defied the odds and together we shall triumph.

Index

www.ingramcontent.com/pod-product-compliance
Lightning Source LLC
Chambersburg PA
CBHW061217270326
41926CB00028B/4669